# PERSPECTIVES ON INTERCULTURALITY

# Perspectives on Interculturality

## The Construction of Meaning in Relationships of Difference

Edited by

*Michal Jan Rozbicki*

PERSPECTIVES ON INTERCULTURALITY

First published in 2015 by
PALGRAVE MACMILLAN®
in the United States—a division of St. Martin's Press LLC,
175 Fifth Avenue, New York, NY 10010.

Where this book is distributed in the UK, Europe and the rest of the world,
this is by Palgrave Macmillan, a division of Macmillan Publishers Limited,
registered in England, company number 785998, of Houndmills,
Basingstoke, Hampshire RG21 6XS.

Palgrave Macmillan is the global academic imprint of the above companies
and has companies and representatives throughout the world.

Palgrave® and Macmillan® are registered trademarks in the United States,
the United Kingdom, Europe and other countries.

ISBN: 978–1–137–48913–5

Library of Congress Cataloging-in-Publication Data

Perspectives on interculturality : the construction of meaning in
relationships of difference / edited by Michal Jan Rozbicki.
pages cm
Summary: "The intercultural occurs in the space between two or
more distinct cultures that encounter each other, an area where
meaning is translated and difference is negotiated. A better, more
systemic understanding of these processes is a major challenge of our
time. Intercultural themes have thus far been mostly pursued within
bounded academic disciplines, but the fact that people often have
multiple, overlapping cultural affinities, and that cultures are inherently
dynamic because they are man-made, not fixed and ahistorical systems,
begs for interdisciplinary approaches. However, scholars are rarely
trained to do so. They are routinely constrained by conventionalized
conceptual languages of their disciplines, by their own apperceptions
and assumptions, and by the incommensurability of frameworks
of knowledge in an increasingly interconnected world. Intercultural
studies are due for reflection and refinement. This volume brings
together international scholars from diverse disciplines to reflect on
the phenomenon of interculturality, and to share the theoretical and
methodological frameworks of interpreting it."—Provided by publisher.
Includes bibliographical references and index.
ISBN 978–1–137–48913–5 (hardback)
1. Cultural relations. 2. Cultural pluralism. 3. Group identity.
4. Intercultural communication. I. Rozbicki, Michal.
HM621.P474 2015
303.48′2—dc23                                                    2014041822

A catalogue record of the book is available from the British Library.

Design by Newgen Knowledge Works (P) Ltd., Chennai, India.

First edition: April 2015

# Contents

## Part I    Conceptualizing Interculturality

## Part II    Interculturality and Social Identity

## Part III    A Global Stage for Interculturality

## Part IV    The Practice of Interculturality

# FIGURES AND TABLES

## FIGURES

## TABLES

# ACKNOWLEDGMENTS

The origins of this book go back to an international conference in St. Louis entitled Perspectives on Interculturality organized in March of 2013 by the Center for Intercultural Studies at Saint Louis University. It brought together scholars from diverse disciplines to explore the conceptual frameworks available for studying the mechanisms of interactions between different cultures. The goal was to assemble a theoretical and methodological toolbox that would help to understand more fully the phenomenon of interculturality, one of the greatest challenges of our times. We wish to thank all participants for contributing the essays that make up this volume, the second in a series on interculturality put together by the Center for Intercultural Studies.

Special thanks go to those who served as session chairs: Monica Eppinger, Julia Lieberman, Hisako Matsuo, David Murphy, and George Ndege, as well as to our inspiring keynote speaker Donal Carbaugh. From the conference to the volume, our work was blessed with steadfast support and encouragement from Mike Barber, S. J., Dean of the College of Arts and Sciences, and Diana Carlin, Associate Vice President for Graduate Education and International Initiatives at Saint Louis University. We also have many debts to graduate students, research fellows, and staff who offered invaluable help with corresponding, coordinating and creating: Cho-Chien Feng, Sara Rodgers, Ted Listerman, Scott McDermott, Amy Wallhermfechtel, and Mary Petri Bokern. Mike Aperauch, Editorial Assistant at Palgrave Macmillan in New York, never failed to impress us with his quiet professionalism in guiding the manuscript on its way to becoming a book.

# INTRODUCTION

# INTERCULTURAL STUDIES: THE METHODOLOGICAL CONTOURS OF AN EMERGING DISCIPLINE

*Michal Jan Rozbicki*

## I

An intercultural encounter is ultimately a relation of difference. It occurs in the space where people with distinct ways of interpreting the world reciprocally negotiate their otherness. It engages a wide spectrum of groups with discrete sub-cultures, identities, social positions, and rules of operation—from associations and professions to corporations, tribes, ethnicities, and nations—with varying levels of involvement and uneven degrees of internal coherence. The intercultural does not need a meeting in the same physical space; people may come into contact with ideas and things that originate in a culture that is not in direct proximity to them. Interculturality may be said to take place when people come into contact with cultural otherness. At that point they become aware that they have been *taking for granted* certain perceptions of reality shared by their own group, that is, that these perceptions are not universal but conventional, generated by their own environment. The responses to this realization may be defensive, adaptive, or coexistential, but whatever form they assume, intercultural relationships are one of the most dynamic forces driving historical change.

Considering that today's relentless and often unpredictable advances of globalization make the understanding of the intercultural process a major intellectual challenge of our time, it is rather surprising that our knowledge of its inner mechanisms remains relatively modest. It is also demonstrably fragmented, with its subfields separated by institutionalized boundaries and methodological particularities of academic disciplines. This despite the fact that a half century of critique of the concept of culture has made significant contributions, including fore-grounding ethnocentrism as a source of research bias across disciplines; incorporating power into cultural studies; and expanding scholarship on cultures beyond nationally or ethno-linguistically defined groups. Likewise, study of processes that transcend group divisions, such as globalization, empire, and neocolonialism, has flourished. Meanwhile, our understanding of the totality of the intercultural process has not kept pace. Intercultural studies are due for reflection, refinement, and systematization. It is not a small undertaking as it requires scholars to cross their own cultural boundaries, move beyond the entrenched paradigms of their disciplines, and—probably the most demanding task—acquire a deep awareness of not only their own epistemological categories but also those of the diverse actors within the intercultural relationship that is being interpreted. Few academics are trained to take up all these errands.

On the other hand, intercultural studies today are aided by the fact that over the past few decades scholarship on culture has become much less parochial and substantially more sophisticated. It is true that it is also philosophically more differentiated than ever, but the positive result of this heterogeneity is that scholars across the world are today light years away from attitudes to the cultural Other epitomized half a century ago in the remark of Hugh Trevor-Roper, a prominent historian of Europe and Britain, who referred to the cultures of certain non-Western societies as "the unedifying gyrations of barbarous tribes in picturesque but irrelevant corners of the globe."[1] Not only Western academics today are much less likely to universalize Western categories of thinking, but also scholars in postcolonial countries are ready to move beyond merely rebuffing such universalizing attitudes—painfully associated with imperialism—and are now recognizing that intercultural misunderstandings are not exclusive to colonizers but a global phenomenon linked to the very nature of cultural identities. A genuine recognition of the peculiarities of each culture's historical formation and of the unique arsenal of meanings that it attaches to people's experience of reality is more widespread across the global community of scholars than ever. There is also the growing realization that although no discipline alone can answer the questions that arise from intercultural encounters, the notion of intercultural studies is big enough to comfortably include most disciplines.

One of the most important arguments for the study of interculturality—which is both a field and an analytical concept—is that it carries substantial intellectual rewards. Perhaps the greatest one of them is that it generates new knowledge. It does so because an encounter between different cultures, as well as an encounter between the scholar and the object of study located in a distinct culture, sets off a phenomenon akin to an act of magic that transforms the stage for all actors. Until the wand of otherness is waved and the familiar fixedness of everyone's culture is thereby dented, people view much of the reality around them—social structure, authority, moral values, notions of taste and beauty, propriety of behavior—as ordinary, natural, and largely unquestioned, "the way things ought to be." They see these "things" as meaningful in themselves. The magic wand exposes these received understandings to be historical, constructed, imaginary, and conventional—prompting creative reflections and innovative inquiries.[2] Common, everyday meanings and academic analytical categories—so deeply naturalized by social practice that they had turned into givens—become sufficiently relativized to generate fresh questions. In a way, this resembles debates among disagreeing parties in a democracy; they help the system to innovate, while a state with one-party rule predictably gravitates toward conformity. Just as education that exposes students only to their own kind is not a very productive one, scholarship that focuses only on self-defined groups does not serve its purpose well.

A comparison to the mechanism of humor may be helpful in explaining this process of triggering innovation. The comical typically occurs when a description of some phenomenon or situation unexpectedly departs from a widely accepted norm. This departure disrupts a commonly practiced—and usually taken for granted—pattern of behavior. It may be a violation of such norms as a "proper" use of language, ways of dressing considered appropriate for one's age, or rules of commonsensical logic. Such violations may be achieved by means of distorting, exaggerating, or contradicting the existing, conventionalized perceptions of reality. The ensuing surprise is more than just a comical episode, even if the reaction (laughter) is a spontaneous, not reflexive, response to a new and surprising association or situation. It is also an epistemological fact. It has cognitive implications because it verifies reality by telling us something new about it. By pointing out contradictions and paradoxes, and thus forcing us to reflect and take a position, this new angle may suggest novel interpretations or uncover unknown attributes of things and people we thought we knew. It may reveal that which is not visible in daily life such as, for instance, elements of the absurd in things that were considered sound and sensible. After all, absurdity occurs when customary order is unsettled, a situation that may produce a comical effect, but it may also breed deep and genuine warning bells. Humor, of course, is not only disruptive; it can also play a conservative role (and in that it also resembles encounters with otherness) when it serves to censure those who violate habitual norms. By ridiculing the transgressors, it helps *reproduce and maintain* the established, distinctive features of a given culture by sustaining people's confidence in communally shared beliefs. However, ridicule is a two-edged sword. It can also be a very powerful political tool for change. This two-sidedness is illustrated by the fact that once people become *used to* previously transgressive (and thus comical) behaviors, these behaviors become "normal" and their humorous capacity evaporates—just as otherness fades away once it becomes domesticated by a culture.[3]

New questions posed by the intercultural—both for historical actors and for academic investigators—require new ways of resolving them, and this necessity can have an immensely revitalizing effect on academic disciplines. For instance, scholars continually talk about the need for expanding horizons through interdisciplinarity, but the reality is that most of them are deeply imbedded in traditional disciplinary specializations where they are held captive by entrenched methodologies and interpretative models. At the same time, they are also discouraged from trespassing on the territories of others by a system of departments that handle research plans, evaluations, tenure, and promotions—usually decided by older, tenured members that tend to be firmly committed to the established paradigms. However, those who take up intercultural studies soon find that they simply must venture outside of their castles in order to grasp the complex, multileveled phenomenon they are studying. They are among the first to appreciate that culture is not simply one of the *dimensions* of old disciplinary fields like political science, economics, or history but a fundamental reality underlying all those fields.

The intercultural process emerges in its full beauty as a vital dynamic of human history when scholarship takes a long-term perspective. Confrontations with otherness bring intellectual ferment, creative tensions, and innovative adaptations—all triggers of culture change. Time flows differently for isolated cultures, able to preserve their localism and their sense of permanence, and for cultures involved in significant encounters with the Other that energize them to alter their ways and grow. An accompanying benefit to the scholar studying this process is its inherent demand for a neutral stance. Much ink has been spilled on the need for objectivity and for suspending one's biases, but doing intercultural studies effectively without such capabilities is practically impossible. Taking sides or injecting the interpreter's ideology all but precludes access to the lived world of otherness.

To successfully chart all these characteristics of interculturality we need a sound interpretive scaffolding that would reveal the intricate nature of this phenomenon. It is an area that begs for theoretical preparedness; without it, we are mostly walking blindfolded. First, epistemological self-awareness of the investigator is a precondition of any success. A scholar who sees himself as a tourist in a foreign land, and not a foreigner in someone's homeland, faces intractable barriers. Second, theoretical knowledge of disciplines other than one's own is crucial because culture cannot be contained within any one discipline, and different conceptual languages are needed to explain the various levels at which actors simultaneously live. Third, we should bear in mind that cultures are primarily local, and that too abstract a language used to describe them cannot capture that localism. Finally, it would not hurt to remember that theories of how culture works are not necessary for it to work. Attention to the *practice* of culture is essential if we are to avoid wasting time puzzling over the issue of why people behave in ways that do not fit *our* theoretical categories, or—worse—trying to force them into these categories. Theory is a result of observing practice, but practice is not applied theory.

There is one more point to be aware of when demarcating intercultural studies as a new discipline: it should not be confused with comparative studies. The latter, still a familiar presence in political science, literary criticism and global history, compare distant, often unconnected societies, groups, and cultures in search of similarities and differences that would generate broader conclusions and enrich the understanding of human practices across the world. Specialists in these areas do not always have training in the theory of culture, which explains why they so often treat it as an supplementary aspect of the subjects being compared (such as, for instance, foreign policy or law enforcement institutions), and not a fundamental context of social life.[4] Consequently, generalized conclusions stemming from such comparative analyses often neglect an important area. For instance, in detecting similarities between policing practices in two distinct countries, they do not sufficiently take into account the fact that they carry very different meanings within their respective societies. On top of the hazards posed by such surface comparisons, there is also the problem that some of the scholar's own categories used in the comparative analysis originate from yet another, third, cultural context. The effect is that the larger "patterns" that are discovered in such studies are not infrequently so removed from the local contexts that they can be said to reside mainly in the mind of the discoverer.[5]

## II

For intercultural studies to bring intellectual dividends, its key analytical category—culture—must be well understood. Since its meaning is highly contested across disciplines, some reflection on its ontology should be a starting point toward putting together a usable definition. The spectrum of interpretations extends from culture as a fixed design, a key that opens all investigative locks, to a postmodern, fluctuating assortment of individual communicative acts.

The fixed design model derives from the classic mid-nineteenth-century works of Jacob Burkhardt, and assumes that culture is a relatively static structure, a set of values that tells its members what to do and how to think, and that it is internally coherent. Such an essentialized concept of culture—an emblematic error of modernity—does not fully take into account that culture is a man-made entity, and that people are active agents, continuously involved in categorizing, permitting, prohibiting, and reorganizing—in short, making changes. Static and timeless understandings of culture—and for that matter its major ingredients such as race, class, or ethnicity—are simply ahistorical. Culture does not have to be coherent to create order in the minds of people. It builds this harmony mainly by means of fictions, symbols, and representations, not by objective descriptions of factual reality. This is why more recent studies have abandoned viewing it as a consistent, self-contained system, and have focused instead on how it constructs its *meanings*.

In the first half of the twentieth century, functional definitions of culture continued the main tenets of Burkhardt's approach by focusing on its ability to integrate societies and to reproduce itself over long periods of time. Less attention was paid to how culture changed and how different groups within society related to it, and more to how its various ingredients served to unite and bond people. In the 1960s, with the coming of the linguistic turn and postmodern epistemology, academic attention shifted from unity and stability to change, fluidity and internal differentiation within cultures. Earlier approaches such as those of Oswald Spengler or Arnold Toynbee—based on macro-scale distinctions between "civilizations"—came to be seen as seriously oversimplified. And yet, the essentializing tradition did not die, and was taken up by several recent scholars. Perhaps the most conspicuous among them has been Samuel P. Huntington, who warned against a clash of civilizations threatening the globe, and promoted the recognition of civilizational distinctions as the best security policy. But even if he was right about the formidable potential of culture to create conflict and tensions, and about the ineffectuality of forced nation-building by the Western powers, the problems of old functionalism resurfaced prominently in his work. The seven key "civilizations" he identified were highly abstract as categories, and suffered from ahistorical fixity.[6] In a similar vein, Francis Fukuyama, reacting to the collapse of the Soviet Union, concluded that the Western system would become the reigning model across the globe, implying that non-Western cultures will evolve accordingly (he has since changed his mind on that point).[7]

The demise of functionalism left the academic arena to views of culture deriving from linguistic and postmodern philosophies. The main stress now shifted to individual "performances" and particular, subjective construction of meaning. Claims to objectivity were met with skepticism as naïve. The functionalist emphasis on integration was criticized for legitimizing power relations, underestimating conflict, and ignoring class inequalities. In its more far-reaching versions, this approach claimed that there are as many meanings of a given text as there are readers.[8] Following this logic, culture cannot legitimately be said to exist, as it is only a collection of stories about one's own social group. To an extent, postmodern skepticism toward the structuralist quest for totalizing concepts and unifying truths has been very valuable. It has directed our interest toward such issues as the construction of reality and symbolic communication, away from the faith that words are mirror images of objective reality, and from concepts of homogeneous national identities with their oversimplified determinism and insufficient allowance for human agency. It drew our attention to the fact that meanings attached by people to reality are neither transparent nor knowable through people's supposedly "objective" interests. It also allowed us to understand better that even within the same culture there are many different ways of experiencing reality, depending on people's membership in different social classes and groups. Identities too are not fixed but fluid and pluralistic; people can hold several, depending on ethnicity, profession, family, and a myriad other factors.[9] All these shifts in thinking about culture have contributed to discrediting the determinism of presumably timeless "laws" and patterns of human history, so ubiquitous from Karl Marx to Claude Levi-Strauss.

But just as the earlier theories made cultures more homogeneous than they are, the postmodern approach may have swung the pendulum too far in the opposite direction and relativized them more than their capability to be relativistic. Some scholars are eager to dismiss the "old and tired concept of culture" when they discover that culture is "imagined" and "not the truth" (something that carries no surprise for historians, for whom such understanding has for long been a basic tenet of their craft).[10] The trouble with the tendency to absolutize contingency in culture is that it leaves out the collectively shaped—and thus to a significant degree *structured and unifying*—context of one's individual and "subjective" beliefs. Even the presumably detached, cosmopolitan and self-reflexive academic who practices such thinking is not able to fully separate from the various categories, norms, ideologies, beliefs and values that structure his interpretation, whether he is aware of them or not. These categories did not originate deus ex machina from the investigators' own mind; they had mostly been absorbed from culture's *historically* developed social, institutional, professional, religious, and other repositories, collectively co-constructed by large groups of actors over time.[11] A notable shortcoming of the postmodern and postcolonial writing has been the belief that we can explain culture, including political and historical patterns, by perusing literary and critical publications only.

A more sociological—and more usable for a wide spectrum of disciplines—view of culture, put forward by British theorist Terry Eagleton, is that it is who people believe they are and what they live for. In this view, culture supplies a shared model for interpreting the meaning of life. In other words, it makes sense of people's existence.[12] It creates a purposeful order for people to navigate a chaotic world. These beliefs are deeply subjective but they are experienced as natural reality. This reality—constituted and co-constructed in the process of communication—should concern us as the subject of our study, and not the question whether it is a reflection of scientistically understood "objective reality." It is found at the core of all cultures, whether those of small professional groups or large societies. Some postmodern scholars, still haunted by the positivist criterion of objective truth, arrive at an unworkable conclusion that because cultures are subjective, imagined, and fluid (and therefore do not represent "the truth"), they do not exist. It is unworkable because if people accept cultural reality as naturally true, and guide their behavior accordingly, its characteristics are sufficiently factual to qualify for existential status. This is particularly important to grasp when studying interculturality because constructed reality may be subjective but it is not capricious, haphazard or an attribute of individuals. On the contrary, it is deeply rooted in long-term, collective experiences of the group.

The storehouse of categories with which people classify and make sense of their life-world is provided by language. Its rootedness in the past is reflected in the fact that one culture's language is not fully translatable into another culture's language because the intricate web of meanings of every speech act had been created by long-term, past experiences peculiar to the group involved. As Alfred Schutz sagely put it, to learn another language truly successfully "one must have written love letters in it; one has to know how to pray and curse in it and how to say things with every shade appropriate to the addressee and the situation."[13] In a sense, responses to life situations—especially to the novelty of otherness—resemble a Rorschach test; people typically interpret them by reaching into the available, preexisting arsenal of categories and concepts. In other words, their acts are subjective, but they think subjectively with acquired, collective sociocultural categories and conventions of interpreting the world that *precede* their individual interpretations. The actor thus shapes the interpretation of reality around him, but this shaping is to a great extent constructed with the norms and precepts drawn from his culture's collective repository. Neither the culture nor the actor determines the meaning of reality independently.

This is precisely why the debate about the relativism of culture— rooted in the traditional opposition between purportedly objective, scientific truth and subjectivism—is not particularly useful for understanding interculturality, and should not concern us too much. Stanley Fish may have gone too far in universalizing the aprioristic nature of belief systems (for which he has been castigated by Terry Eagleton), but his point that no one is able to fully separate oneself from one's norms and categories of thinking—internalized over time from one's social group—is sound.[14] There are at least three good reasons why it is accurate: these norms typically become naturalized, they are then held as taken-for-granted truths, and as such they are used mostly prereflexively. When William Penn argued that society must be ordered hierarchically because it is the same pattern we see in nature, his certainty was unequivocal. He was not saying "I tentatively think that hierarchy ought to exist in society."[15] He was saying "this norm exists naturally among people just as it exists among animals and planets; it is part of who we are." For a student of seventeenth-century Quaker culture, there is no need to ponder whether Penn's statement is a "naïve concept of reality." Such a dismissal presupposes that, unlike Penn, the investigator stands for objective reality, even though his own cultural categories have fashioned his narrative in the same way as Penn's categories fashioned his. Even if we agree that absolutely knowable reality is not accessible, we can still happily study—in nonnaïve ways—diverse versions of reality without losing sight of certain more generalized, durable, and systemic patterns. Some scholars have usefully suggested that this can best be done by making an effort to distinguish the informative from the persuasive and the ideological in texts.[16] To achieve this, it is important not to focus, as is so often done, exclusively on the communicative sphere and speech acts, to the point of excluding socioeconomic factors from the analysis of cultures.

In light of the above, a question inevitably arises: what to do with the fact that preexisting, shared meanings ("culture") influence society, but at the same time people are active agents who not only use but also change these meanings? One of the most fruitful approaches to this phenomenon has been proposed by Anthony Giddens, who sees social practice as a combination of two forces: cultural structures that channel and guide people's actions, and individually initiated actions that are nevertheless constrained by cultural structures.[17] Reality is thus constantly constituted by people who actively and creatively perform meaningful acts, but these acts are neither entirely individual nor entirely determined by the culture. They are rooted in collective history that produced cultural structures (norms, forms of power, categories of thinking, social status, gender roles, etc.). These individual acts are not in an antagonistic relationship to the established structures; on the contrary, such acts are enabled and legitimized by them. Scholars studying an intercultural relationship would thus be engaging with three realms: they would be using their own categories to interpret a scene where two other worlds are already interpreting each other by means of their own categories. Put differently, the scholar's pre-assumptions mediate in constructing his two investigated subjects, who, upon their mutual encounter, had already constructed each other with the help of *their* pre-assumptions. Without an acute awareness of this convergence of three different metalanguages and its interpretive consequences, scholarship on interculturality cannot be effective.

Prejudgments construct meanings, and without proper attention to meanings that human groups ascribe to their lives the intercultural process is impossible to capture. The trouble with the current, atomized view that a cultural act has as many meanings as there are readers is that it sidelines an area of inquiry that is crucial to accessing the significance of this very act—the context of people's communicative sphere—beliefs and views of world order that *generate* meanings. A banknote is just a piece of paper unless people believe that it represents value that can be used in transactions. A flag is just a piece of cloth unless people collectively perceive it as a symbol of their state or nation or group. Cultures exist through symbolic representations. In order to carry meaning, these representations first have to be shared, not individually originated. A single person on a desert island cannot construct money, because money operates as a social relation. People gradually acquire such shared understandings of reality by mutual communication. This hermeneutically oriented understanding of culture—first spelled out by Martin Heidegger and later developed by Hans Gadamer—has the virtue of being both intellectually productive and usable by a variety of disciplines, a point that prominently applies to intercultural studies.[18]

The above suggests that the presumed antagonism between stability (Burkhardt, functionalists) and fluidity (postmodernism, performance theory) of culture is a red herring. Culture is not an outside, fixed system that guides people's behavior, and can be reduced to a set of abstract rules, but a dynamic phenomenon. It exists as a form of social discourse and as such is continually transforming itself as people oscillate between the received habits and the practical needs of their environment. It is multilayered and shifting, but it also contains distinctive clusters of shared traits that are structured and fairly durable. People are neither socially determined robots, nor do they merely follow culture's dictates; they are constantly *improvising* to balance contingency and convention.

The lasting power of conventions lay in the fact that they represent people's distinctive identities, historically derived from their *unique and collective experiences*. Furthermore, cultures naturally seek structure and coherence because their raison d'être is to make sense of the world and to create order. This does not mean that they are consistent, homogeneous, bounded, or permanent, only that they seek stability by instituting customary norms of thinking about the world. This historical component of culture has a significant integrating capacity that should not be taken lightly. Downplaying it makes behavior that is culturally driven appear more individual and subjective than it actually is. Just as the fact that cultural differences exist does not negate certain traits that human beings have in common, the fact that some of people's experiences are culturally determined does not mean that all their experiences are. By the same token, just because cultures are fluid and constantly change does not mean that they do not contain longlasting, shared attributes. This is why in studying them a historical dimension is just as indispensable as an anthropological one. Greg Dening of the Melbourne School of history once observed that the historian gives voice to the dead, and the interculturalist gives voice to the Other. Both share an acute awareness that the strangers they write about exist independently of our knowing about them.[19]

# III

Two further points that are crucial to any research on interculturality need to be emphasized. The first is that people do not naturally take an intercultural perspective. On the contrary, they naturally take an indigenous, ethnocentric perspective. People do not "misread" otherness; to call it misreading already presupposes an alternative possibility of "reading" it properly, but people typically do not have the knowledge to do so. Pierre Bourdieu has once pointed out that all recognitions are to some degree mis-recognitions because no one is able to *fully* see the other objectively, outside of one's own knowledge.[20] The second point to note is that no social acts are initially intercultural. Of the two distinct groups gazing at each other on their first meeting, each is interpreting the other in terms of its own culture. Their encounters only assume the attributes of intercultural facts when subjected to intercultural analysis.[21]

This is important for appreciating the fact that for most people, the experience of life is primarily local. People do not live in the world. They live in *their* societies, communities, professional groups, and kinship networks.[22] No one has a global epistemological capability. As Alfred Schutz has shown, people inherently seek for themselves a cultural home, a place where they can take shelter in familiarity, typicality, acceptance, and belonging, and where they can enjoy the reassuring comforts of shared, taken-for-granted meanings.[23] Everyday, local life is the central reality for them, because it is most tangible, immediate, and recognizable. Early modern Englishmen who for the first time observed the customs of East coast American Indians did not feel they were in an intercultural relationship; instead they saw these customs as "absurd and ridiculous."[24] Even a moment's reflection must lead us to the conclusion that such a perspective on cultural strangers is far from being a relic of the past. In today's world, however much interconnected by ubiquitous electronic media, people still live primarily in their home cultures. It is not very likely that a Nairobi native can wake up one day and say "I no longer have any links to Kenya, I now feel I belong in Norway." Cultural universals are few, and upon close examination they usually turn out to be other people's previously local beliefs and ways—adopted, domesticated, and converted into normalness by the receiving group. This new normalness, however, first had to be internally negotiated through interactions and conversations among its members who filtered it through their preexisting, locally shaped frameworks of typicality, rationality, and expectations.

This brings us to one of the most frequently discussed but also most routinely misunderstood issues involving interactions between different cultures—the so-called ethnocentricity that people display toward those not of their own kind. The term is fairly imprecise and comprises attitudes ranging from plain hostility and intolerance to "misreading" other people by interpreting them strictly in terms of one's own cultural norms (usually by stressing a *lack* of such norms among the Other). It is most frequently used in a morally charged sense as an indicator of a failure to treat others on their own terms and to value them equally as fellow human beings. In this approach, culture emerges as a prison of sorts that hems people in its web of meanings, and engenders bias that *prevents* them from appreciating those who are different (as if such appreciation were a *natural* course of things, only thwarted by cultural insularity). A prominent example can be found in the writing of Tzvetan Todorov, who, having reconstructed the semiotic access that Hernando Cortez had gained into the Aztec worldviews, condemned him sharply for having "never abandoned" his own culture's self-evident assumptions of normativity.[25] In a similar vein, Kenneth A. Lockridge, writing on the eighteenth-century colonial Virginia planter William Byrd II, deplored his tireless pursuit of metropolitan, English cultural norms, and concluded that it was an example of culture serving as a restraining "cage."[26]

On closer reflection, however, ethnocentrism appears to be neither a cage nor an anomaly. It is not merely an undesirable characteristic overlaid on a group's culture when it confronts difference. It is intrinsic to culture. While in its more extreme forms it may surface as aggression, racism, or political supremacy, it represents the historically embedded, preconscious, taken-for-granted perspective that enables people to make sense of reality. No one can simply leave behind these deeply ingrained tools of understanding the world, as one would escape from a cage. The interpretation that people give to a case of otherness—or to any text, for that matter—is neither fixed nor determined by culture (in fact, it varies within cultures and sub-cultures, depending on such factors as, for instance, gender or class), but it is initially *made possible* by the preexisting tools absorbed from the social environment.[27] Understood this way, a degree of ethnocentrism (or prejudice, in its etymological sense derived from Latin *prejudicium*, a judgment formed in advance) is a *prerequisite* of recognizing and understanding the world, a kind of basic epistemological toolbox. This is not to say that such recognitions and understandings are not distorted. On the contrary, they are *always* distorted (prejudiced) because nobody holds prejudgments that are timeless or universal.

Subjective prejudgments are the lifeblood of the intercultural process, and a little ethnocentricity is not necessarily a dangerous thing.

Too much ethnocentricity, however, can be hazardous—not only to relations between different peoples but also to the health of scholarship. In the latter case, it often takes the form of presentism. The resulting distortions are especially noticeable in studies of past cultures, where actors in distant centuries are censured for not conforming to the values or ideology held by the historian (even as they do conform to the conventions and expectations of the actor's contemporaries).[28] Putting aside the inadvertently humorous aspect of presenting the *conventional* behavior of these actors as an aberration, it does illustrate nicely the enormous power of taken-for-granted prejudgments over our attempts to reconstruct other people's reality. Some scholars have gone to great lengths to devise a theoretical apparatus to prevent such distortions. For instance, German historian of culture Jörn Rüsen has proposed a sophisticated model of "universal history rooted in a concept of humankind" that would prevent methodological ethnocentrism by stressing normative equality rather than asymmetrical interpretations, contingency and discontinuity rather than teleological continuity, and polycentric approaches rather than centralized perspectives.[29] These are all laudable efforts, but one should not lose sight of two things: that theoretical constructions of their cultures by present-day academics were not on the minds of the people who populated those past cultures (while their inherently "ethnocentric" perspectives were), and that all people, including scholars, have and always will continue to harbor prejudgments rooted in their *own* experiences. In the case of scholars, an additional obstacle to accessing the worldviews of past actors they are studying is the fact that the interpreter, *unlike the actor*, is often aware of the outcome of the actor's actions, and so the interpreter's perspective tends to be more unified and comprehensive. A keen awareness of the ubiquitous and stealthy presence of such prejudgments must be at the very top of the interculturalist's toolbox.

Finally, an aspect of ethnocentricity that is often obscured is that it can be beneficial when it helps to preserve diverse cultural identities. These identities should be protected not only because people have a right to uphold their own values (even if they do not agree with the values of other groups) but, more importantly, because attempts to eradicate cultural identities peculiar to individual groups and societies in the name of some sort of global homogeneity can be perilous. Such unity would necessarily have to be based on an idea of harmony peculiar to some, but alien to others. It would have to be achieved by an imposition of the values of some cultures at the expense of other cultures, a practice eerily resembling neocolonialism. Forced homogeneity is a more likely source of conflict than the coexistence of diverse, even incompatible, cultures because it tends to generate a vicious cycle of authoritarianism and resistance.

## IV

One general postulate for students of interculturality that emerges from the foregoing lines of argument is that they must make an effort to cope with a major interpretative issue: the yawning gap between the current academic approaches that tend to de-essentialize culture, and the lived world of people's everyday existence where essentializing cultural tenets is crucial to making sense of life. How to accurately capture the actors' commonsensical, shared assumptions that are deemed truths, even absolute ones, in the language of relativism? After all, the actor is an insider and the scholar is an outsider; the latter has only a modest capability to *experience the subjectivity* of the former, even if his professed goal is to do just that. It stands to reason that to achieve any success, he must attempt to put himself in the same commonsensical mode of thinking as the actor who is being studied. Yet, the currently prevailing analytical categories strongly advocate de-essentializing the actor's culture, making the scholar's attempts to capture it difficult, if not problematic.

The above problem is not just the result of the well-known difference between academic, theory-infused knowledge and practical, everyday, "commonsensical" knowledge. It is also in part a by-product of certain distinctive features of the academic sub-culture. There is ample evidence in history that intellectuals are often the first to break with their group's *inside* knowledge and become open to adapting "foreign" ways. For instance, Hsu Chi-yü, a nineteenth-century Chinese writer and provincial governor, at first subscribed to the locally prevalent view of Westerners as contemptible "barbarians" with "unfathomable" behavior. But having come into prolonged contact with them in Canton and Fukien, he wrote a book about the non-Chinese world, *Ying-huan chih-lueh* (1848), in which he conspicuously transcended his former epistemological insularity, and not only described the technological and commercial advantages of the Western world but also the consequences of its expanding power for China's place in global politics. He was well ahead of his compatriots; it took a long time before his views became widely shared.[30] Academics are by nature inclined to have more distance to their own sociocultural reality and to be more cosmopolitan than others. In postmodern, Western societies like the United States they, like many others, confidently "shop" for their needs among many options, from cuisines and dress styles to churches, without being overly reliant on conventions. The result is that they at times have difficulty appreciating just how powerful is the hold of traditional culture on ordinary people (both at home and abroad), how much they depend on their group for identity, and how high the cost of noncompliance with established norms may be.[31] Extending one's own outlook to all people can blur the investigator's gaze in ways that are not immediately apparent, and lead to serious misconstructions of other cultures. It is not infrequent that one comes across a study premised on extending to the whole world the concept of a "postmodern individual," who is no longer clear as to where he belongs because culture has become so fluid that it practically "evaporated." It is a view that in its de-essentializing zeal itself essentializes one perspective—that from a Western ivory tower.[32]

This gap between abstract academic theorizing about culture's intangibility to the point of its nonexistence and the fundamental essentialism and timelessness of lived, grassroots cultures remains a gray area of scholarship that the emerging field of intercultural studies must address. Instead of belatedly continuing to spend so much energy on invalidating the fixity of cultures—a genuine problem when it was still a rigid given—it would be more productive to focus on the fact that it is *fictions* that are the most solid—and, accordingly, quite durably fixed—building blocks of culture. Their durability is nourished by the need for stable categories that enable people to fashion an orderly world. Many longstanding organizations, institutions, and political parties are not only founded on fictions, but would not even exist without them. Whole classes of people widely recognized as such today did not have a presence in the public mind until they came to be represented by their spokesmen as groups whose members supposedly possessed certain essentialized attributes—a particular worldview, a political agenda, a common interest, or a practiced trade. These otherwise fictional entities—"the working class," "the trade union," "the nation"—do not exist as mere speech acts, perceptions, or metaphors of human experiences, but are firmly linked to socioeconomic circumstances, and actually make group *action* possible.

# V

To study the intercultural is to study difference, and difference is not a product of the present. Assumptions and beliefs that have achieved the status of taken-for-grantedness are the outcome of history. They have been instituted by past experiences of peoples or groups. The flaw of the positivist, rational choice theory lay in the assumption that Reason—presumably universal—has a primary role in affecting behavior as it reacts to various individual situations that demand resolution. In reality, Reason's ability to surmount and displace historically established and mainly prereflexive knowledge is much more limited. Conventionalized knowledge is relished and defended because it is a source of order. The traditional juxtaposition of such supposedly "irrational" knowledge and the logic of "objective" Reason does not contribute much to our understanding of the former. Instead, it prevents us from fully appreciating the fact that assumptions and beliefs internalized from the society or group *enable* one's consciousness by providing explanatory strategies of responding to the world.

If we can agree on this, we should be cautious about two analytical models in the humanities and social sciences: those that underplay the epistemological role of conventionalized prejudgments, and those that make light of the continuous changeability, multidimensionality, and hybridity of culture. The two most common are the *totalizing* framework, and the approach ascribing primacy to the *political* aspects of culture.

Poststructuralist, neo-Marxist, class, race, gender, postcolonial, and hegemony studies have all employed these models to a smaller or greater extent, guiding much of scholarship toward interpretations based on often overly *universalized*, oppositional relationships between large, *politically* defined groups. Because such macro-scale categories not infrequently come across as durable, even timeless, structures that merely resurface in different times and places, they make slowly accruing, grassroots-level cultural change less noticeable. More importantly, because they typically insist on categorizing fragments of society into antagonistic segments, they make interactions, exchanges, adaptations, borrowings, and hybridity among these segments barely visible, even though such crossings and transfers are widespread and substantial, rather than exceptional. For instance, people may identify with a trans-national religious group as well as with their local ethnic group. Immigrants may hold two cultural identities simultaneously. Social praxis cuts across macro categories. The antagonistic model may work well for revealing power relations, but it is not very efficient in interpreting interculturality. This is not to say that cultural domination or class conflict are not important as analytical categories, only that they are never total, the dominated are never merely passive actors, and interactions between the dominant and the subaltern are never a one-way street. Adopting an intercultural per-spective provides an excellent opportunity to move beyond the reduc-tionism of traditional, totalizing models.

One caveat is in order here. Although large-scale categories like power relations cannot explain culture, they make sense when cultural capital is institutionalized by the rulers to facilitate domination over others. For instance, John Davis, a mid-nineteenth-century East India Company official in China, noted with astonishment how effectively the government of Canton exploited traditional prejudices against Europeans, calling on the Chinese to "rule barbarians by misrule, like beasts and not like native subjects" and to treat them "as if they were really a degraded order of beings."[33] Yet, a view of this episode through a large-scale prism such as the structure of power relations alone, without attention to the complex historical genesis of Chinese cultural identity and perceptions of outsiders, simply cannot offer a full explanation.

Another area where the Innovative promise of interculturality may yield productive results lies in its potential to revitalize the traditional understanding of multiculturalism. The original goal of multicultural-ism was to recognize and promote the value of diversity, and to pro-tect ethnic groups against nativism, nationalism, and other forms of cultural domination by majorities. It put faith in cultural pluralism as a means of strengthening liberal democracy, just as liberal democracy, by recognizing and accommodating political interests of minorities, offers equality of citizenship. The hope was that removing the pres-sure to assimilate will in time result in greater unity through shared civic values. In retrospect, however, these worthy goals have pro-duced unintended consequences. Steady emphasis of public discourse on separateness did little to encourage breaking down the barriers of difference. Politicians exacerbated this problem by practicing identity politics that artificially homogenize and stereotype group members in order to mobilize electorates. Furthermore, the focus on indefinitely sheltering and preserving group identities suggests that such identities are static rather than dynamic, an ahistorical emphasis that disregards the fact that they are not fixed and cannot be enduringly preserved because they are constantly modified by encounters with outside reali-ties. It also tends to draw attention away from an impartial study of cultural mixing and transfers, processes that have taken place even under the most oppressive systems, such as colonialism or slavery, and in today's globalizing world have accelerated exponentially.

Many of these dilemmas can be addressed by a new and vigorous emphasis on interculturality in public discourse. There is an urgent need for a common conceptual language that is not based solely on the experiences of one's own group, that underscores mutual dependency and shared interests, and that fosters responsibility to the whole society rather than only to one's own sociocultural sphere. Interculturalism can provide such a language because it requires openness and is focused on dialogue and interaction. This is why educational systems are increasingly recognizing the fact that exposing students only to their own kind does not encourage a deeper acceptance of cultural diversity, and are introducing appropriate changes, usually under the broad rubric of "internationalization." Some scholars, such as Kwame Anthony Appiah, have concluded that traditional multiculturalism has reached a point where it "often designates the disease it purports to cure," and propose replacing it with an enlightened and democratic "cosmopolitanism" that encourages respect for difference. One might note, however, that in charting this promising and open-minded vision Appiah engages in a bit of wishful thinking in assuming that different cultures have enough *in common*—especially shared moral standards—that "cosmopolitan curiosity" will eventually lead them to learn more about things foreign. In reality, the often seemingly similar standards carry different meanings in different cultures. For an academic philosopher focused on theory, the Other may be merely an "imaginary stranger," but for people at grassroots level, as world news reports remind us daily, the strangeness is not only real—subjectively, to be sure—but it is also an important tool of affirming their own, local identity. It would therefore seem that, to be effective, cosmopolitanism should not be conceived as an alternative to localism (just as it should not be envisioned in terms of homogenized global unity, where the great diversity of humans would be centrally ruled by a few). It is important to realize that like interculturality, cosmopolitanism—whether based on universalistic morals or Kantian common humanity—does not come naturally. Appiah rightly emphasizes that it has to be dynamically promoted and actively constructed by people in real interactions and conversations across borderlands created by cultural disparities.[34] Only then will they come to an understanding that everyone is simultaneously a local and a stranger. It is in this sense that the study of interculturality can and should serve as a gateway to a future global community that has learned to live with difference.

# VI

The 13 essays that follow reflect on the various facets of interculturality identified above. Michael D. Barber discusses the phenomenology of cultural presuppositions, and uses humor to illustrate the essentialism of such prejudgments in interracial relations. Reflecting on the role of mobility as it relates to interculturality in studies of religions, Paul Kollman proposes several theses: on the impact of metaphorical mobility, on the struggle between locatedness in a sacred center and the idealization of intercultural mobility, and on adaptations of global religions to local identities. Teruyuki Tsuji examines the unsettled issue of reconciling ethnography and historiography in order to illustrate the value of a historicized ethnographic approach for bridging the enduring chasm between theory and lived culture. Brien K. Ashdown, Judith L. Gibbons, and Yetilú de Baessa assess the value of social identity theory and intergroup contact theory with respect to interethnic ethnic relations in Guatemala. Focusing on the knotted cord as a symbolic representation invoking memories of the Pueblo Revolt of 1680, Tracy Brown shows how it contributed to the perpetuation of a space of trauma among both the Pueblos and the Spaniards well into the late eighteenth century, as they forged collective identities and discourses about themselves and each other centered on the shared threat signified by the cord. William P. Childers considers the inquisitorial visit in sixteenth-century Spain as a laboratory for intercultural dialogue, and for attempts to construct a proto-national, homogeneous, Counter-Reformation identity, different from that of any of the historic social groups in Iberian society. Nilanjana Bardhan and Miriam Sobré-Denton set out to create a concept of cosmopolitanism, translated into the vocabulary of intercultural communication, in order to create a framework for an ethical, global citizenship that moves beyond multiculturalism. Using South Korea as a case study, Mun-Cho Kim proposes a culture-driven theory of globalization, where the logical sequence of the existing economy-driven globalization theory is inverted, as an alternative perspective. He also outlines a cosmopolitan sociology as the frame of analysis to advance this approach. To examine the challenges to interculturality in emerging global cities, Henrik Gert Larsen and Leslie Wolowitz center their attention on electronic media as an ethnographic source, and analyze hundreds of thousands of website posts by Western expatriates in Shanghai to uncover the construction of their attitudes toward the Chinese. Jennifer Hale-Gallardo scrutinizes attempts to incorporate indigenous medicine into the Mexican health care system as a case study of institutionalizing and politicizing the intercultural process. Irmina Wawrzyczek combines tourism studies, media studies, and cultural studies to investigate how British media promotions of tourist destinations in Poland serve as mediators of intercultural contact, and to probe how they impact the knowledge of the Other. Finally, to explore the limitations, motivations, and directions of interculturality as it develops in students of second languages, Kara McBride and Jingyun Gu investigate how language learners construct the meanings of their encounters with another culture, and how cultures are manipulated as they are translated in classrooms.

## NOTES

1. Hugh Trevor-Roper, *The Rise of Christian Europe* (London: Thomas and Hudson, 1965), 9.
2. On similar events that suddenly relativize political structures, see Claude Lefort, *Democracy and Political Theory* (Minneapolis: University of Minnesota Press, 1988), 93.
3. Bohdan Dziemidok, *O komiźmie* [The comical] (Warsaw: KiW, 1967), 131, 33–36.
4. Patrick Chabal and Jean-Pascal Daloz, *Culture Troubles: Politics and the Interpretation of Meaning* (Chicago: University of Chicago Press, 2006).
5. See, for example, Peter Kolchin, *American Slavery and Russian Serfdom* (Cambridge: Belknap, 1987); and Nancy Schoemaker, *A Strange Likeness: Becoming Red and White in Eighteenth-Century North America* (New York: Oxford University Press, 2004).
6. Samuel P. Huntington, *The Clash of Civilizations and the Remaking of World Order* (New York: Simon and Shuster, 1996).
7. Francis Fukuyama, *The End of History and the Last Man* (New York: Avon Books, 1992).
8. Hayden White, *Metahistory: The Historical Imagination in Nineteenth-Century Europe* (Baltimore: Johns Hopkins University Press, 1975).
9. This point is made well by Amartya Sen, *The Argumentative Indian* (London: Allan Lane, 2005), 350.
10. Fred Dervin, "Researching Identity and Interculturality: Moving Away from Methodological Nationalism for Good?" in *Intersecting Identities and Interculturality: Discourse and Practice*, ed. Regis Machart et al. (Newcastle upon Tyne: Cambridge Scholars Publishing, 2013), 10, 16.
11. See Donal Carbaugh, Michael Berry, and Marjatta Nurmikari-Berry, "Coding Personhood through Cultural Terms and Practices: Silence and Quietude as a Finnish 'Natural Way of Being,'" *Journal of Language and Social Psychology*, 25, 3 (2006): 203–220, on how Finns co-construct one of their common cultural traits.
12. Terry Eagleton, *The Idea of Culture* (Oxford: Blackwell, 2000), 131.
13. Alfred Schutz and Arvid Brodersen, *Collected Papers Vol. II: Studies in Social Theory* (The Hague: Martinus Nijhoff, 1976), 101.
14. Stanley Fish, *Is There a Text in This Class? The Authority of Interpretive Communities* (Cambridge: Harvard University Press, 1982). For a critical

commentary on Fish's theories, see Terry Eagleton's review of Stanley Fish, *The Trouble with Principle* in the *London Review of Books*, 22, 7 (2000).

15. William Penn, *Some Fruits of Solitude* (London: T. Sowle, 1706), 91–93.

16. Jerzy Topolski, "A Non-Postmodernist Analysis of Historical Narratives," in *Historiography between Modernism and Postmodernism*, ed. Jerzy Topolski (Amsterdam and Atlanta, GA: Editions Rodopi, 1994), 9.

17. Anthony Giddens, *New Rules for Sociological Method* (London: Hutchinson, 1976).

18. Martin Heidegger, *Being and Time* (New York: Harper & Row, 2008, originally published in German, 1927); Hans Gadamer, "Hermeneutics and Social Science," in *Cultural Hermeneutics* 2 (Dordrecht: D. Reidel Publishing Company, 1975), 307–316.

19. "A Library Sailor: An Interview with Greg Dening," *Limina: A Journal of Cultural and Historical Studies*, 7 (2001): 2.

20. Pierre Bourdieu, *The Logic of Practice* (Stanford: Stanford University Press, 1980), 68.

21. Martine Abdallah-Pretceille (ed.), *Les métamorphoses de l'identité* (Paris: Economica, 2006), 480.

22. On the relation between the local and the global in the case of history, see Wolf Schäfer, "Historical Feasibility and Environmental Reality," in *Conceptualizing Global History*, ed. Bruce Mazlish and Ralph Buultjens (Boulder: Westview Press, 1993), 48–49.

23. Alfred Schutz, "The Stranger: An Essay in Social Psychology," *American Journal of Sociology*, 49, 6 (1944): 499–507.

24. Clayton C. Hall (ed.), "A Character of the Province of Maryland," in *Narratives of Early Maryland, 1633–1684* (New York: Scribner's, 1910), 369.

25. Tzvetan Todorov, *The Conquest of America: The Question of the Other*, trans. Richard Howard (New York: Harper, 1984), 248.

26. Kenneth A. Lockridge, *The Diary and Life of William Byrd II of Virginia, 1674–1744* (New York: W. W. Norton, 1987), 151.

27. Hazard Adams and Leroy Searle (eds.), "Hans Georg Gadamer," in *Critical Theory since 1965* (Tallahassee: Florida State University Press, 1986), 839.

28. For a probe into the interpretative consequences of ahistoricism, see Michal Jan Rozbicki, *Culture and Liberty in the Age of the American Revolution* (Charlottesville: University of Virginia Press, 2011), 17–33.

29. Jörn Rüsen, "How to Overcome Ethnocentrism: Approaches to a Culture of Recognition by History in the Twenty-First Century," *History and Theory*, 43 (2004), 118–129.

30. Fred W. Drake, "A Mid-Nineteenth-Century Discovery of the Non-Chinese World," *Modern Asian Studies*, 6, 2 (1972), 209, 224. I wish to thank Professor John Carroll of the University of Hong Kong for drawing my attention to this source.

31. On identity, see Jessica Abrams, John O'Connor, and Howard Giles, "Identity and Intergroup Communication," in *Cross-Cultural and Intercultural Communication,* ed. Gudykunst (Thousand Oaks: Sage Publications, 2003), 215. On transgressing norms, see Brent T. Ruben, "A System-Theoretic View," in *Intercultural Communication Theory: Current Perspectives,* ed. William B. Gudykunst (Beverly Hills: Sage Publications, 1983), 140.
32. Dervin, *Intersecting Identities and Interculturality,* 20.
33. John Francis Davis, *China: A General Description of that Empire and Its Inhabitants; with the History of Foreign Intercourse Down to the Events which Produced the Dissolution of 1857* (London: John Murray, 1857), vol. 1, 297.
34. Kwame Anthony Appiah, *Cosmopolitanism: Ethics in a World of Strangers* (New York: W. W. Norton, 2006), xiii–xviii, 97–99.

# Part I

## CONCEPTUALIZING
## INTERCULTURALITY

# 1

# APPERCEPTION, THE INFLUENCE OF CULTURE, AND INTERRACIAL HUMOR

## Michael D. Barber

Recent discussions of passive synthesis and genetic and generative phenomenology have revealed a very different Edmund Husserl than the standard one—a new Husserl much more aware of how, prior to reflection and beneath the control of the ego, experiences, and aspects of experience are synthesized in us and social groups and cultures leave their imprint on us. In this chapter, I will explain how apperception in Husserl's view provides a locus in which cultural influences make their entry into our experience. I will focus on how apperception facilitates the "culturalization" of experience in Husserl's *Die Lebenswelt: Auslegungen der vorgegebenen Welt und ihrer Konstitution*.[1] I will describe what apperception is, its development and function in experience, its role in the transmission of culture, and its place in intercultural exchange. I believe that because Husserl recognized how passive-synthetic apperception is pervasively at work in us, he returned over and over again to the importance of phenomenological reduction as a philosophical method for the reflective recovery of what is taken for granted. Finally, to illustrate how apperceptive expectations work in intercultural exchange and to illustrate how humor and intercultural exchange can play a role analogous to reduction in enabling us to appropriate our apperceptive intentionality, I will consider some humorous exchanges between me and an African-American friend, whose cultural background differs from mine. I should add that I take "race" in this essay to be what Anthony Appiah has called a "metonym for culture."[2]

## APPERCEPTION: ITS GENERAL SIGNIFICANCE

Of course, the root of "apperception" involves a combination of "ad" (to) and "perception," and hence apperception signifies all we bring to perception. Husserl calls apperception a "perceiving-to-perceiving perception" that involves a transference of past experience to what is occurring in the present.[3] This idea of apperception as "adding to" perception appears very clearly in a passage in *Die Lebenswelt*:

> It is evident that in this way every concrete life-world experience, as apperception ad-perceiving "meaning-predicates," must contain a kernel content of the perceivable. Correlatively everything of the life-world under its more or less mediate-layered predicates of "valid-for" (meaning predicates) has as the purely perceivable a last substrate.[4]

This passage might lead one to suspect that Husserl begins with a confrontation between the subject and object, with the meaning predicates all on the side of the subject who brings them to bear on an object that is absolutely free of meaning. Such a view, however, would not square with the text of *Die Lebenswelt*, which insists that "In the pre-given world objects are normally outfitted with trusted cultural predicates; they are concrete typical cultural objects."[5] Even to get at "mere nature,"[6] a process of *Abstufung*, de-layering, or *Abbauen*, unbuilding, is needed in which we leave out of sight all subjective meaning-features, feeling and valuing predicates, and anything having to do with how an object stimulates our drives or instincts.[7] By stripping off these meaning-predicates in reflection, one reaches the "pure perceivable," an "ultimate substrate," "pure nature."[8] Ironically, even to get the pure thing, devoid of meaning-predicates, in order to determine how our meaning-predicates are brought to bear on the world or transferred to it in apperception, one has to dismantle through reflection layers of meaning-predicates that have already been bestowed on objects.

For Husserl, apperception, what we bring to the base-level perception of a pure object recovered via a process of *Abbildung*, can depend on the experience of *one* object *one* time, since that experience equips us with meaning-predicates that will be brought to bear when we encounter an object like it in the future. He writes,

> If I recognize a strange animal, I acquire not only a knowledge of this individual as this, which I can always again remember and which I can return to again for perception at my pleasure, renewing my knowledge and proceeding in new directions. As often as later I meet

once again an individual other animal, never seen before, but of the same type, I grasp it in my first look as an animal of this type, that is, I apperceive it with all its properties, which I have actually acquired for myself in the earlier experience, and this apperception occurs wholly immediately through "apperceptive transference" on the ground of analogy.[9]

Consequently, we would have to say that we do not just experience individual objects but grasp them through types that can be applied flexibly to analogous objects in the future, which of course will be like the originally experienced object but different from it in some ways and, therefore, not identical with it.

Furthermore, in some sense, the earlier experience of the animal or any object is not thematically present when I encounter a like animal or object later. In fact, the previous experience can pass out of my thematic focus and assume a place within the nonthematized horizon that will accompany me in future experiences in which I am focused on something else. Husserl describes this horizon, into which a present experience sinks as an "unconscious background"[10]; but in this horizon there are possibilities that eventually can be wakened by experience in the present, that can be relived in intuitive memory, or that can enter into synthesis with a new perception, with that new perception now presenting itself as a perception of the same thing which had been earlier perceived. The earlier experience thus remains as something still valid for me. As Husserl puts it, "The first validity establishes a horizon of continual validity,"[11] with the possibility that the encounter with a similar object can reactivate the expectations generated by the earlier situation. What had been part of my horizon suddenly will be evoked out of the horizon of my experience to apply to what is now my thematic focus. All our outer experience of new objects establishes an original pattern of experience (they are *urstiftend*)[12] that can be brought to bear on any future situation (if aspects of that future situation are analogous to what I have experienced before). It is conceivable that even if I encounter something new, I transfer to it predicates of previous experience insofar as I take it to be at least minimally a "thing" or an "object,"[13] since I have previous experiences of things and objects. Something known creates an apperceptive type available for the experience of analogous objects.[14]

In all apperception and the genesis of it, the coincidence of one similar being paired with another in coexistence or succession plays a defining role. Dorion Cairns once correctly commented, "The ultimate generalization is that the fundamental tendencies of mental life are tendencies to identify and assimilate."[15] Again, "there is a fundamental tendency to believe in the *likeness* of everything to everything else."[16] Hence, in encountering what is present, whatever it may be, an object, a color, a texture, a pattern of acting, it will remind us of what we have previously experienced as carried forward in the nonthematized horizon of our perceptual activity, and what we have experienced will be brought to bear on what we are experiencing. Of course, analogical connections need not imply that what in the present is analogous to what one is reminded of is identical with what one previously experienced. A red square can remind me of a previous red circle, even though the shapes of the objects are very different. Such assimilations take place through passive synthesis, automatically, beneath the level of the controlling I or theory. Hence Cairns believes, for instance, that on a lower level we can experience the world as expressing a mind (by apperceptively transferring our own spiritual properties to the world, as animists do), as when we say that "Mother Nature is angry." We do this, even though on the theoretical level we may be hard-nosed scientists who reject all animism.[17]

The apperceptive transferences of which Husserl speaks take place at the lowest levels, with data joining with similar other data to produce higher-level unities in a passive, associative manner, as occurs, for instance, when the experience of the object at one time and place leads me to expect that its identity will be continuous across the manifold of new experiences. Hence, when I experience a unity such as a dog, despite the passage of time or the different acts in which the dog engages (eating, playing, etc.), I approach each new experience with the expectation that the dog will continue as a unity through a manifold of experiences. In this regard, it is to be noticed that one does not only apply a type or a meaning-predicate (e.g., "dog"), but also with the application of that meaning-predicate, there are future expectations that this dog will behave in a manner like dogs. In addition and beyond the constitution of an individual unity, pairs of objects alike in some way function together such that a present object evokes transferences from past experience of an object to which it is similar in a kind of pairing (*Paarung*) that takes place automatically, beneath the level of the controlling I. In fact, I live in continual apperceptive transferences.[18]

Although Husserl insists that we experience things directly, he does state that the meaning-predicates apperceptively evoked by and applied to an object are cultural in nature, and hence we experience things as typewriters, synagogues, or dogs—all of which terms and meanings draw on a cultural heritage. "Cultural things are seen as things in their thingly qualities, but they alike (*zugleich*) are apperceived as cultural formations in their cultural properties."[19] Objects are fitted out (*ausgestattet*) in one's everyday environment (*Umwelt*) with cultural predicates that are trusted and typical.[20] If one's encounter with a single object is able to set up a type to be apperceptively applied to a future similar object, how much more efficient are the cultural types which one acquires via education, imitation, and other mechanisms of secondary passive synthesis and which give one an extensive network of types that enable one to assimilate a wide variety of objects, without having to proceed one by one.

## PHENOMENOLOGY, INTENTIONALITY, AND APPERCEPTION

Phenomenological method has been presupposed by the above account of apperception. Phenomenological method basically involves adopting a disciplined reflective stance, known as the phenomenological reduction, toward one's lived experience with the result that the intentional acts aimed at the world and the objects given to those acts can be clearly seen and analyzed. Since one focuses carefully on how the objects given to those acts appear, without committing oneself to or making focal their existence, the objects are spoken of as "phenomena" and hence the method as "phenomenology."

What one discovers, when undertaking the phenomenological reduction, is a whole field of diverse kinds of previously anonymous intentional orientations that aim at the world and objects given within it. Examples of intentional orientation include an act of perception that aims at the object perceived, or an act of valuing aiming at an object desired, or an action aimed at an outcome that my act of will aims at realizing. Besides such intendings or encounterings, which involve individual acts and can often be expressed in belief statements that are oriented toward the world, our bodies and their movements are mutely directed toward the world, as Maurice Merleau-Ponty has shown, and hence when one leans on a desk or steps on an icy sidewalk—bodily intending takes place, without much intellectual activity being involved. Apperception, then, the transference of horizontal past experiences on to the present with anticipations about the future, represents another kind of intentionality. In addition to the types we apply to objects, the roles we play or the social norms we observe engender in us a large reserve of mostly unconscious, nonthematized, horizonal expectations about how we or others ought to act or think that we bring to bear in apperceptive fashion on present situations, which often evoke or activate such expectations.

Only by the careful attention to the conscious processes that phenomenological reduction fosters, would Husserl have been able to garner the insights into apperception and its passive-synthetic features that we have seen in the previous section. Husserl's recognition of the pervasive passive-synthetic ways in which we are oriented to the world, beneath the levels of the thematizing ego, no doubt informed his repeated emphasis on the need for reflection on our anonymous conscious processes, particularly through the reduction. In addition, his account of experience that involves intentional orientations and passive syntheses presents an alternative to causal accounts that view experience as causally produced, as a matter of responses elicited by stimuli, in the same way that one physical object impacts another.

Alfred Schutz describes how intentional activity in a complex interlocking is deployed in the relationship between persons when he writes in his *The Phenomenology of the Social World*:

> Furthermore, as I watch you, I shall see that you are oriented to me, that you are seeking the subjective meaning of my words, my actions, and what I have in mind insofar as you are concerned. And I will in turn take account of the fact that you are thus oriented to me, and this will influence both my intentions with respect to you and how I act toward you. This again you will see. I will see that you have seen it, and so on. This interlocking of glances, this thousand-faceted mirroring of each other, is one of the unique features of the face-to-face situation. We may say that it is a constitutive characteristic of this particular social relationship.[21]

When two parties from differing cultures associate with each other, there is the possibility that each can undergo an experience akin to the phenomenological reduction, which, as described by Maurice Merleau-Ponty, "slackens the intentional threads which attach us to world and thus brings them to our notice."[22] In fact, Howard Schwartz and Jerry Jacobs, in *Qualitative Sociology*, argue that something like the reduction occurs whenever one associates with cultural "troublemakers," such as immigrants, strangers, or novices—those who do not share one's cultural suppositions, who do not have the same expectations of how one is supposed to act, who often place them and their guaranty in question, and, especially, who make the cultural insider aware that he or she even has such cultural suppositions at all.[23] Alfred

Schutz comments on the "objectivity" of the stranger that makes him a troublemaker.

> The deeper reason for his objectivity, however, lies in his own bitter experience of the limits of "thinking as usual," which has taught him that a man may lose his status, his rules of guidance, and even his history and the normal way of life is always far less guaranteed than it seems. Therefore, the stranger discerns, frequently with a grievous clear-sightedness, the rising of a crisis which may menace the whole foundation of the "relatively natural conception of the world," while all those symptoms pass unnoticed by the members of the in-group, who rely on the continuance of the customary way of life.[24]

The phenomenological method, or analogates of it, such as association with those of a different culture, is particularly well-suited for bringing to light intentional expectations or anticipations that bear the mark of our distinctive cultures, for revealing how culture anonymously pervades our every action, and for illuminating in intercultural exchanges our own cultural anticipations and their differences from those of another.

The humor, which my African-American friend shared with me, also depends on intentionality insofar as it consists in some expectations that are "exploded," that is, they meet unanticipated outcomes. Hence the jack in the box that pops out of a box as a soft melody leads to its denouement evokes laughter on the part of those who did not anticipate that the winding down melody would lead to this surprising outcome. There is slapstick humor involved when someone throws a pie at an intended victim who ducks with the result that the pie hits someone nobody thought would be hit. A repeated theme in comedic plays involves actors disguising themselves as someone of the opposite sex and finding themselves pursued by someone of that sex in a plot that is headed for a massive disappointment of expectations. Humor in interracial or intercultural settings is to be expected since repeatedly in such settings those who are culturally different from each other hold suppositions, types, and expectations that are brought apperceptively to bear on the other person and culture and that are frequently upset or thwarted. It is often only when such expectations are thwarted that we recognize that we even had them in the first place; and hence humorous intercultural encounters function like the phenomenological reduction in bringing intentional orientations out of anonymity. To conclude, I will consider a few examples of how my African-American friend deployed humor to explode and reveal expectations on a more cognitive plane, then in role reversals, and finally with regard to more *embodied* cultural intentionalities.

## EXAMPLES: COGNITIVE EXPLODING OF
## EXPECTATIONS, ROLE REVERSALS,
## EMBODIED CULTURE

Once I mentioned to me friend that I had seen the movie "Once Upon a Time When We Were Colored," which portrayed earlier times when racial prejudice was more obvious and African-Americans were characterized as "colored." My friend, though, objected, "I still *am* colored, Mike." I suspect that my anticipation was to commence a conversation about past racial domination beyond which I was thinking that we had progressed and beyond which the movie positioned itself insofar as it looked back toward the past. My friend's objection, however, threw in abeyance my anticipation about such a discussion, especially if that anticipation may have included the idea that racial features are no longer that significant. My friend's objection, I believe, reflected his deep experience of being a black man in a predominantly white society with a long history of racial prejudice in which his morphological features clearly identify him and are not erasable. My expectation was exploded by his interpreting the phrase ("when we *were* colored") as ignoring the experience he has day in and day out of *now* being black in a predominantly white society—an experience which is not my own, has little purchase on my own thinking, and which I can at best imagine. My expectation was exploded by his deep-rooted experience, which I could begin to glimpse and which revealed for me whole gaps in experience that characterized me as a white person of European descent in a predominantly white society. My exploded expectations revealed something of what it was to be black and showed me that I was white, with all its interpersonal and cultural implications.

As an example of role reversal, he raised through humor questions about the fair treatment that whites may have been led to expect by their own cultural experience. At one of his basketball games, a white player in a game in which all the other players and referees were black, complained to my friend about a referee's call. My friend jokingly informed him, "Look you are the only white person out here on the court—you can't expect a fair call." His playful comment here highlighted the white player's expectation that he would have been treated fairly, especially by referees, regardless of his or their race. At the same time my friend's comment undermined that expectation by suggesting, tongue-in-cheek, that racial loyalties trump any notion of impartiality. But even more, his comment suddenly and imaginatively placed that white player in the situation that African-Americans often occupy insofar as they, as a minority member in a dominantly white setting, from sports events to court situations, can often wonder whether they have received or will receive a "fair call" when the white majority dominates or whether a pretense to impartiality might actually conceal racism. In this case, my friend not only referred to a long history of racial injustice, but actually questioned whether there might not be something inevitable to racial injustice, as if the African-American referees could not help making calls in favor of African-Americans, as if representatives of different races, when in the majority, are congenitally incapable of being fair to those of the other race. In questioning the expectation for fairness regardless of race and transposing the experience of whites and blacks, he once again gave the white person a taste of African-American experience and suggested to him (and me) that the fairness that we whites often experience and expect could be based on the fact that we belong to the racial majority—a possibility that we might not even suspect. Once again, the revelation of the black perspective illuminates how white persons might be occupying a cultural standpoint with expectations and blindspots of which they might be unaware.

It should also be pointed out, though, my friend's humorous comment had the effect of diminishing the racial polarization he at first seems to present as inevitable. After all, it is the black players and referees who he, a black person also, suggests are prejudicial here, and there is a kind of self-effacement going on here, as if my friend was admitting that blacks, too, engage in the very prejudices they resent in whites. In addition, my friend was reassuring the white player that the call was in fact unfair, building a bridge with him by agreeing on its unfairness. Finally, by assimilating the white player's experience with the long history of prejudice African-Americans have encountered, it was as if my friend was inviting the white player to enter a bit into the black experience even if only in playful imagination, as if the white player's doubts about the fairness of the call (and my friend's playful suggestion that the call had covert racial motivations) had brought him into a kind of unity with blacks, thereby dissolving the separation between blacks and whites that my friend had suggested were inevitable.

Racial segregation both springs from and accentuates cultural differences, and these cultural differences leave some of their most noticeable marks upon our bodies. My friend perceptively observes the bodily differences that show up in our gait or bodily movements or pronunciation—behaviors over which we have little deliberate control. For instance, my friend imitates my manner of speaking by pronouncing words with extreme precision, "Do you have the ten dollars?" "Have you purchased the White Castles?" Of course, his exaggerated precision, which exceeds my own, yields humor because his precision goes farther than anyone familiar with my less precise pronunciation would expect. In addition, imitations reflect a structure of humor by blowing up what one expects, as when comedians imitate a politician for instance, with the humor consisting in the surprising and unexpected dissonance one experiences in hearing the politician's pronunciation and voice modulations appear in a different person, who, on his or her own, would be expected to speak in a different manner. My friend once remarked that when I speak, I pronounce even the silent vowels and consonants—an image humorous because of its exaggeration and very impossibility. Of course, the precision of one's pronunciation is not something that one is often aware of insofar as one uses language to refer to objects or for other linguistic purposes, as Wittgenstein has shown. One's intentional direction toward objects or purposes blinds one to the linguistic activity, such as pronunciation patterns, through which one is directed to those objects or purposes. Not only are these pronunciation patterns generally invisible, but the bodily movements that realize these pronunciation patterns, the interaction between teeth, tongue, mouth, and breathing proceed beneath the level of deliberate consciousness. The pronunciation patterns themselves, rooted in bodily movements beneath conscious control, can be drawn out of obscurity, though, through the observations of someone whose bodily linguistic behaviors have been shaped by a different cultural (and family) environment. The intercultural interlocutor once again reveals to us the ways through which we intend our world and to which we are often oblivious.

My friend and I are often surprised at the different vocabulary words that emerge in our conversations, or by the pronunciation of different words. One of our standing jokes is that my pronunciation of the adjective "terrible" is inferior to my friend's pronunciation of that adjective as "turrible." The latter pronunciation seems more in line with the situations that the adjective is meant to characterize.

The scrupulosity exhibited in my use of language, reflecting how the cultural context in which I was raised has impressed itself on my body, also appears in other bodily motions. For instance, my friend has pointed out repeatedly that I, like many other white people he knows, when we press on the remote control to lock or unlock our cars, aim the control at the car, in contrast to my friend who does not aim, but relaxedly presses on it in his pocket without aiming it. Just as our language, the vocabulary that emerges, or the pronunciation patterns we deploy reveal the way that our culture and upbringing have impressed themselves on bodily movements, so also the punctiliousness or casualness of our bodily intending of the world (e.g., pointing the remote at the car) reveals how cultural influences saturate our bodies long before we reflect on them. The very exposure of what we do not even notice about ourselves is surprising and strikes us as humorous. Often it is only in an intercultural and interracial encounter of the type that I am describing that what is taken for granted becomes visible. For this reason, Schwartz and Jacobs compare hanging out with those of another culture as a variant of phenomenological reduction, which, according to Merleau-Ponty "slackens the intentional threads which attach us to the world and thus brings them to our notice."[25]

## Notes

1. Edmund Husserl, *Die Lebenswelt: Auslegungen der vorgegebenen Welt und ihrer Konstitution, Texte aus dem Nachlass (1916–1937)*, ed. Rochus Sowa, *Husserliana*, vol. 39 (Dordrecht: Springer, 2008).
2. Anthony Appiah, *In My Father's House: Africa in the Philosophy of Culture* (New York: Oxford University Press, 1992), 45.
3. Husserl, *Die Lebenswelt*, 431.
4. Ibid., 517–518.
5. Ibid., 62, 516.
6. Ibid., 30.
7. Ibid., 267.
8. Ibid., 517–518.
9. Ibid., 442–443.
10. Ibid., 364.
11. Ibid., 1.
12. Ibid., 2.
13. Ibid.
14. Ibid., 16, 27, 114, 364.
15. Dorion Cairns, "Applications of the Theory of Sense-Transfer," in *Animism, Adumbration, Willing and Wisdom: Studies in the Phenomenology of Dorion Cairns*, ed. Lester Embree (Bucharest: Zetabooks, 2012), 57.
16. Ibid., 68.
17. Ibid., 54, 68, 72, 80; Husserl, *Die Lebenswelt*, 419, 452.
18. Husserl, *Die Lebenswelt*, 431–432, 451.
19. Ibid., 411.
20. Ibid., 62, 62n.1.
21. Alfred Schutz, *The Phenomenology of the Social World*, trans. Frederick Lehnert and George Walsh, Introduction by George Walsh (Evanston: Northwestern University Press, 1967), 170.
22. Maurice Merleau-Ponty, *The Phenomenology of Perception*, trans. Colin Smith (London: Humanities Press, 1962), xiii.

23. Howard Schwartz and Jerry Jacobs, *Qualitative Sociology: A Method to the Madness* (New York: The Free Press, 1979), 262–264.

24. Alfred Schutz, *Collected Papers 2: Studies in Social Theory*, ed. Arvid Brodersen (The Hague: Martinus Nijhoff, 1964), 104.

25. Merleau-Ponty, *Phenomenology of Perception*, xiii.

# 2

# TOWARD FOUNDATIONS FOR INTERCULTURAL STUDIES: CONSIDERING MOBILITY STUDIES AND THE STUDY OF RELIGION*

## *Paul Kollman*

When trying to create foundations for a new discipline—in this case, intercultural studies—I am convinced it is better to be bold and clear, even if wrong, than cautious and vague, even if right. Clear statements encourage productive disagreement, an important step for the emergence of genuine insights, especially when compared to hedged about, vague truisms universally and hastily agreed to since they risk so little. A well-expressed, easily understood error can, I believe, be an important, retrospectively verified step in the march toward insight, even if unintended.

The theses presented here seek to be clear statements of this sort, statements that, even if proved unhelpful or wrong, will advance the development of intercultural studies. They link two emerging disciplinary fields: *intercultural studies* itself, the topic of the essays in this volume, and *mobility studies*. I will contend that these two fields would benefit from close dialogue with each other for they are natural allies in seeking to make sense of important facets of social experience, especially today. In describing and defending the complementarity and potential mutual enrichments of intercultural studies and mobility studies, examples will come from religious studies, the subject of my own academic work.

Both intercultural studies and mobility studies have appeared recently and both have a somewhat tenuous foothold in the contemporary academy. Intercultural studies, a field for which these essays

seek to develop what Michal Rozbicki calls "a theoretical and methodological toolbox," has an emerging institutional place in the academy,
with a number of centers of something like "intercultural studies" at
mostly Christian universities in the United States, and several others in
Europe. There is also a *Journal of Intercultural Studies* now in its 33rd
volume, published in Australia at Deakin University.

Mobility studies also appeared rather recently. In the past few years
a number of publications have sought to theorize in a more systematic way the notion of mobility. In 2006 there appeared a journal
called *Mobilities*, which continues publication twice a year. Stephen
Greenblatt's 2010 edited volume *Cultural Mobility: A Manifesto* also
struck a chord, issuing a call to undertake "mobility studies" as a self-
defined endeavor. Perhaps in response, in 2011 appeared a new peer-
reviewed journal entitled *Transfers*, with the subtitle *Interdisciplinary
Journal of Mobility Studies*. Its website promises "cutting-edge research
on the processes, structures and consequences of the movement of
people, resources, and commodities."[1]

The adjectives that identify each emerging field mark out a rather
ambiguous semantic place, illustrative of the indeterminate disciplinary status each occupies. Both words, "mobility" and "intercultural,"
though conceptually isolable, tend to adhere to something else, so
that they represent properties or domains rather than distinct entities. They are not what philosophers of science like Ian Hacking have
called "natural kinds"[2]—that is, more or less, entities that have an
existence apart from being perceived—but instead take their meaning
in relationship to what they modify.

The adjective "intercultural," for instance, implies a domain that
foregrounds realities implicated when things linked with "cultures"
meet—for instance, individual persons and communities, languages,
personal and social habits. "Mobility," unlike "intercultural" a noun,
nonetheless in the discipline that Greenblatt and others want to establish, mobility studies, refers especially to the mobility associated with
persons and realities often subsumed under the term "culture" linked
to persons. (Among the most common referents for "mobility studies" emerging from a casual web search, however, is research on traffic
patterns, not Greenblatt's concern!)

Mobility and interculturality can be difficult to define and delimit
precisely. On the one hand, mobility implies the simple capacity for
motion of any sort, and interculturality implies a multiplicity of cultures overlapping or interacting. On the other hand, both can be
specified, too. Mobility can demarcate motion between self-defined
states—actual physical spaces (from New York to Chicago) or socially

defined roles (from single to married, or unemployed to employed, sinful to forgiven, for example). Interculturality is at times invoked with particular "cultures" in mind—German culture and that of Turkish immigrants to Germany, for example. And one can have mobility and interculturality in the first, very literal sense—ability to move, the reality of some in-between-ness, culturally speaking—without the *capacity* for mobility or embracing interculturality in the way that matters to those discerning such capacities—toward greater wealth or more holiness, for example, or toward greater comfort in cultural interstices.

Those familiar with contemporary religious studies know that the concept "religion," like mobility and "the intercultural," is not without its ambiguities. Yet though its status as a distinct subject has undergone considerable deconstruction recently,[3] religion nonetheless exists—more than interculturality or mobility—as an entity *without* needing to adhere to something. Religions have a thing-ness that mobility and interculturality lack.

More importantly for this chapter, religion also represents a particularly apt subject with which to consider the mutual implications of mobility studies and intercultural studies. After all, scholars have long studied religions in ways that take their mobility and interculturality very seriously, largely because religion is treated by most scholars as an aspect of culture. The global spreads of Christianity, Islam, and Buddhism, the three archetypal missionary religions, for example, have been covered in immense volumes in many languages. One common theme has been their variety due to cultural differences as the faiths have traveled.[4]

That said, even those who stress religion's distinctiveness vis-à-vis culture—for either theological or other reasons—have also attended to its mobility and interculturality. For example, investigations of sacred place and sacred time have been a standard topic in religious studies, and in many such studies, movements between and among spaces and times defined as sacred and those defined as profane (unsacred) have received special attention. Attention to mobility in relation to sacred space and time has been a career-maker, famously so for giants in religious studies Emile Durkheim and Mircea Eliade, as well as many who have followed their quite divergent approaches. And over the past half century, there are many important studies of "new religious movements," in Africa and elsewhere—often linked with cultural assertion, political resistance, and religious innovation. For their part, Christian theologians have also long examined their faith's mobile reach and capacity to find a home in—and transform—differing cultural milieus.

This chapter offers six theses about mobility studies and intercultural studies in relationship to the study of religion. The first two address the *present* as offering a particular set of reasons to consider intercultural studies and mobility studies together, with religious data serving to make the case. The second two consider how mobility and interculturality might be considered in looking back more or less into the *past*, where both were regularly at work in religions even when unrecognized. The final two theses will suggest likely prospects for how intercultural studies and mobility studies can fruitfully interact, that is, how our scholarly tools might help yield insights into a mobile and intercultural religious *future*.

*　*　*

The *first thesis* seems relatively uncontroversial: There is particular value in putting religion, interculturality, and mobility in a single analytical frame today because *religions possess unprecedented and very obvious physical and intercultural mobility in the present*, so much so that acknowledging their kinetic adaptability has almost become a reflexive impulse among scholars.

As Stephen Greenblatt notes in the introduction to the aforementioned *Cultural Mobility*, radical mobility has long been a feature of human life.[5] And certainly religions have not become intercultural and mobile only recently, for many had an impressive geographical reach long before the present. Buddhism, for example, reached across the Himalayas into China and elsewhere in eastern Asia, into southeast Asia and insular and peninsular Asia, a few centuries after the supposed dates of Siddhartha Gautama's life. Christianity, too, reached from Ireland and Spain into China and India, and from Ethiopia to the Netherlands, already by the sixth century, while Portuguese and Spanish sailors and missionaries made Christianity a truly global religion starting in the sixteenth century. And already in its first nine centuries, Islam spanned three continents, reaching from Morocco to Indonesia, the Balkans to Ethiopia, becoming the predominant religion in the area that some evangelical Christians today call the "10–40 window" to indicate the place, speaking of latitude and longitude, that Christian mission ought to prioritize.

Despite their mobile and intercultural past, religions today—that is, a large collection of facets including religious actors, discourses, ideas, practices, and objects—are mobile and intercultural today in ways they have not been in the past, and to degrees and at a pace that they have not been in the past. The traditional missionary religions of Islam, Christianity, and Buddhism, global for centuries, are today nearly everywhere in ways not seen before the middle of the twentieth century. Mark Noll lists some of the transformations in Christianity over the past half century: more Christians in church on a given Sunday in China than in all of Europe, and more Anglicans in Kenya than Episcopalians and Anglicans in the United Kingdom, Canada, and the United States combined; more Catholics at church in the Philippines than in any European country, with Europe's largest ordinary Sunday congregation being a Pentecostal church in Kiev with a Nigerian pastor.[6] Muslims and Buddhists with historical perspective could no doubt express equal bewilderment at how their religious identities take shape in diverse settings: large mosques in London, Buddhist monasteries in Brazil. Equally everywhere are many religions that have mostly been quite localized in their self-understanding, or at least have had less expansive missionary energy, such as Hinduism, Confucianism, Judaism, and the traditional religions of Africa.

Anthropologist Thomas Csordas sees the importance of both *portable practices* (e.g., the rosary, Islamic chanting, Buddhist meditation) and *transposable messages* (salvation through Christ, the ineffability of the Qur'an, the illusory nature of much common experience) in fostering religions' migratory tendencies—for the purposes of this chapter, for religions to be intercultural and mobile. Csordas helpfully identifies four archetypal ways that religions move from one place or one culture to another. Each helpfully begins with the letter "m": missionization, the migration of peoples, the mobility of cosmopolitans, and mediatization. Each has played a part in the unprecedented mobility and interculturality of religions today.[7]

African Christianity's current transformations epitomize changes in each of the manners of interculturality and mobility that Csordas identifies. With regard to *missionization*, standard historical perspectives on Christianity in Africa rightly see modern Catholic and Protestant missionary efforts as prioritizing sub-Saharan Africa for concerted evangelization. Thousands of north Atlantic-based missionaries sought to convert Africans beginning in the latter nineteenth century, continuing to the present, though today with more shorter-term and many fewer lifelong expatriate missionaries on the ground. Increasingly, however, African Christians are themselves serving as missionaries, both in places where Christianity is perceived as quite young—for example, New Guinea and the Amazon—and where it is old or seen as disintegrating, such as in London or Toronto. African missionaries in latter such places evangelize both their fellow Africans and ever more (as in the Kiev church noted above) those perceived to be "native," whose prior religious adherences have faltered.

*Migration* now takes African Christians all over the world as well, replicating patterns that took enslaved Africans to what was in European eyes the New World already in the sixteenth century, and in considerable numbers beginning in the early eighteenth century. These days independent churches founded in Nigeria, Ghana, and the Democratic Republic of Congo, for example, have branches all over the world. Equally new has been the nature of those arriving, who epitomize the *mobility of cosmopolitan elites* that Csordas identifies as a typical way for religions to spread. Nigerian evangelists used to train at places like Oral Roberts University in Oklahoma; now they teach there, epitomizing the wealth and social power the prosperity gospel they sometimes preach can promise. The Vatican's missionary office Propaganda Fide divided up Africa as mission territory from the seventeenth century; now it has African cardinals overseeing important church offices.

Csordas' fourth mode, *mediatization*, represents the factor that recently has spurred some of the most far-reaching transformations, and which likely will continue to situate sweeping changes. Whether it be meditation practices linked to Falun Gong, Islamic chanting broadcast to passengers on buses and ferries, cassettes and radio messages with biblical and Qur'anic interpretations and applications, or Nigerian Pentecostal soap operas, the profound potential for the mediatization of religious discourses and images means myths and rituals, stories and practices move about with unprecedented speed, insinuating themselves into more and more places and cultures.

In light of these modes of mobility and interculturality in portable practices and transposable messages, French political scientist Olivier Roy joins many in noting the new autonomy of religion, linked to secularization and globalization. Contemporary market conditions of religion allow unprecedented export and circulation of religious discourses and practices, along with consequent deterritorialization of what used to be deemed local, and a related de-ethnicization of many religious identities. Such religious identities are newly mobile and newly intercultural.[8]

*Thesis two* seeks to respond to what might be called "Greenblatt's restriction." In his edited volume, Stephen Greenblatt concludes with a "mobility studies manifesto." Its first principle warns against using mobility in a metaphorical sense. Mobility must be taken in a literal sense, Greenblatt insists, for only with physical movement does metaphorical movement make sense.[9]

Greenblatt's attempted embargo against over-attention to non-physical approaches to mobility in mobility studies—his insistence that actual physical mobility be the *sine qua non* of the sub-discipline he proposes—would seem to prohibit mobility studies from taking an interest in many internal religious discourses about personal mobility and related interculturality, since these do not always foreground, or even include, ordinary physical understandings of mobility. One could also extend Greenblatt's literalist stricture for mobility studies to intercultural studies, seeking its own potential limiting condition. One might ask: if mobility studies should, following Greenblatt, insist on actual physical movement as a necessary condition, should intercultural studies require something like clearly defined "cultures" that are interacting?

For approaches to religion, such self-imposed limits create difficulties for these new disciplines. Would Greenblatt include in mobility studies, for instance, the phantasmagoric spectral voyages that defined the shamanic identities of those whose visionary experiences made them religious virtuosi in Asiatic Siberia? Shared shamanic practices like these—not obviously predicated on objective physical mobility—helped create a pan-regional religious framework that shaped Amerindian religions from Alaska to Patagonia as well.[10] What about the woman who, I was told, once crashed into a church roof in Nigeria? Her clatter led the worshippers to look out alarmed, then climb up to rescue her. They gathered her into their congregation, where she explained that she was a witch who had been flying by when she was struck down into the church—so that she might be saved. This is also an intercultural moment of sorts—as local beliefs about witchcraft meet a Christian church. Or is this in fact a new culture that emerges as Africans make Christianity their own? And physical movement was at least claimed. The question arises, however: is it sufficiently mobile in a physical sense to meet Greenblatt's threshold?

Perhaps one way to answer the challenge implicit in Greenblatt's restrictive impulse from the point of view of religious interculturality and mobility per se lies in accepting that—and here's the second thesis—*For many religions a remembered experience of actual physical mobility is foundational—often with intercultural experiences paramount—but mobility in the metaphorical sense is even more central to their identity.*

In a great many religious systems, as David Shulman and Guy Stroumsa note, physical mobility has been a metaphor for religious transformations of self, and religious transformations of the self are metaphorized through images for actual physical mobility.[11] For those

within such religious self-understandings, previous physical mobility,
by establishing the religious foundations for their own self-understanding, are not metaphorical, but actual, though they might not
be in a way that objective observers would accept. Arguably they ful-
fill Greenblatt's stringent demand, however, despite the fact that the
physical movement alluded to is remembered rather than enacted in
a physical way. Thus perhaps Greenblatt's rigorous caution gains a bit
of flexibility.

Yet the changes in individual believers, often understood through
metaphors linked with mobility, differ from other ways that religious
transformations might be considered. The third thesis addresses how
religions understood in a collective way have, in the past, evaluated
their mobility and intercultural capacity. These days, many believers
value the intercultural capacity and mobility of religions, and implicitly scholars seem to agree that to be mobile and culturally agile is an
advantage for a religion. Mobility, cultural and physical, in relation to
religion today carries a positive valence, generally speaking. Capacity
for substantial mobility and adaptability is linked in the contemporary
lexicon to a host of other properties and terms mostly with a positive value—for example, power, modernity, hybridity, *creolité*, cosmopolitanism, and agency. Some scholars have traced the genealogy of
this valorization of intercultural gracefulness and mobility. Joan-Pau
Rubiés, for example, charts the rise in early modern Europe of the cult
of the "empirical traveler" whose personal experience lay at the core of
the claims to the truth of the discourse.[12]

This has not always been the case, for many world religions have
possessed a more complex and interesting assessment of mobility and
cultural diversity. There are two apparently contradictory aspects to
this. First, in general, religions that were perceived to be monocul-
tural and stable have been more highly valued than religions that were
mobile and culturally diverse. Nomadic or unsettled peoples practiced
religions easily labeled primitive, and their often slower conversions
toward so-called world religions were seen as evidence of the underdeveloped state of their religious sensibilities. At the same time, those
scattered among others in diaspora and shaped by others' cultures and
religions risked contamination of their religions. Thus having their
own place has been a value for religious people. Second, however, a
period of wandering or intercultural mixing has also been an important liminal reality in many religions' self-understandings.

This paradox shapes the ways believers in most world religions have
come to tell the story of their own religion's beginnings. Certainly,
achieving a fixed place for religious identity and a single cultural

identity has generally been valued. Thus in many officialized religious narratives, mobility and intercultural mixing were things they eventually were glad to overcome by achieving a settled, fixed place to call their own, so they could be culturally distinctive. They understand themselves as having arrived at a certain achieved status by establishing their identity so they no longer needed to be mobile and interdependent—that is, they arrived *as religions* by *ending* their mobility and cultural mixing. It is easy enough to cite such sacred centers: Jews with Zion/Jerusalem; Christians with Jerusalem, and later Rome, Constantinople, Moscow, perhaps even Geneva and Canterbury; all Muslims with Jerusalem and Mecca, some as well with Karbala and Qum; Buddhists with Bodh Gaya and other sites where body parts of Buddha are revered.

At the same time, even when adherents of these religions procured a clearly defined sacred place and often as well a structured sacred calendar—both establishments grounding their identity as religions—they also often trace their origins to a particular experience of mobility and cultural fluidity when they *lacked* such a clear sacred place and an organized sense of sacred time. This remembered mobility and versatility—sometimes chosen, often forced by historical circumstances—has since become a touchstone for their identity, one often treated with nostalgic reverence that sometimes even relativizes the value of the settled place that those who belong to the religion think of as their own.

One thinks of Abraham's journey, the Exodus, the Exile, and more recently a variety of diasporas and returns for Jews; the first and second Hijras from Mecca—to Axum and later to Medina—and then the return to Mecca for Muslims; the Buddha's years of wandering as he discerned the Four Noble Truths; Jesus' wandering as an itinerant preacher, Christians suffering persecution and praying in catacombs prior to the legalization of their religion by the Roman Empire. In each case the settling that ended the mobility—while not regretted exactly—has been seen at times to occasion a loss or at least softening of religious idealism.

It is not only older religions—or the central traditions of such religions—that manifest this paradoxical pattern. The Christian conversion of Uganda is one of the great success stories of missionization. It saw large-scale conversions to Christianity among both Protestants and Catholics starting in the late nineteenth century. Both groups idealized a history of their persecution—by pagans and by Muslims for both, and for the Catholics, also by Protestants—in ways that made their eventual settling down into respectability something to be celebrated. Yet memories of exile, wandering, and uncertainty have remained important in their self-understanding. Similarly, Zimbabwean Pentecostals linked to certain prophets likewise delight in having their own places to pray, and they call such a place a *sowe*, which has come to mean their church. Yet *sowe* is prototypically the Shona word for "wilderness," and the adoption to their own liturgical space reminds them how their prophets and early followers struggled against persecution, seeking refuge in marginal land where they could worship in peace.[13]

One can find similar patterns among Mormons—who rejoiced in reaching Utah but idealize the years it took to get there—and even in American civil religion, which long has emphasized the pilgrims' struggle to reach Massachusetts and found "a city on a hill." And some African-American Christians already in the latter nineteenth century wistfully remembered the hidden ways they lived their faith prior to emancipation, idealizing the courage of their forebears.

The *third thesis* seeks to name this paradox regarding mobility and interculturality that lies at the heart of the history of many religious traditions—*namely, a common coexisting struggle within religions for fixity or locatedness in a sacred center where religio-cultural unity was achieved, on the one hand, and an idealization of intercultural mobility, on the other.* As a consequence, even when believers celebrate their identity through the establishment of places uniquely their own, mobility and cultural mixing, either forced or voluntary, remains a central aspect of the stories they use to identify themselves. Many religions manifest this complex dialectical relationship between opposing ideals: of pure settled identity, on the one hand, and, on the other, an idealized mobile (often moral) purity.

The fourth and fifth theses consider how religions have been and are being studied in light of their interculturality and mobility. Interestingly, at first glance many theoretical books on religion today seem disconnected from these aspects of religion, for one feature of contemporary scholarship in religious studies is the burgeoning of intrapsychic theories about religion. Some of these prioritize cognitive processes or evolutionary mental and/or social advances associated with religious belief and practice that gave religious practitioners subtle advantages as time went by.[14]

Along with this cognitivist-intrapsychic-evolutionary trend, however, there have also been two different scholarly approaches to religion that respond to its interculturality and mobility more directly, which will serve as a fourth and fifth thesis. The *fourth thesis* addresses what has been the most common way to think about religion's adaptive and agile nature, namely a variety of studies over the past half century or so that *show how putative global religions adapt to take on local identities in various new cultural settings.* There now exist a plethora of terms and related cases that show the permutations of Christianity, Islam, Buddhism, Judaism, Hinduism, and other religions in particular times, places, and circumstances. Judging from what is studied, mobility of religion in the strict sense—the capacity for someone to be a Hindu in Hyderabad or Houston, a Buddhist in Bangkok or Boston—is not nearly as interesting or important as the adaptive capacities that religious believers show in settling in new places. That is to say, it is not only mobility that is interesting, but also lability, malleability, ductility or adaptability.

Given the abundance of studies of localized global religious identities and the human capacities to be religiously at home in myriad circumstances, the intellectual yield from such projects—in terms of larger conceptual insights—might be approaching exhaustion. Of central importance to the history of such religions, however, has been the way such local manifestations can call into question aspects of the larger tradition that have often been assumed to be essential to it. This can happen when new believers' discourses and practices erode the obviousness of the previously assumed central aspects, enhance the importance of what was seen as marginal, or reclaim the forgotten. Thus, since insights into particular cases no doubt remain to be achieved, the potential *political* yield of such studies remains very substantial, as local communities discover their own distinctiveness in religion to the larger religious traditions in which they participate.

The *fifth thesis* turns to efforts made to consider religion as a whole from its mobile and intercultural nature. It recognizes that *several recent attempts at comprehensive theories of religion have prioritized the mobility of religion and linked interculturality. It also, however, has a caveat: none have achieved widespread acceptance.*

Most important among theories of this sort, in my opinion, is that of Thomas Tweed, which focuses directly on mobility as foundational to religion. In his 2006 study entitled *Crossing and Dwelling: A Theory of Religion,* Tweed defines religions as "confluences of organic-cultural flows that intensify joy and confront suffering by drawing on human and suprahuman forces to make homes and cross boundaries."[15] Tweed's theory builds on his own fieldwork in Miami, which examined in particular the role of an annual procession with a statue of the Virgin Mary in the social and religious life of the Cuban-American community.[16] His work epitomizes the sorts of work identified in thesis four, the many studies underscoring the creative agency of religious believers, yet he is one of only a few scholars to develop a theory of religion making central its mobility and interculturality.

A sixth and final thesis considers the intentional effort to make mobile and intercultural something like religion. Such practices, often decried by those wary of how evangelization can undo cultural integrity, reinforce colonial and imperial practices, and legitimate the erasure of local identities, nonetheless are ubiquitous in the modern world. Regardless of whether we like them or not, they deserve study. Thus *thesis six: Studies of mobility, interculturality, and religion cannot be confined to the deliberate spreading of religion by some adherents, but neither should such efforts—in Christian terms, missionary activity—be ignored, for they are a central feature of many widespread religions.*

In seeking to link mobility studies and intercultural studies through a discussion of religion through these six theses, I hope to have shown their usefulness to one another, and to have highlighted their mutual implications.

★   ★   ★

By way of conclusion, it is worth noting how the notion of culture is a point of reference in intercultural studies and mobility studies, as well as in the contemporary study of religion. Thus all three fields have to face the commonplace insight into culture: despite our regular invocation of term, the concept of culture as long used in common parlance—as coherent, bounded, and able to be mapped neatly on an identifiable people—has become untenable. Yes, there can be something collective that a group of people share that is nonbiological—a language, set of customs, bodily habits, a whole slew of other attributes—yet individuals appropriate that amorphous collectivity in distinct ways, shaped by particular experiences, some linked to gender, age, and class, others rather more idiosyncratic. And what people share in common is not acted upon in the same ways, for a variety of reasons. Island populations and otherwise more or less isolated "tribes" who undergo novel meetings with heretofore unknown people—classic instances of intercultural contact, and traditionally the sites for anthropology's nineteenth- and twentieth-century theory-building—have been relatively few, even if historically momentous, and are getting fewer. Much more common examples of interculturality, past and present, are equally prone to fluidity and confusion, misrecognition and uncertainty, but involve a variety of other systems of meaning and practice, including religion and other ideologically freighted sources of social identity.

In light of this, an important benefit of linking mobility studies and intercultural studies lies in the way they are positioned to develop notions of culture that acknowledge its problematic past without ignoring the importance of the domain culture marks out. Both fields implicitly foreground culture's performative nature, the way its capacity to define human belonging and difference responds to personal and collective agency in distinct circumstances, instead of unfolding in programmed behavior. This seems to me another reason for the importance of the two fields, and for their necessary and potentially very fruitful interaction.

## NOTES

* Chapters that have led to what is here were given in two other venues. First, I was invited to speak at Columbia University by Valentina Izmirlieva and Karen Barkey in November 2011, addressing the notion of mobility in relation to religious studies. I am grateful to them and others present at that event for their helpful comments. I also thank those present at the conference at St. Louis University in February 2013, where a revised version was presented along with the others here collected in this volume. Again, I appreciate comments given on that occasion.

1. Accessed September 3, 2012.
2. Ian Hacking, "Natural Kinds," in *Perspectives on Quine*, ed. Robert B. Barrett and Roger F. Gibson (Cambridge, MA: Blackwell, 1990). Apparently Hacking himself now has doubts about the concept of natural kinds. See the brief discussion at http://www.kli.ac.at/events/event-detail/1315346400/natural-kinds-in-philosophy-and-in-the-life-sciences-scholastic-twilight-or-new-dawn, accessed May 9, 2013.
3. Timothy Fitzgerald and William T. Cavanaugh are among recent scholars who have challenged conventional understandings of religion. See Timothy Fitzgerald, *The Ideology of Religious Studies* (New York: Oxford University Press, 2001); Timothy Fitzgerald, *Discourse on Civility and Barbarity: A Critical History of Religion and Related Categories* (New York: Oxford University Press, 2007); William T. Cavanaugh, *The Myth of Religious Violence: Secular Ideology and the Roots of Modern Conflict* (New York: Oxford University Press, 2009).
4. Robert L. Montgomery is one of the few scholars who have compared the spread of these missionary religions. See his 2007 work *The Spread of Religions: A Social-Scientific Theory Based on the Spread of Buddhism, Christianity, and Islam* (Hackensack, NJ: Long Dash Books).
5. Stephen Greenblatt (ed.), *Cultural Mobility: A Manifesto* (New York: Cambridge University Press, 2010), 2–3.
6. Mark A. Noll, *The New Shape of World Christianity: How American Experience Reflects Global Faith* (Downers Grove, IL: InterVarsity Press, 2009), 20–21.

7. Thomas J. Csordas, "Introduction: Modalities of Transnational Transcendence," *Anthropological Theory*, 7/3 (2007): 259–272.

8. Olivier Roy, *Holy Ignorance: When Religion and Culture Part Ways* (New York: Columbia University Press, 2009), 163–185.

9. Greenblatt, *Cultural Mobility*, 251–252.

10. Mircea Eliade, *Shamanism: Archaic Techniques of Ecstasy* (New York: Bollingen Foundation, 1964).

11. David Shulman and Guy G. Stroumsa, "Introduction: Persons, Passages, and Shifting Cultural Space," in *Self and Self-Transformation in the History of Religions* (Oxford: Oxford University Press, 2002), 3–16.

12. Joan-Pau Rubiés, "New Worlds and Renaissance Ethnology," *History and Anthropology*, 6, 2/3 (1993): 157–197.

13. Isabel Mukonyora, *Wandering a Gendered Wilderness: Suffering and Healing in an African Initiated Church* (New York: Peter Lang, 2007); Matthew Engelke, *A Problem of Presence: Beyond Scripture in an African Church* (Berkeley: University of California Press, 2007).

14. Such theories take many forms, ranging from Stewart Guthrie's postulation of a hyperactive agency detection device within us that explains anthropomorphism in religion, to very recent approaches that examine actual neuro-biological processes within the cerebral cortex. Another approach associated with French sociologist Danièle Hervieu-Léger defines a religion as a chain of memory that unites people to one another and to a shared past—again prioritizing the mental work that religion entails. For a good summary of recent theories of religion, see: Michael Stausberg, *Contemporary Theories of Religion: A Critical Companion* (New York: Routledge, 2009).

15. Thomas Tweed, *Crossing and Dwelling: A Theory of Religion* (Cambridge: Harvard University Press, 2006), 54.

16. Thomas Tweed, *Our Lady of the Exile: Diasporic Religion at a Cuban Catholic Shrine in Miami* (New York: Oxford University Press, 1997).

# 3

# TOWARD THE MATERIALITY OF INTERCULTURAL DIALOGUE, STILL A "MIRACLE BEGGING FOR ANALYSIS"

*Teruyuki Tsuji*

## INTRODUCTION

Creolization (in the sense of cultural mixing or crossover) is a "miracle begging for analysis. Because it first occurred against all odds between the jaws of brute and absolute power, no explanation seems to do justice to the very wonder that it happened at all."[1] The wonder has now apparently been demystified. With the poststructuralist turn, renewed attention to political dynamics in cultural production has unearthed submerged yet persistent interstices within culture, formerly imagined as a seamless system. The interstices have revealed ways in which cultural domination is never completed. Culture is not merely a manifestation of institutional and material reality, constraining and coercing human actions, consciousness, and reflections. Instead, culture is the key avenue for shaking or even breaking the "iron jaws of power." Power is not "absolute," however "brute" it may be.

The "precariousness of power"[2] could have given us greater insight into the various consequences of intercultural dialogue. However, the particular conditions, although they make this epistemological shift possible, have restricted the scope of research on alternative constructions to certain dimensions of the intercultural dialogue. In metropolitan centers, the students of culture have shifted the focus of their research from the "fictitious distance" between traditional others and our rational selves to the "alternative distance" between those who represent and those who are being represented. In decolonizing societies, on the other hand, the colonized intellectual and political elites strove to reformulate the colonial past into a sequence of events of a subaltern ideological struggle that proceeded teleologically to sovereignty. The precariousness of power became a conceptual ground common to the metropolitan and postcolonial aspirations for an alternate history, and, as a result, it framed a certain academic-cum-ideological movement of the production of knowledge. How have subordinate individuals and groups retained their cultures against stigmatization and assimilationism in colonial and postcolonial contexts? What implications have the subalterns and their cultural elements had for necessarily asymmetrical intercultural dialogues? How and what impact have they had on the outcomes? These questions are designed to subjectify cultural production, deconstructing the distance between the traditional *them* and the rational *us*, and ultimately rewriting history with former *others* as the major authors.

These questions emphasize the potential of cultural interstices to serve as a terrain for past, present, and future cultural politics—a battle waged by the underprivileged against ideological incorporation. In this construction, cultural combination is often defined as antithetical to integration, as opposed to mixing which is idealized as a universal totality. Meanwhile, "shared" culture has become "a myth, a fabrication, a mystification-the collective misrepresentation of someone's particular interests"[3] and the traditional search for structure has been branded as politically incorrect.[4] The exploration of cultural combination began as a critique of cultural essentialism; now it is cultural combination that has been essentialized.

Cultural combinations—and people's perception and performance of them—are shaped and reshaped within a certain kind of power relation, "rather than as prescriptive, predicting a priori what those relations ought to be."[5] The interactions among individuals and groups of different cultural identities are richer, busier, and more "wondrous" than the simplistic and optimistic perspective of the counter-hegemony narrative. Although power inevitably operates and causes political tension in cultural production, cultural politics empirically turns out to be multidimensional and resistance becomes polymorphous, as the acts of establishing hegemony lead to a nested form of hegemonic relations. Politics and pragmatics involved in cultural idealism and survival become entangled, leading to a constellation of agencies in which creativity produces (and reproduces) a complex form of cultural combination. The possible outcomes do not necessarily live up to the academic ideal of social justice. Cultural production will remain opaque to our view until the contexts of intercultural dialogue are more thoroughly explored, revisiting the how and when questions.[6]

This chapter draws upon what may be referred to as *longue durée* ethnography, which combines original ethnographic observations with historical analyses in order to explore intercultural dialogue and the subsequent cultural combination. An ethnographic case study, examined in light of particular sociohistorical conditions of cultural production, is followed by critical reflections on conceptual assumptions in the study of intercultural dialogue. First, the case study problematizes the premise that self-contained, distinct origins exist prior to their interactions, which has prevented our logical thinking outside a sequential, evolutionary reading of *purity* and *mixing* in the process of intercultural dialogues. Second, the analysis of the case questions the emphasis on a conception of agency as creative and free from self-contradiction, which has typically characterized the study of intercultural dialogue. Finally, the chapter points out that these conceptual emphases endure as a response to the dialectic of hopelessness regarding the colonial past and the hope of breaking with it.

## CASE STUDY: THE DEVOTION TO THE MARIAN STATUE IN TRINIDAD

*La Divina Pastora*, affectionately called by her adherents *La Divin* or "Mother," is a statue of a dark-complexioned Virgin Mary, a Catholic tutelary saint, which resides in the Catholic Church in Siparia, a southern town in the southern Caribbean island of Trinidad. Since the late nineteenth century, *La Divin*'s reputed miraculous power of curing "sickness"—broadly defined by devotees as physical, emotional, and material problems—has inspired passionate devotion from those of religions other than Catholicism.

Each year, between the afternoons of Maundy Thursday and Good Friday, thousands of non-Catholic—predominantly Hindu—pilgrims crowd the Church in Siparia and offer passionate prayers to *La Divin*. The scenes of devotion are visibly Hindu: many pilgrims, particularly women, are dressed in traditional South Asian-derived attire and wear a *tika* mark on their foreheads. They take along their newborn baby boys and let them receive their first haircut before the statue (the Hindu belief is that doing so in the divine presence brings fertility). The pilgrims shower offerings, including money, flowers, and rice grains on the statue as they do to *murtis* (effigies of Hindu gods/goddesses) during *puja* or other Hindu rites. Concluding their devotions, the pilgrims pour half a bottle of sweet [olive] oil into barrels set beside the statue. They take home the other half of the bottle, believing it has the power of curing [the] sick. On their way out of the site, most female devotees approach female lay ministers, affectionately calling them "mother," to request *jharay*, a Hindu practice of private consulting concerning "sickness."

On the third Sunday after Easter, however, the Church overflows with Catholic pilgrims, who make equally fervent devotion to the same statue. After Mass with eulogies on *La Divin*, the assembly goes in procession throughout Siparia. The statue, which was formerly carried on a portable shrine by parishioners, is now carried at the head of the procession tied to the roof of a car. After the procession is done, the statue is placed alongside the chapel's central altar for prayers and offerings offered from pilgrims. Many pilgrims from distant parishes—even from abroad—attend the Mass at the Siparia Church on this particular day, because *La Divin* is temporarily moved out of the gated shrine where she usually rests, which allows the pilgrims to have a closer audience with the Mother. An equally important motivation, particularly among female devotees, is to obtain the sweet oil, which they also believe cures sickness.

## PERFORMING WITH THE STATUE: PURITY AS SINE QUA NON

In Trinidad, a former British colony born of plantation-based exploitation, the "articulated discourse" of religion and race[7] has normalized notions that South Asian-descended populations are "unfit to be true Christians"[8] and that they would permanently insulate themselves from creolization process because of their primordial attachment to inferior, non-Christian religious expression, particularly Hinduism. Moreover, the context of postcolonial Creole nationalism has highlighted, not deconstructed, these notions of religion as representative of the abiding alterity of the people of South Asian origin. South Asian religious and intellectual elites appropriated this articulated discourse of race and religion to verify their cultural authenticity in rivalry with the political metadiscourse of nationalism, which idealizes the adaptability of European- and African-derived races and cultures.[9]

This discussion requires an exploration of why and how this statue has persisted as a shared agent of empowerment across ethnoreligious bounds in the colonial and postcolonial politics of race and cultural il/legitimation in this multireligious society. In fact, from the early twentieth century, the articulated discourse of race and religion had caused the Catholic elites to demand that the Siparian Catholics, the custodians of the statue, ban Hindu pilgrims from the Church. At the same time, Hindu elites urged lay Hindus to stay away from this image of Virgin Mary.[10] In the present study, however, a combination of ethnographic and archival research has revealed that *La Divin*, located at the intersection of various power relations, has inspired and enabled the Siparian Catholics to decline the Catholic central authorities' request. Instead, the leaders and parishioners in Siparia undertook measures to continually accommodate Hindu/non-Catholic devotees while guarding the immaculateness of *La Divin* as a Catholic Mother.

First, the Siparian Catholics have worked to set a temporal separation between Hindu/non-Catholic and Catholic devotions. The primary concern of the Catholic elites was that the Hindu/non-Catholic devotion usually extended through the night of Maundy Thursday and often delayed the beginning of the Good Friday Mass. Siparian Catholics started to set stricter temporal limits on the Hindu/non-Catholic devotion to the statue. Meanwhile, they urged lay Catholics to discontinue their custom of offering prayers to the statue on Good Friday and to stay away from the Church until Hindu/non-Catholic devotees removed themselves shortly before the Good Friday Mass. As a result, Hindu/non-Catholic devotions increasingly turned from a spontaneous and discursive phenomenon to a temporally circumscribed and scheduled event, then and now popularly called the "Coolie Fête."

Second, Siparian Catholics have placed the statue outside the sanctuary during the Coolie Fête. The spatial rearrangement of the statue started at the completion of the older chapel building in 1906 (when Siparia became an independent parish). In the older chapel, the statue was enshrined at the top of a high altar, and it was never taken down except for the annual Catholic Mass for *La Divin*, which came to be known as the "Siparia Fête" in contrast to the Coolie Fête. The current chapel, completed in 1960, installed a shrine dedicated to the statue at the same level as the pews, which allows devotees, Catholic or non-Catholic, to have a closer physical interaction with the statue. In response, the then-parish priest requested that the parishioners move the statue out of the chapel, and place her in the courtyard of the adjacent Catholic school when Hindus make their annual procession. Since then, on Maundy Thursdays and Good Fridays, the statue has never been offered payers within the sanctuary, although her location has constantly shifted.

Third, Siparian Catholics have fitted the statue up for different dresses between when she receives Hindu/non-Catholic devotees and when she presents herself before Catholic pilgrims. In the early twentieth century, they dressed the statue with new clothing, and made up her face with cosmetics before the Siparia Fête. After the completion of the present sanctuary, which allowed physically closer devotion to Hindu/non-Catholic pilgrims, the caretakers have increased the frequency of ceremonial change of the statue's outfits. Since the 1970s, the statue's clothing was changed before and after the Coolie Fête, in addition to the traditional dressing for the Siparia Fête. At the same time, the clothes used during the Coolie Fête became thrown away and would never be reused because, according to the caretakers, they were always "tainted with oils showered by Hindus."

Today, each year, on Easter Wednesday, the day prior to the Coolie Fête, Siparian Catholics work to embody what they refer to as "their [Hindu/non-Catholic] Mother," moving the statue out of the sanctuary and fitting her with clothing made for the Coolie Fête. When the Coolie Fête is over, they restore the statue as *La Divin*, "our [Catholic] Mother," placing her in her shrine within the sanctuary and dressing her with virgin robe and gown. In 2002, looking up at the statue, now located in the chapel and dressed for Easter Sunday, one of the caretakers stated with a sense of fulfillment and relief, "Now she happy to go see her son."

The parishioners in Siparia stress that this statue has always been a shared agent of empowerment across ethnoreligious boundaries due to their tolerance to otherness, which is both innate to the theological foundation of Roman Catholicism and characteristic of the diverse religious landscape of this Caribbean society. However, they have remained attentive to inconsistent ethnoreligious influences, which potentially compromise *La Divin*'s Catholic self. In the past, whenever Siparian Catholics perceived that the Catholic-ness of *La Divin* was becoming blurred, they have actualized further the ethnoreligious divisions and hierarchies, rearranging the statue in space and time, and changing the statue's clothes more often and more ceremonially. The Catholics' historical performance related to the statue has constantly addressed their original—and continuing—concern for cultural legitimacy. By making the statue available for Catholic and Hindu/non-Catholic devotions on different dates, at different places, and in different dresses, they have successfully sanctified *La Divin* as a manifestation of Virgin Mary. This has been the Siparian Catholics' rationale for tolerating and accommodating the Hindu/non-Catholic devotion to the statue within their cultural domain.

## "OUR MOTHER" AND "THEIR MOTHER": SYNCHRONIZING AND CO-AUTHENTICATING THE ORIGINS

Catholics' adoration of *La Divin* dates back to the eighteenth century, long before Hindus discovered the curative power of the statue. Since the late nineteenth century, the Hindu devotees have worshipped the statue, often calling her by different names, such as *Soparee Ke Mai* ("Mother of Siparia"). As argued in prior studies, the statue's Indian-like bodily features, such as her long dark hair that hangs down to her waist and her copper-colored complexion, may have motivated Hindus to identify the statue as an apparition of a Hindu goddess. However, what has given substance to *Soparee Ke Mai*, and to the practices and conscience centered on her, were the Catholics' ceremonial performances related to the statue, rather than manifestations of the Hindus' constant devotion. In the process, a unified spiritual community emerged, revolving around the statue as an indispensable counterpart of *La Divin*, "our Mother," in circular reference for each other's legitimation.

On Easter Wednesday in 2003, a female caretaker explained why she arrayed the statue for Hindu and non-Catholic devotees: "She goes out see them ... [as] their Mother in next two days. So she has to get all dressed up and wear more thorough makeup," indicating her intention to prepare the statue for Coolie Fête even more elaborately than for the Siparia Fête. Completing the arrangement by expertly painting the statue's face, she related in a triumphant tone: "Last year, a young Hindu woman came see their Mother and asked she blessing for a baby, baby boy. It worked! She came back this year with lots of offerings in return. It really works, you know. *My* Mother is great, isn't she?" More than this caretaker, the parishioners of today frequently adduce concrete episodes of how well "their Mother" has cured their sickness in attempting to evince the virtues of "our Mother." As a result, the supposedly distinct ethnoreligious origins, which are personified by the Mothers, have synchronized and formed a relation of circular reference for each other's authenticity.

More than vindication for *transgressing* Catholics to accept Hindu/non-Catholic devotions, the interstices between the Mothers—racialized representations of ethnoreligious origins—have served as a way for *transgressing* Hindus/non-Catholics to ensure their salvation at the statue within the Church without compromising their ethnoreligious identities. The lay Hindus' attachment to the image of Virgin Mary has also been considered as a heterodox representation within the elite-defined Hindu Orthodoxy. The entanglement of politics and pragmatic ritual practices has transformed *La Divin* into "our Mother" to consecrate the statue's Catholic identities, and embodied "their Mother" as consecrated without the bounds of the elite-defined Hindu Orthodoxy. Hindu devotion has increasingly authenticated "their Mother" as a representation of their own spirituality, thereby subconsciously engaging in the consecration of "our Mother." The Catholics' original arrangements have come to constitute a "life-endowing ritual" that has rendered the Mothers and both Fêtes more real and more powerful in conjunction with the processes they constantly activate.[11]

## The Statue that Performs: The Entanglement of Faith, Things, and Practice

Exemplified by the statue's clothes, which complete the statue's transfiguration between distinct ethnoreligious selves, the Siparian Catholics' power, political intentions, and creative faculties have conditioned the development of the worship of the statue. The Catholics have always intended to sanctify *La Divin* by dressing the statue in different outfits. Focusing on the materiality of the statue, however, the Catholics' practices have transformed the statue into an agentic and indexical object, which engages the devotees' spirituality and sociality. The mutual engagement between agencies of the statue and devotees has thus spiritualized the materiality of the statue and materialized the spirituality of the devotees.[12]

Clothing the statue has clothed it with abilities to cure devotees' sickness by moving between their social categories and hierarchies. The Catholics' ceremonial practices of contrasting and transposing the tangible and visible images of the statue have articulated their own belief that the statue autonomously changes identities according to devotees' individuality, such as their religious background, mode of prayers, and types and seriousness of their "sicknesses." And the historical "fact" that the statue has granted devotees' prayers without causing intercultural contentions has increased devotees' attachment to the statue and her virtues to cure sickness and confer salvation. At the same time, contextual identification has embedded the statue in social and material networks peculiar to Trinidad, where such identification is a required competence if one is to accommodate oneself to daily migratory processes, and to participate in the sociopolitical flows of multireligious and multiethnic Trinidad.[13] As a result, the statue has become "more real, more divine, and more interiorized"[14] and her performance of "curing sickness" has carried more conviction. What matters in connection with the statue's mobility is that the caretakers have insisted on the statue's material intermediacy, which is irreducible to either of the specific categories in the traditional black/white color-grading continuum. Instead, they often define the statue's bodily intermediacy with particular reference to the Indian-like features, despite the fact that African-descended populations have historically constituted a majority of Trinidadian Catholics. The statue is Marian, the most womanly representation, and is associated with stereotyped images of female identity, changeable with clothing and make-up. Together, these bodily characteristics of the statue may be said to have facilitated the devotees' classificatory objectification of the statue's subjects.

## An Alternate History: The Disembodiment of Intercultural Dialogue

The ethnographic case in this chapter has questioned the validity of the conceptual assumptions that predominate when intercultural dialogue is studied. These assumptions have been associated with the enduring desire for an ideological and intellectual break with the colonial past, and correspond with the two major approaches used to achieve this end. Vindicating what was disdained in the colonial past and redocumenting the colonial past per se—avenues to an alternate history—have facilitated and directed the production of ethnographic and historical knowledge.

The bastardization of mixed parentage in the colonial era obsessed with purity resulted in a "psycho-affective equilibrium,"[15] which established a counternarrative that attributes the creativity and fecundity of race and culture to their creoleness against self-contained pureness. The consequent obsession with "mixedness" has replicated, rather than deconstructed, a sequential, evolutionary reading of purity and mixing, which had rationalized the colonial degradation of the mixed. Subsequent theories have often downplayed the inevitable contradiction of racial and cultural production caused by peoples' simultaneous pursuit of these apparently inconsistent qualities. Driven by colonial past and urged by global social transformations today, people have often strived to simultaneously (even consistently) achieve racial and cultural pureness *and* "mixedness" for the sake of their status in ever-mixing sociopolitical processes. This chapter has illustrated such a parallel quest of pureness and mixedness in a particular sociohistorical context.

In Trinidad, since the late nineteenth century, the Hindus' discovery of the statue's curative power has inspired multilayered ideological and cultural politics in asymmetrical relations across and within Christian and non-Christian bounds. Placed at the intersection of various power relations, *La Divin* both forced and enabled Siparian Catholics to undertake pragmatic practices to sanctify the Catholic-ness personified by *La Divin* while accommodating Hindu/non-Catholic devotees in order to benefit from their devotional gift-giving. The entanglement of politics and pragmatism embodies the statue's two racial manifestations, "our Mother" and "their Mother," as representative of inconsistent ethnoreligious origins. At the same time, it incorporates these manifestations into mutual references affirming each other's genuineness. With the creation of mutually exclusive, yet coterminous Mothers, the symbols, practices, and consciences of competing ethnoreligious origins, which would have otherwise remained isolated, have formed a micro-community, and the dynamics of Hindus'/non-Catholics' transgression and the Catholics' responsive politics of identities have become important to the reproduction of this community. Within this community, the followers of the respective Mothers must simultaneously reproduce their ethnoreligious authenticity while engaging in a continuing practice of mixing with their counterparts. The Mothers will only retain their virtue and efficacy to cure sickness if they remain separate within an integrative whole. Catholic and Hindu/non-Catholic devotees have never shared a Mother; but they have shared Mothers.

Historiography seeking to view the colonial past in a new light has often concentrated on correcting supposed misrepresentations created by the colonizers' one-sided narration, rather than on increasing knowledge of the past.[16] The result is that the colonial past has been reimagined away from conscious and *actor-centered* perspectives of the colonized, particularly their working-class segments, in order to align the past with selective counterevidence. This historiography has served as an impetus to transform the designators for mixing (e.g., "Creole," "hybrid") from descriptive terms for linguistic and biological phenomena to concepts of general sociocultural experience.[17] This has historicized intercultural dialogue and mixing, drawing our attention to the fact that they predated the postcolonial transference of state and political institutions. However, the actuality of intercultural dialogue has been disembodied because of the underlying desire to demonstrate that human agency was creative and purposive, and consciousness was free from self-contradiction even in the face of brute colonialism. This is well exemplified by the trajectory of the notion of creolization. Creolization as a sociocultural concept originally focused on "interculturation" in order to propose that intercultural dialogue necessarily involved an interactive and cross-fertilizing process.[18] Selectively employed to unearth the submerged yet persistent cultures of the subaltern, however, the concept presented a rigid description of the relations between class and culture, as if they were predictable and universal.[19]

The Catholics' acts of contrasting and transposing the statue's material arrangements were and are intended to sanctify the integrity of *La Divin* from inconsistent ethnoreligious influences. However, the Catholics' practices have come to form an essential part of a "life-endowing ritual" that imbues the statue with agency, in conjunction with the Hindus' unceasing *transgressive* devotional practices (enabled by their own acts of separation). The resulting cross-religious collaboration developed the conception that the statue switches between competing ethnoreligious identities by her own volition, and therefore grants the prayers of devotees of any religious background—thus averting contentious cultural politics. The mobility of the statue resonates with the popular oral traditions among the devotees that the statue has a real, walking, transfiguring body. Their practices of rearranging the statue's placement and changing her dresses have facilitated and anchored the efficacy of the statue. These practices have created and recreated visible and tangible images of the statue, which have simultaneously created and recreated the devotees' spirituality and sociality. The creativity of this interreligious custom of sharing the statue resides in and emanates from the entanglement of the agencies of devotees, things (the statue and other relative objects, such as clothing), and existing social relations, a sphere where intentionality and unintentionality become intertwined.[20]

## TOWARD THE ACTUALITY OF INTERCULTURAL DIALOGUE

It is the result of a political process that the "intercultural" has come to occupy a central position in research on postcolonial societies. Intercultural dialogue has drawn increasing attention as part of broader academic-cum-political agenda based on a dialectic of mutually enhancing sentiments—hopelessness regarding the colonial past and hopefulness for a break with it. This dialectic of hope and hopelessness has involved analytical antitheses, such as mixing and purity, intentional and unconscious, divisive and organic, and creative and undermining. Creolization, hybridization, and other concepts of mixing have gained the status of *grandes idées* or even "master tropes," with increasing currency in academic and popular discourses within this epistemological context.[21]

The creativity of the devotional practices surrounding the statue of *La Divin* has historically resided in, and emanated from, situations where these analytically contrasted qualities and dimensions formed a relational texture. As suggested by this case study, the real challenge is that neither a theory of the mutual constitution of prior forms nor a complete deconstruction (if at all possible) of classificatory concepts such as culture, subject and object, and "mixedness" and pureness, seem to be effective strategies for elucidating the nature of intercultural dialogue. Instead, it is when intercultural dialogues involve the structural relations of specific agencies, they require developing a more concrete interpretation than the usual abstractions (such as an assemblage of free-floating events or a perpetually changing process of meaning-making that imply a lack of structure). At the current moment, a reconciliation of ethnography and historiography seems to be the best path to the materiality of intercultural dialogue. What is important is to cut our observations free from the dialectic of hope/hopelessness, which has so often transformed deconstruction as an applicable form of semiotic analysis into deconstructionism as an end unto itself.[22]

## NOTES

1. Michael-Rolph Trouillot, "Culture on the Edge: Caribbean Creolization in Historical Context," in *From the Margins: Historical Anthropology and Its Future*, ed. B. K. Axel (Durham, NC: Duke University Press, 2002), 189.

2. Sara Suleri, *The Rhetoric of English India* (Chicago: University of Chicago Press, 1992), 23.

3. Christoph Brumann, "Writing for Culture: Why a Successful Concept Should Not Be Discarded," (Special Issue: Culture—A Second Chance?) *Current Anthropology*, 40 (1999): S1–S27; Marshall Sahlins, "Two or Three Things that I Know About Culture," *Journal of the Royal Anthropological Institute*, 5, 3 (1999): 299–421.

4. Pnina Werbner, "Introduction: The Dialectics of Cultural Hybridity," in *Debating Cultural Hybridity: Multi-Cultural Identities and the Politics of Anti-racism*, ed. P. Werbner and T. Modood (Atlantic Highlands, NJ: Zed Books, 1997), 1–26.

5. Aisha Khan, *Callaloo Nation: Metaphors of Race and Religious Identity among South Asians in Trinidad* (Durham, NC: Duke University Press, 2004), 5.

6. Richard Price, *Travels with Tooy: History, Memory, and the African American Imagination* (Chicago: University of Chicago Press, 2008);

Richard Price and Sally Price, "Shadowboxing in the Mangrove," *Cultural Anthropology*, 12, 1 (1997): 3–36; Trouillot, "Culture on the Edge: Caribbean Creolization in Historical Context," 189–210.

7. Khan, *Callaloo Nation: Metaphors of Race and Religious Identity among South Asians in Trinidad.*

8. Viranjini Munasinghe, *Callaloo or Tossed Salad? East Indians and the Cultural Politics of Identity in Trinidad* (Ithaca, NY: Cornell University Press, 2001), 197; Viranjini Munasinghe, "Theorizing World Culture through the New World: East Indians and Creolization," *American Ethnologist*, 33, 4 (2006): 549–562, 553.

9. Munasinghe, ibid.; Khan, *Callaloo Nation: Metaphors of Race and Religious Identity among South Asians in Trinidad*; Aisha Khan, "Creolization Moments," in *Creolization: History, Ethnography, Theory*, ed. C. Stewart (Walnut Creek, CA: Left Coast Press, 2007), 237–253; Aisha Khan, "Good to Think? Creolization, Optimism, and Agency," *Current Anthropology*, 48, 5 (2007): 653–673.

10. Teruyuki Tsuji, *Hyphenated Cultures: Ethnicity and Nation in Trinidad*. PhD Diss., Florida International University, Miami, FL, 2006; Teruyuki Tsuji, "Mothers—Hyphenated Imaginations: The Feasts of *Soparee Ke Mai* and *La Divina Pastora* in Trinidad," in *Indian Diaspora in the Caribbean*, ed. K. Mahabir (New Delhi: Serials Publications, 2010), 169–191.

11. Peter L. Berger, *The Sacred Canopy: Elements of a Sociological Theory of Religion* (Garden City, NY: Doubleday, 1969); Lynn Meskell, "Objects in the Mirror Appear Closer than They Are," in *Materiality*, ed. D. Miller (Durham, NC: Duke University Press, 2005), 51–71.

12. Alfred Gell, *Art and Agency: An Anthropological Theory* (Oxford: Oxford University Press, 1998); Julius Bautista and Anthony Reid, "Introduction: Materiality in a Problematically Plural Southeast Asia," in *The Spirit of Things: Materiality and Religious Diversity in Southeast Asia*, ed. J. Bautista, South Asian Program Publications (Ithaca, NY: Cornell University Press, 2012), 1–10; Meskell, "Objects in the Mirror Appear Closer than They Are," 2005.

13. Charles V. Carnegie, "Strategic Flexibility in the West Indies: A Social Psychology of Caribbean Migration," *Caribbean Review*, 11, 1 (1982): 10–13, 54; Tsuji, *Hyphenated Cultures: Ethnicity and Nation in Trinidad*; Tsuji, "Mothers—Hyphenated Imaginations: The Feasts of *Soparee Ke Mai* and *La Divina Pastora* in Trinidad."

14. Meskell, "Objects in the Mirror Appear Closer than They Are," 58.

15. Franz Fanon, *The Wretched of the Earth* (New York: Grove, 1963), 148.

16. Fanon, *The Wretched of the Earth*, 1963; Charles V. Carnegie, *Postcolonialism Prefigured: Caribbean Borderlands* (New Brunswick, NJ: Rutgers University Press, 2002).

17. See, for example, Mervyn C. Alleyne, "Acculturation and the Cultural Matrix of Creolization," in *Pidginization and Creolization of Languages: Proceedings of a Conference Held at the University of the West Indies,*

*Mona, Jamaica, April 1968*, ed. Dell Hymes (Cambridge: Cambridge University Press, 1971), 169–186.

18. See, for example, Edward Brathwaite, *Contradictory Omens: Cultural Diversity and Integration in the Caribbean* (Mona: Savocou Publications, 1974).

19. Robert C. Young, *Colonial Desire: Hybridity in Theory, Culture, and Race* (New York: Routledge, 1995); Robert C. Young, *Postcolonialism: A Historical Introduction* (Hoboken, NJ: Wiley-Blackwell, 2001); Charles Stewart, "Creolization: History, Ethnography, Theory," in *Creolization: History, Ethnography, and Theory*, ed. C. Stewart (Walnut Creek, CA: Left Coast Press, 2007), 1–25; Khan, *Callaloo Nation: Metaphors of Race and Religious Identity among South Asians in Trinidad*; Khan, "Creolization Moments"; Khan, "Good to Think? Creolization, Optimism, and Agency."

20. Daniel Miller, "Materiality: An Introduction," in *Materiality*, ed. D. Miller (Durham, NC: Duke University Press, 2005), 1–50; Michael Rowlands, "A Materialist Approach to Materiality," in *Materiality*, ed. D. Miller (Durham, NC: Duke University Press, 2005), 72–87; Berger, *The Sacred Canopy: Elements of a Sociological Theory of Religion*; Gell, *Art and Agency: An Anthropological Theory*; Meskell, "Objects in the Mirror Appear Closer than They Are"; Bautista and Reid, "Introduction: Materiality in a Problematically Plural Southeast Asia."

21. Trouillot, "Culture on the Edge: Caribbean Creolization in Historical Context"; Stewart "Creolization: History, Ethnography, Theory"; Khan, "Creolization Moments"; Khan, "Good to Think? Creolization, Optimism, and Agency."

22. Naoki Kasuga, "*Ima naze rekishi ka*" [Why history matters now], *Bunkajinruigaku*, 69, 3 (2004): 373–385; Khan, "Good to Think? Creolization, Optimism, and Agency."

# Part II

# Interculturality and Social Identity

# 4

# GROUP IDENTITY AND ATTITUDES IN GUATEMALA: THE ROLE OF ETHNIC INTERCULTURALITY

*Brien K. Ashdown, Judith L. Gibbons,
and Yetilú de Baessa*

For most of its history, the field of psychology has been tied to the cultures of the countries in which it originated—the United States and the nations of Western Europe.[1] As a result, psychology is culture-bound (limited to the findings, evidence, and assumptions of the United States and Europe) and culture-blind (overlooking and disregarding the influence of culture on human behavior).[2] A psychology that is intercultural in nature is necessary to overcome both of those shortcomings. The fields of cross-cultural psychology, indigenous psychology, and intercultural psychology can further a science of psychology that is global and at the same time acknowledges local differences in human psychology.

Creating a global psychology requires an awareness of diversity and increased interculturality, not only between different groups and cultures, but also within individuals. Increasingly, individuals define themselves as bi- or multicultural, incorporating the traditions, values, and identities of more than one heritage. In contrast, psychology and other social sciences often focus on creating distinct groups of individuals in order to make comparisons—especially between gender and ethnic/cultural groups. Constructing these distinct groups aids with analyses and interpretations, but it also creates arbitrary boundaries and ignores the rich variety of experiences of individuals.

Group identity and group attitudes have been the focus of a great deal of psychological theory and research. However, the exploration of interculturality in identity and group membership is still underdeveloped. Advancing the understanding of interstitial individuals, those who do not fall neatly within a group, will provide opportunities to better understand multiple identities and how they are instantiated in behavior and attitudes. This can be done without having to ignore between-group comparisons. The study of intergroup relations, theories, and interculturality is particularly valuable in the unique cultural context of Guatemala, where research could reveal insights regarding the global applicability of those theories and at the same time advance our understanding of interculturality.

## PSYCHOLOGICAL THEORIES OF GROUP IDENTITY AND ATTITUDES

### Social Identity Theory

Social Identity Theory postulates that people identify themselves as a member of a group and then assess and consider their group, called the in-group, more favorably than other groups, called the out-group(s).[3] The reason for in-group favoritism (or, possibly, out-group derogation) is that by favoring the in-group, individuals boost their own self-identity and self-esteem. Viewing ourselves as members of a group provides a clear, distinctive, and valid identity, which is important in telling us who we are and where we belong.[4]

Social Identity Theory can be applied not only to ethnic intergroup relations, but also to interactions between other social groups that differ by religion, nationality, or even some arbitrary factor. For example, school children assigned to groups distinguished and classified solely by shirt color demonstrated a clear bias for in-group members compared to out-group members.[5]

The logic of Social Identity Theory suggests that if in-group favoritism leads to out-group derogation, then racism, bias, and discrimination can be explained in terms of group membership. However, some have claimed that in-group favoritism does not automatically lead to out-group derogation. One can prefer his or her in-group without actively hating or disliking the out-groups.[6] It is clear, then, that Social Identity Theory alone is not sufficient to explain all aspects of group identity and attitudes, and that other theories also explain crucial components of these constructs.

### Self-Categorization Theory

Tajfel suggested that the salience, or prominence, of group membership influences the consequences of group identity in any given situation.[7] Turner and his colleagues[8] further developed this hypothesis as a major component of Self-Categorization Theory.[9]

Self-Categorization Theory posits that an individual's sense of self and identity is organized in a hierarchical fashion.[10] As in Social Identity Theory, self-identity is based on relationships, group membership, and comparisons. However, what distinguishes Self-Categorization Theory from Social Identity Theory is the greater emphasis on identity salience. Not all social identities have equal influence in all social contexts; for example, an individual may place greater importance on her gender than her ethnicity. Another individual may have a strong religious identity, and less salient gender, professional, and ethnic identities.

One of the major constructs of this theory is the meta-contrast principle, which states that individuals compare between-group differences to within-group differences.[11] Large meta-contrasts suggest that the between-group differences are much greater than the within-group differences, critically distinguishing between the two groups. The greater the meta-contrast, the greater the likelihood that that particular group categorization will become salient and important to the individual.[12]

A key condition of the meta-contrast principle is the social context in which the comparison of between-group and within-group differences takes place. For example, if a group of ethnically diverse people is asked to discuss their spiritual beliefs, religious membership will likely become the salient group categorization. This is because the differences within religious groups will be seen as less sizable than the differences between religious groups. However, if the conversation shifts to a topic such as affirmative action, ethnic group (or perhaps political group) membership might become the salient group categorization. This is because the salience of group identity is reliant upon the context, and will change as the context changes.[13] There are clear differences between Social Identity Theory and Self-Categorization Theory, such as the emphasis placed on group salience and social context. Both theories, however, underscore the importance of group membership and comparisons between groups in explaining group identity and group attitudes.

## Model of Ethnic Identity Development

Based on the theoretical and empirical work of James Marcia[14]—which in turn was based on the work of Erik Erikson[15]—Jean Phinney proposed a new framework for considering ethnic identity, especially among ethnic minorities.[16] The theory is developmental, and posits stages and processes for development of an ethnic identity. Originally a three-stage model, the theory now focuses primarily on two processes derived from Erikson's and Marcia's work: exploration and commitment.[17]

Exploration is a process in which individuals invest time and effort to learn about their ethnic group via conversing with other group members, reading histories or biographies, or participating in sociocultural activities. Commitment, also referred to as resolution,[18] refers to achieving a strong sense of belonging to one's ethnic group, along with an understanding of the role that that ethnic identity will play in one's life. Phinney claims that exploration and commitment to an ethnic group identity are characteristic of the life stage of adolescence, but can remain an important developmental task for adults as well.[19]

Based on her theoretical work, Phinney developed the Multigroup Ethnic Identity Measure (MEIM),[20] and a later revised version (MEIM-R),[21] to measure ethnic group identity. Using those measures (as well as some others), higher levels of ethnic identity achievement have been related to psychological well-being, including high self-esteem, and negatively related to externalizing symptoms, such as rule breaking and stealing.[22] One should note, however, that while the relationship between ethnic identity and psychosocial adjustment tends to be positive, some of the research findings are mixed.[23]

A strong ethnic identity is also associated with positive evaluations of both one's in-group and out-group.[24] Phinney claims that the more secure an individual feels in her or his own ethnic identity, the more likely that she or he will accept and value out-group members.[25] Phinney's claim is consistent with the multicultural hypothesis put forth by Berry[26]—that people who have a positive and secure sense of their own cultural identity will be more tolerant of and positive toward other cultural groups.

One of the benefits of having a strong ethnic group identity might be an increased willingness to interact with members of other groups. Indeed, Phinney and others[27] found that the more individuals interacted with out-group members (in conjunction with a strong sense of their own identity), the more likely they were to have positive attitudes toward the out-group. This view, known as Intergroup Contact Hypothesis, was first popularized by Gordon Allport.[28]

## Intergroup Contact Hypothesis

Although the belief that contact with out-group members would reduce prejudice had been present since the 1930s,[29] Allport is usually credited with espousing intergroup contact as the way to reduce ethnic prejudice. In his now classic work *The Nature of Prejudice*,[30] he cautioned that for intergroup contact to be effective certain conditions must apply:

> To be maximally effective, contact and acquaintance programs should lead to a sense of equality in social status, should occur in ordinary purposeful pursuits, avoid artificiality, and if possible enjoy the sanction of the community in which they occur. The deeper and more genuine the association, the greater its effect. While it may help somewhat to place members of different ethnic groups side by side on a job, the gain is greater if these members regard themselves as part of a *team*. (454, emphasis in original)[31]

Since the publication of Allport's book, research on the Intergroup Contact Hypothesis[32] has proliferated.[33] For example, Phinney and others[34] found that the more often adolescents interacted with outgroup members outside of school, the more positive were their views of those out-group members. In addition, research has linked Self-Categorization Theory to the Intergroup Contact Hypothesis. Attitudes toward out-group members are more favorable when group categories remain salient during the intergroup contact.[35]

The Intergroup Contact Hypothesis and the other three theories of group identity and attitudes described above are only a subset of such theories.[36] However, they provide a starting point from which to explore the cross-cultural applicability of the theories, as well as to investigate the role of interculturality in a unique, intercultural context such as Guatemala.

## THE INTERCULTURAL CONTEXT OF GUATEMALA

Since the arrival of the Spanish conquistadors and Catholic Church[37] in the sixteenth century, inequality and discrimination have been a hallmark of ethnic group relations in Guatemala. Early distinctions were made between those of indigenous Maya heritage and those of European (mostly Spanish) heritage.[38] That distinction continues today,[39] where currently in Guatemala there are two primary ethnic groups: those who make a strong claim to Maya heritage and are known as Indigenous peoples and those who make a claim to European heritage, called Ladinos (who are often of mixed-heritage but perceived as nonindigenous).

This ongoing distinction leads to continuing discrimination against the Indigenous peoples.[40] The discrimination reveals itself in great discrepancies in health, economics, politics, and education—Ladinos have more access to health care, accumulate more wealth, and attain higher levels of formal education than Indigenous peoples.[41] For example, the GINI coefficient (a measure of economic inequality in which higher numbers indicate more disparity) for Guatemala is the world's tenth highest, recorded at 55.1 as of the year 2007 (the most recent year this information is available).[42] For comparison, the United States' GINI coefficient is 45.0, making it the forty-first highest recorded in the world, and Sweden's is 23.0, the lowest recorded in the world.[43] The issue of economic disparity is also an issue of ethnic disparity, as roughly four of every five Indigenous peoples in Guatemala live in poverty, compared to approximately two of every five Ladinos.[44]

Guatemala's Human Development Index (HDI), a measure of a country's progress in health, education, and standard of living, was .62 for the year 2014. This places it in the medium human development category with the rank of 125 of 187 countries. Guatemala has an HDI lower than the average for Latin America and the Caribbean (which is .74) and slightly above the average for other medium category countries (.61).[45] Even though Guatemala is in the medium category, it should be noted that the HDI for the country as a whole is higher than it is for Indigenous groups,[46] meaning that Indigenous peoples experience less progress in health, wealth, and education than does Guatemala as a whole. For example, when the HDI of Guatemala is adjusted for in-country inequalities, it drops to .42, a loss of 32.8% from the non-adjusted HDI, underscoring the level of inequality among ethnic groups in Guatemala.[47]

As part of the 1996 peace accords that ended more than 30 years of civil war defined by violence against the Indigenous peoples, equal treatment for Indigenous people was prescribed.[48] Unfortunately, the country's government has been slow to implement these provisions, as Indigenous people still suffer from the disparities mentioned above.[49] Inequality and bias are also apparent in social attitudes. Some Indigenous peoples see their group membership and identity as disadvantageous. For example, a majority of interviewed Quiché children (members of an Indigenous group from the Guatemala highlands) answered negatively when asked if they liked being Indigenous, and some were ashamed of their ethnic identity.[50] In another study, an Indigenous woman claimed that Indigenous people were afraid to speak their own languages because the Ladinos do not like it.[51]

A poll by local Guatemalan media in 2005 found that a majority of respondents, both Indigenous and Ladinos, agreed that Indigenous people face discrimination in every-day situations.[52] For example, respondents claimed that lighter-skinned people and Ladinos have an easier time finding employment and are better treated in government offices than darker-skinned and Indigenous people. In addition, attitudes between the two cultural groups were mutually negative.[53] Research in academic journals has displayed much the same picture of in-group favoritism and mutually negative attitudes between the two cultural groups.[54]

It should be noted, though, that attempts to address these issues are being carried out. Conversations about ethnic and cultural relations are becoming more common via media outlets, such as daily newspapers.[55] Historical, cultural, and anthropological groups, such as El Centro de Investigaciones Regionales de Mesoamérica, are focusing on the issue by way of museum exhibits, book series, and public lectures. A recent exhibition in the national airport in Guatemala City, aimed at demonstrating the diversity of Guatemalans, was titled "Guatemala Diversa" [Diverse Guatemala]. The exhibition consisted of larger-than-life photographs of Guatemalans who differed by origin (ethnicity), age, gender, and social condition. The government is also involved in such discussions. There is a presidential commission charged with investigating racism and discrimination, the Comisión Presidencial contra la Discriminación y el Racismo contra los Pueblos Indígenas en Guatemala (CODISRA).[56] One hopes that these efforts, while slow in arriving and slow in progression, are the forerunners of significant and important change.

These issues of modern discrimination and the historical bases for establishment of the ethnic groups in Guatemala make it an appropriate setting for the study of group identity and bias.[57] As in all parts of the world, ethnicity and race in Guatemala are socially constructed categories. Ethnicity in Guatemala has been described as a "fiction of bipolarity" (translated from the Spanish).[58] Specifically, the concept of "Ladino" is diffuse and not well defined.[59] Although the term refers to anyone who claims some European heritage and does not adopt a Mayan identity, the lack of a unified history and absence of unifying cultural symbols limit the strength of identification. As a nation, Guatemala uses images drawn from its Mayan heritage to promote its international image; these include ancient Mayan pyramids and persons dressed in "traje," the traditional attire of the Maya.

Unsurprisingly then, ethnic group identity in Guatemala is relatively fluid.[60] Because so many of the markers of ethnic group identity in Guatemala are cultural in nature (language, attire), it is possible for individuals to shift from one group to the other. This can be done by speaking a different language (e.g., speaking Spanish instead of a Maya language), wearing nontraditional or Western clothes, associating with particular groups of people, or by simply claiming a different identity. The fluidity of group membership makes Guatemala an especially appropriate setting to examine the meaning of interculturality and its relation to ethnic attitudes.

If individuals can transition from one group to another, it might make their group identity less important to them due to a sense of transience. On the other hand, it might make group identity even more important because the group members feel like they must actively work to maintain their identity. Either of these consequences could impact the level of interculturality of Guatemalans. People who are more variable in their group identity or those who see themselves as a mix of both heritages would need to expend effort in order to be proficient in both groups.

Another reason why Guatemalan society provides an interesting context for the exploration of these constructs is because the difference between the powerful group (Ladinos) and the subordinate group (Indigenous peoples) is not one of numbers, but one of power. Ladinos make up approximately 58% of the population while Indigenous Maya persons make up approximately 40% of the population.[61] This creates a society that relies on the acceptance and transmission of cultural ideologies to maintain societal hierarchies over such a large subordinate group.[62]

The unique situation of ethnic group identity in Guatemala, along with the new and increasing prevalence of dialogue about these issues, combine to create a dynamic situation in which to explore the interculturality of group membership (both within and between groups). It proffers the opportunity to move beyond investigating group identity and attitudes based on in-group or out-group memberships and to include an exploration of the interculturality of Guatemalans. This is particularly useful in the context of the psychological theories of group identity discussed above.

## Application of Theories in Guatemala

One of the first steps we took in exploring group identity in Guatemala was to develop an innovative method to measure the variability of group membership.[63] We presented participants with a 15-cm line, anchored with "purely Indigenous" on the left and "purely Ladino" on the right. Participants were instructed to put a mark on the line where they believe their group identity best fit. The participants' marks were then measured from the left, simply so that higher numbers indicated a greater claim to Ladino heritage (and, alternately, lower numbers indicated a greater claim to Indigenous heritage).

Measuring group identity in this manner provides participants with the chance to claim their own heritage rather than be forced to put themselves into "boxes," ethnic categories predetermined by researchers. It also allows researchers to investigate participants' ethnicity in at least two different ways. First, their ethnicity can be explored as a continuous variable from Indigenous to Ladino. This allows individuals to locate themselves between the labeled groups and to endorse an intercultural identity.

Second, participants' self-reported ethnicity can still be used to create grouping variables, or ethnic categories, based on the distribution of the continuous variable. In the studies where we have utilized this method of measuring ethnic identity,[64] the distribution of the continuous ethnicity variable breaks into three distinct groups: Ladinos (who put their marks on the far right side of the line), Indigenous (who put their marks on the far left side of the line), and those we might call Interculturals (who put their mark somewhere in the middle of line). Creating these groups allows researchers to explore group differences on variables, such as in-group favoritism or out-group derogation.

Utilizing this method of collecting information about Guatemalan's ethnic group identity, we have been able to explore the theories of group identity discussed previously among university students and adolescents in Guatemala, as well as investigate the way that interculturality may (or may not) correspond to those theories. We have focused on those age groups because, as stated above, group identity is seen as an important developmental task for adolescents[65] and young (also called emerging) adults.[66] Our findings indicate that while age-group differences do exist, there are interesting parallels with respect to interculturality.

In several studies both adolescents and emerging adults held more favorable attitudes toward their own ethnic group. Statistical analysis revealed in-group favoritism among Ladino and Indigenous people: Ladinos expressed more positive attitudes toward other Ladinos than toward Indigenous, and Indigenous people expressed more positive attitudes toward other Indigenous people than toward Ladinos.[67]

However, those with an intercultural identification were unique. Their attitudes toward the two ethnic groups fell in-between the attitudes of Ladinos and those of Indigenous. They did not express more positive attitudes for either Indigenous or Ladinos.[68] Interculturality seems to have played the role of tempering Intercultural peoples' attitudes toward both groups. In other words, according to Social-Categorization Theory, for Interculturals the ethnic group might be less salient. The meta-contrast between within-group differences and between-group differences may not be large enough to make ethnic group categorization salient and relevant.

In a study of adolescents' ethnic identity,[69] we worked with participants in two locales: Tecpan, a town of approximately 22,000 people in the highlands of Guatemala with a relatively large population of Maya Kaqchikel people, and Antigua, a tourist destination that is a more diverse urban setting, with a population of about 40,000. Among adolescents in Tecpan, the majority claimed Indigenous heritage, while the majority of adolescents in Antigua claimed Ladino heritage. Those who claimed an intercultural heritage were more likely to live in Tecpan than in Antigua.

In-group favoritism was more prominent in Tecpan than in Antigua and more prominent for Indigenous peoples than for Ladinos. The differences between the communities reinforce the idea that context matters—one of the basic claims of Self-Categorization Theory.[70] In-group favoritism was highest for Indigenous peoples where the majority of the people were Indigenous. In a predominantly Indigenous town such as Tecpan the language, attire, and other signs of ethnic identity are marked, so that ethnic identity assumes salience. In other words, consistent with Self-Categorization Theory, the salient and prominent Indigenous group developed more favorable in-group attitudes because of a large meta-contrast (larger between-group than within-group differences).

In Antigua, where the majority of individuals claim Ladino heritage, attitudes toward Indigenous peoples were unrelated to participants' own ethnicity. On one hand, this appears to contradict both Social Identity Theory and Self-Categorization Theory (both of which assert that a person's own group identity will influence his or her attitudes toward in- and out-group members). On the other hand, though, it does provide support for the Intergroup Contact Hypothesis.[71] Living in the urban, more diverse Antigua leads to more contact among members of different ethnic groups, and this contact in a heterogeneous context might reduce negative out-group attitudes and/or in-group favoritism. The greater in-group favoritism among Indigenous people (independent of the geographical setting) may be related to the cohesive historical record of Mayan culture, along with visible markers, such as language and dress, that extend to the present time. Ethnic identity may be more salient for cohesive groups with well-established boundaries.

Not only does ethnic identification influence in-group and out-group attitudes, but the strength of that identity also influences attitudes. Recall that Phinney[72] claims that people who strongly identify with their own ethnic group will have more positive attitudes toward both the in-group and the out-group than will those who do not identify with their group as strongly.

Phinney's hypothesis bears out in Guatemala. Using the MEIM[73] as a measure of the strength of ethnic identity, we found that the more strongly individuals identified with their ethnic group—regardless of whether they identify themselves as Ladinos, Indigenous, or Interculturals—the more positive their attitudes toward both in-group members and out-group members.[74] When people feel confident in their own ethnic identification, they may feel less need to favor the in-group and derogate the out-group in order to supplement their personal self-esteem.

## Conclusion

What these research findings suggest is multifaceted. The most important finding is that ethnicity in Guatemala is not well represented by "boxes." Significant numbers of individuals locate themselves in the interstitial spaces, and may be described as Interculturals. Interculturals occupy a unique position with respect to group identity and attitudes. Their attitudes toward other groups are different from those who claim mainly Indigenous or Ladino heritage. Because they fail to show derogation of either Indigenous or Ladino others, their viewpoints may harbinger a future of less prejudice and discrimination.

A second implication is that no single theory is sufficient to explain ethnic group identity and group attitudes. Rather, various aspects of the data support different theories—suggesting that a more complex and comprehensive theory would better represent group relations in Guatemala.

The findings also reinforce the importance of social context in influencing the salience of group identities, and that salience in turn influences group attitudes. Those relations are consistent with Self-Categorization Theory.[75] Individuals who live in a more diverse and heterogeneous community showed less out-group derogation and in-group favoritism, supporting the main claim of the Intergroup Contact Hypothesis.[76]

However, in-group favoritism still prevails, as people tend to have more positive attitudes toward individuals who are similar to them, consistent with Social Identity Theory.[77] Further complicating the picture is the finding that the more confident people are in their own ethnic identity, the less likely they are to demonstrate group bias, as theorized by Phinney.[78]

Further steps could be taken to explore the impact of group saliency more thoroughly within the context of Social Identity Theory and Self-Categorization Theory—perhaps by measuring Interculturals' attitudes toward other Interculturals. If Interculturals showed in-group favoritism by having more positive attitudes toward other Interculturals than they do toward Ladinos or Indigenous peoples, it would lend great support to Social Identity Theory, even when accounting for the influence of interculturality on the theory.

In addition, future research and theoretical writing should focus on expanding beyond ethnicity. For example, do the current theories of group identity hold true as sufficient explanation for groups other than ethnic groups, such as gender groups, religious groups, or national groups? All of these are types of cultural groups in which interculturality will play a role. In addition, they are all types of identities that interact, or intersect, with one another. Future explorations should address this intersectionality, and the way in which interculturality impacts the way different types of group identity interact on an individual and societal level.

Furthermore, qualitative methods, such as interviews and focus groups, should be used in conjunction with and in addition to quantitative methods. Qualitative methods allow for more detailed, rich, and fuller descriptions of peoples' lives, experiences, beliefs, and encounters.[79] The utilization of qualitative methods will lead to a deeper understanding of people's experiences with and understanding of their own interculturality and its effects on society and individuals.

Focusing on and better understanding the role that interculturality plays in the lives of people will not only lead us toward a more global psychology, but toward a more global understanding of the human experience. It will bring us closer to the goals of being neither culture-bound nor culture-blind, and developing a science of psychology that integrates perspectives and observations from around the world.

## Notes

1. John W. Berry, "Achieving a Global Psychology," *Canadian Psychology/Psychologie Canadienne*, 54 (2013): 55–61.
2. Ibid.
3. Henri Tajfel and John Turner, "The Social Identity Theory of Intergroup Behavior," in *Psychology of Intergroup Relations*, ed. Stephen Worchel and William G. Austin (Chicago: Nelson Hall, 1986), 7–24.

4. Russell Spears, "Group Identities: The Social Identity Perspective," in *Handbook of Identity Theory and Research*, ed. Seth J. Schwartz, Koen Luyckx, and Vivian L. Vignoles (New York: Springer, 2011), 201–224.
5. Rebecca S. Bigler, Cristia S. Brown, and Marc Markell, "When Groups Are Not Created Equal: Effects of Group Status on the Format of Intergroup Attitudes on Children," *Child Development*, 72 (2001): 1151–1162.
6. Frances E. Aboud, *Children and Prejudice* (Oxford: Blackwell, 1988); Gordon. W. Allport, *The Nature of Prejudice* (New York: Doubleday Anchor Books, 1958); James L. Gibson, "Do Strong Group Identities Fuel Intolerance? Evidence from the South African Case," *Political Psychology*, 27 (2006): 665–705.
7. Spears, "Group Identities: The Social Identity Perspective," 201–224.
8. John C. Turner, "Towards a Cognitive Redefinition of the Social Group," in *Social Identity and Intergroup Relations*, ed. by Henri Tajfel (Cambridge: Cambridge University Press, 1982), 15–40; John C. Turner and Others, *Rediscovering the Social Group: A Self-Categorization Theory* (New York: Blackwell, 1987).
9. Spears, "Group Identities: The Social Identity Perspective," 201–224.
10. Ibid.
11. Ibid.
12. Ibid.
13. Ibid.
14. James E. Marcia, "Identity in Adolescence," in *Handbook of Adolescent Psychology*, ed. Joseph Adelson (New York: Wiley, 1980), 159–187.
15. Erik H. Erikson, *Identity: Youth and Crisis* (New York: Norton, 1968).
16. Jean S. Phinney, "Stages of Ethnic Identity Development in Minority Group Adolescents," *The Journal of Early Adolescence*, 9 (1989): 34–49.
17. Adriana J. Umaña-Taylor, "Ethnic Identity," in *Handbook of Identity Theory and Research*, ed. Seth J. Schwartz, Koen Luyckx, and Vivian L. Vignoles (New York: Springer, 2011), 791–810.
18. Ibid.
19. Jean. S. Phinney, "Ethnic Identity in Adolescents and Adults: Review of Research," *Psychological Bulletin*, 108 (1990): 499–514.
20. Jean S. Phinney, "The Multigroup Ethnic Identity Measure: A New Scale for Use with Diverse Groups," *Journal of Adolescent Research*, 7 (1992): 156–176.
21. Jean S. Phinney and Anthony D. Ong, "Conceptualization and Measurement of Ethnic Identity: Current Status and Future Directions," *Journal of Counseling Psychology*, 54 (2007): 271–281.
22. Seth J. Schwartz, Byron L. Zamboanga, and Lorna Hernandez Jarvis, "Ethnic Identity and Acculturation in Hispanic Early Adolescents: Mediated Relationships to Academic Grades, Prosocial Behaviors, and Externalizing Symptoms," *Cultural Diversity and Ethnic Minority Psychology*, 13 (2007): 364–373.
23. Umaña-Taylor, *Handbook of Identity Theory and Research*, 791–810.

24. Phinney, "Stages of Ethnic Identity Development in Minority Group Adolescents," 34–49.

    Jean S. Phinney, Debra L. Ferguson, and Jerry D. Tate, "Intergroup Attitudes among Ethnic Minority Adolescents: A Causal Model," *Child Development*, 68 (1997): 955–969.

25. Ibid.

26. John W. Berry, "Cultural Relations in Plural Societies: Alternatives to Segregation and Their Sociopsychological Implications," in *Groups in Contact: The Psychology of Desegregation*, ed. Norman Miller and Marilyn B. Brewer (Orlando, FL: Academic Press, 1984), 11–29.

27. Phinney, Ferguson, and Tate, "Intergroup Attitudes among Ethnic Minority Adolescents: A Causal Model," 955–969.

28. Allport, *The Nature of Prejudice*.

29. John F. Dovidio, Samuel L. Gaertner, and Kerry Kawakami, "Intergroup Contact: The Past, Present, and the Future," *Group Processes & Intergroup Relations*, 6 (2003): 5–20.

30. Allport, *The Nature of Prejudice*.

31. Ibid.

32. Dovidio, Gaertner, and Kawakami, "Intergroup Contact: The Past, Present, and the Future," 5–20.

33. Thomas F. Pettigrew, "Intergroup Contact Theory," *Annual Review of Psychology*, 49 (1998): 65–85.

34. Phinney, Ferguson, and Tate, "Intergroup Attitudes among Ethnic Minority Adolescents: A Causal Model," 955–969.

35. Rupert Brown, James Vivian, and Miles Hewstone, "Changing Attitudes through Intergroup Contact: The Effects of Group Membership Salience," *European Journal of Social Psychology*, 29 (1999): 741–764.

36. Seth J. Schwartz, Koen Luyckx, and Vivian L. Vignoles, *Handbook of Identity Theory and Research* (New York: Springer, 2011), 2 vols.

37. Richard H. Adams, "The Conquest Tradition of Mesoamerica," *The Americas*, 46 (1989): 119–136.

38. Programa de las Naciones Unidas para el Desarrollo Humano, "Diversidad Etnico-Cultural: La Ciudadanía en un Estado," in *Informe Nacional de Desarrollo Humano 2005* (New York: United Nations System, 2005).

39. Richard H. Adams, "The Conquest Tradition of Mesoamerica," 119–136.

40. Programa de las Naciones Unidas para el Desarrollo Humano, "Diversidad Etnico-Cultural: La Ciudadanía en un Estado"; Manuela Camus, *Ser Indígena en Ciudad de Guatemala* [To be indigenous in Guatemala City] (Guatemala City: Facultad de Latinoamericana, 2002); Judith L. Gibbons and Brien K. Ashdown, "Ethnic Identification, Attitudes, and Group Relations in Guatemala," *Psychology*, 1 (2010): 116–127.

41. Programa de las Naciones Unidas para el Desarrollo Humano, "Diversidad Etnico-Cultural: La Ciudadanía en un Estado."

42. Central Intelligence Agency, "Distribution of Family Income: GINI Index," *The 2013 World Factbook*, https://www.cia.gov/library/publications/the-world-factbook//rankorder/2172rank.html

43. Ibid.
44. Programa de las Naciones Unidas para el Desarrollo Humano, "Diversidad Etnico-Cultural: La Ciudadanía en un Estado."
45. United Nations Development Programme, "Sustaining Human Progress: Reducing Vulnerabilities and Building Resilience," in *Human Development Report 2014*, http://hdr.undp.org/en/countries/profiles/GTM
46. Programa de las Naciones Unidas para el Desarrollo Humano, "Diversidad Etnico-Cultural: La Ciudadanía en un Estado."
47. United Nations Development Programme, "Sustaining Human Progress: Reducing Vulnerabilities and Building Resilience."
48. Lillian Comas-Diaz, M. Brinton Lykes, and Renato D. Alarcón, "Ethnic Conflict and the Psychology of Liberation in Guatemala, Peru, and Puerto Rico," *American Psychologist*, 53 (1998): 778–792.
49. Programa de las Naciones Unidas para el Desarrollo Humano, "Diversidad Etnico-Cultural: La Ciudadanía en un Estado."
50. Stephen M. Quintana and Theresa A. Segura-Herrera, "Development Transformations of Self and Identity in the Context of Oppression," *Self and Identity*, 2 (2003): 269–285.
51. Walter E. Little, *Mayas in the Marketplace: Tourism, Globalization, and Cultural Identity* (Austin: University of Texas Press, 2004).
52. Programa de las Naciones Unidas para el Desarrollo Humano, "Diversidad Etnico-Cultural: La Ciudadanía en un Estado."
53. Ibid.
54. Brien K. Ashdown and Others, "The Influence of Social and Individual Variables on Ethnic Attitudes in Guatemala," *Psychology*, 2, (2011): 78–84.
55. Frank La Rue Lewy, "Resurgimiento del Criollo [Resurgence of the native born]," *Prensa Libre*, last modified April 25, 2013, http://www.prensalibre.com/opinion/Resurgimiento-criollo_0_907709250.html
56. http://www.codisra.gob.gt
57. Ashdown and Others, "The Influence of Social and Individual Variables on Ethnic Attitudes in Guatemala," 78–84.
58. Camus, *Ser Indígena en Ciudad de Guatemala*.
59. Charles R. Hale, *Más Que Un Indio: Racial Ambivalence and Neoliberal Multiculturalism in Guatemala* (Santa Fe, NM: School of American Research, 2006).
60. Ricardo Falla, *Juventud de una comunidad maya Ixcán, Guatemala* [Youth in a Mayan community Ixcán, Guatemala] (Guatemala City: AVANCSO and Editorial Universitaria de la Universidad de San Carlos de Guatemala, 2006); Little, *Mayas in the Marketplace: Tourism, Globalization, and Cultural Identity*.
61. Programa de las Naciones Unidas para el Desarrollo Humano, "Diversidad Etnico-Cultural: La Ciudadanía en un Estado."
62. Felicia Pratto and Others, "Social Dominance Orientation and the Legitimization of Inequality Across Cultures," *Journal of Cross-Cultural Psychology*, 31 (2000): 369–409.

63. Gibbons and Ashdown, "Ethnic Identification, Attitudes, and Group Relations in Guatemala," 116–127.
64. Ibid.; Ashdown and Others, "The Influence of Social and Individual Variables on Ethnic Attitudes in Guatemala," 78–84.
65. Phinney, "Stages of Ethnic Identity Development in Minority Group Adolescents," 34–49.
66. Jeffrey Jensen Arnett, *Emerging Adulthood: The Winding Road from the Late Teens through the Twenties* (New York: Oxford University Press, 2004).
67. Gibbons and Ashdown, "Ethnic Identification, Attitudes, and Group Relations in Guatemala," 116–127; Ashdown and Others, "The Influence of Social and Individual Variables on Ethnic Attitudes in Guatemala," 78–84.
68. Ibid.
69. Judith L. Gibbons, Brien K. Ashdown, and Yetilú de Baessa, "Interculturality among Ethnic Groups in Guatemala," Presentation, Perspectives on Interculturality, St. Louis, MO, February 2013.
70. John C. Turner and Others, *Rediscovering the Social Group: A Self-Categorization Theory.*
71. Allport, *The Nature of Prejudice.*
72. Phinney, "Stages of Ethnic Identity Development in Minority Group Adolescents," 34–49; Phinney, Ferguson, and Tate, "Intergroup Attitudes among Ethnic Minority Adolescents: A Causal Model," 955–969.
73. Phinney, "The Multigroup Ethnic Identity Measure: A New Scale for Use with Diverse Groups," 156–176.
74. Brien. K. Ashdown, Judith L. Gibbons, and Yetilú de Baessa, "Ethnic Group Attitudes and Identity among Guatemalan Adolescents," Presentation, Annual Conference of the Society for Cross-Cultural Research, Charleston, SC, February 2011.
75. John C. Turner and Others, *Rediscovering the Social Group: A Self-Categorization Theory.*
76. Allport, *The Nature of Prejudice.*
77. Henri Tajfel and John Turner, "An Integrative Theory of Intergroup Conflict," in *The Social Psychology of Intergroup Relations*, ed. William G. Austin and Stephen Worchel (Monterey, CA: Brooks/Cole, 1979), 33–48, 7–24.
78. Phinney, "Stages of Ethnic Identity Development in Minority Group Adolescents," 34–49.
79. John W. Creswell, *Qualitative Inquiry and Research Design: Choosing among Five Approaches* (Thousand Oaks, CA: Sage, 1998).

# 5

# Fear of the Knotted Cord: Pueblo-Spanish Relations after the 1680 Revolt

## Tracy L. Brown

The Pueblo Revolt of 1680 was one of the most successful indigenous revolts of the colonial period in all of Latin America. The Pueblos succeeded in expelling all Spaniards from their homeland in New Mexico—a feat few other indigenous groups were able to accomplish in the New World. It was so well known that it sparked other Indian rebellions—to the extent that Spanish authorities feared that the "flames of rebellion" would "engulf the entire northern frontier" of New Spain (or what is now called Mexico).[1] Soon after Diego de Vargas had regained nominal control of New Mexico (1692), he intercepted a cord of maguey fiber with four knots in it that was being sent from pueblo to pueblo. A knotted cord had been passed around in August of 1680 to alert Pueblo communities that the revolt was imminent. Thus, the knotted cord that Vargas intercepted was "an eerie echo of the 1680 rebellion" and was an indication that the Pueblos were ready to go to war with the Spaniards once again.[2] The reconquest—called "bloodless" up to that point due to Vargas' diplomacy and ability to negotiate Pueblo submission—turned violent.

By the turn of the eighteenth century, Spanish authorities had put down another attempted revolt in 1696; but their control over Pueblo communities continued to be tenuous at best. It was in this context that rumors of yet another impending revolt began to circulate in Santa Fe in 1702 because a knotted cord was (allegedly) spotted being passed around in the pueblo of Zuni. This time, however, no actual knotted cord was ever intercepted or located. It did not matter—just the rumor that a knotted cord had been seen in Zuni was enough to spark fears of an impending revolt. Vargas sent Spanish authorities to investigate. While they were unable to locate any substantial evidence that a revolt was indeed being planned, Vargas' reaction to the rumor demonstrates that suspicion of Pueblo people remained high in the decades that followed the 1680 revolt.

Pueblo people understood this to be the case. In the sparse documentation concerning Zuni in 1702, members of the pueblo consistently reassured Spanish authorities that they were "happy living as Christians" and had no "bad intentions" toward the Spanish.[3] Whether or not Zuni people were actually "happy living as Christians" is not something that can be definitively known; but the records do reveal that Pueblo people were clearly aware of the meaning that the Spaniards would read into the appearance of the knotted cord and that they tried their best to deflate Spaniards' suspicions of them.

Many articles and books have been written about what caused the 1680 revolt, and how the revolt was carried out.[4] But there is nothing in the historiography about how (or if) the revolt shaped post-revolt Spanish-Pueblo relations (or "interculturality") in the eighteenth century. The documentation from Zuni in 1702 reveals that this interaction can be best characterized as a tenuous balancing act where Pueblos worked to, at the very least, maintain a peaceful public façade in the face of Spanish accusations that they were secretly planning revolts. It is clear that Spanish civil authorities were suspicious of Pueblo people, and that Pueblo people knew this and did their best to try and calm Spanish fears and suspicions.

Perhaps it is not surprising that Spanish authorities were still suspicious of Pueblo communities in 1702. Even though the 1680 revolt had happened 20 years before, Spanish authorities really only had Pueblo communities under tenuous control for 9 years by the time of the incident at Zuni. However, further research in the eighteenth-century documentation reveals that such suspicions did not dissipate as the century wore on; and that, in fact, Pueblo Indians were just as suspicious of Spanish authorities as Spanish authorities were suspicious of them. I cannot review in detail the entire corpus of eighteenth-century documents in this short chapter. But, even a brief summary of the documentation reveals that Pueblos and Spaniards were, literally, afraid of each other in the eighteenth century. For example, between 1700 and 1720 out of a total of 24 investigations conducted in Pueblo communities, 13 were either revolt or "secret meetings" investigations (6) or "witchcraft" and/ or "idolatry" investigations (7).[5] I include witchcraft and idolatry in my count because Spaniards believed that the practice of witchcraft and idolatry (as they defined it, of course) was not only immoral but could also lead to general insubordination and, ultimately, revolt. In addition, there is documentation which indicates that five Tewa Indians were held for ten months in jail in 1703 without explanation.[6] They were eventually freed after filing a complaint against the governor of New Mexico. Because they were Tewa—Indian communities that fully supported and played a central role in the 1680 revolt—my guess is that the governor suspected that they were planning another revolt or that they were "witches" and jailed them. Also of interest are letters (not full investigations) from Spanish authorities complaining generally about the Pueblos being "bellicose" or planning to kill their friars.[7]

Between 1720 and 1821 (the end of the colonial period), there are periods where the documentation is very, very thin (especially 1750–1780). Nevertheless, complaints about Pueblos planning revolts, conducting secret meetings, holding "dishonest" dances, or simply hiding their "bad intentions" exist to the end of the colonial period. Of particular interest is the extensive revolt investigation that was carried out in the Tewa pueblos in 1793 (again, those communities that fully supported the 1680 revolt).[8] Despite intensive efforts by Spanish authorities, no evidence that a revolt was in the works was unearthed during this investigation. In fact, no evidence of revolt—beyond rumor—was ever unearthed in any eighteenth-century investigation of Pueblo communities. Spaniards were suspicious of any Pueblo gathering, and investigated evidence of "secret meetings" to the end of the colonial period; but they were never able to locate any evidence that a revolt was actually being planned.

As for the Pueblos, they regularly expressed the fear—even late into the colonial period—that Spaniards were planning to attack and kill them. This is true even though there is no evidence to indicate that Spaniards, in actuality, were planning such attacks. In 1720, for example, Spanish authorities conducted an investigation into peyote use at Taos that quickly evolved into a "secret meeting" investigation. During this investigation, Taoseños complained that an individual from Hopi had brought peyote to their pueblo and that several individuals had ingested it and then seen visions of the New Mexico governor attacking the pueblo; but that the governor of Parral had deterred him from carrying out the attack.[9] At the end of the century (1819), we find similar complaints emanating, again, from Taos. As in the 1720 case, Taoseños complained that a Spanish solider named Matías Medina had misled them to believe that many Spanish troops were coming—not to attack them, but to take their belongings and food.[10] They had been ordered by the governor of New Mexico to build an adobe wall and to send him a list of all their belongings without any explanation. Medina told them that the wall they were building was to hold grain; and that the lists of belongings would be used to remove those belongings from them for the troops.

I do not think it was the 1680 revolt per se that was at the bottom of the fears expressed by Taoseños in the Matías Medina investigation; rather, it was a return to a situation similar to that which had led up to the revolt that they feared. Prior to the 1680 revolt, Spaniards relied upon Pueblo people and communities to provide them with food and other necessities. Of course, Pueblo people could not provision Spanish communities; Pueblos were sedentary agriculturalists living in a desert. As such, they lived in a precarious economic balance where one poor crop could lead to famine. Thus, Spanish insistence that they provide them with basic necessities— which included taking supplies by force or waging war against communities that refused their requests—decimated Pueblo food stores leading to famine. This, in addition to other grievances including the persecution of those who participated in traditional religious practices or refused conversion, is what led Pueblo people to revolt in 1680.[11] To me, the Taoseños testimonies reveal a fear of returning to a situation where they would be attacked for not providing food, supplies and labor to Spaniards or for not converting to Christianity. There is no doubt that other Pueblo people shared this fear—in addition to memories and stories passed from generation to generation about the revolt itself.

There are two reasons that I find it surprising that the suspicions and fears that are apparent in the documentation for this period did not dissipate as the century wore on. First, none of the investigations ever turned up hard evidence that either Pueblos were planning to revolt or Spaniards were planning to attack them once the reconquest was finished; yet, suspicions and fears lingered to the end of the colonial period. Second, these findings do not correlate with the argument made by historians of colonial New Mexico that, in fact, Pueblos and Spaniards had a much less contentious relationship in the eighteenth as compared to the seventeenth century. John Kessell describes the eighteenth century as a period of "pragmatic accommodation" between Spaniard and Pueblo (as opposed to the seventeenth century which, he argues, was marked by "crusading intolerance" on the part of both church and civic authorities with regard to Pueblo traditions—especially their religious traditions). The reason historians give for this shift in attitude on the part of Spaniards was, in fact, the

Pueblo revolt: neither Spaniards nor Pueblos wished to repeat that experience. This "pragmatic accommodation" gave way to an almost familial-like social interaction as the two groups formed ties via ritual god-parentage and in their defense of the province against raiding by nomadic peoples which was especially intense at mid-century.[12]

If Spanish-Pueblo interaction was so familial-like, what sense can be made of the evidence I have presented here regarding the fears and suspicions apparent in the eighteenth-century documentation? It is clear that Spanish-Pueblo "interculturality" in the eighteenth century was much more complicated than has been described in the historiography for the province up to this point in time. Despite the rather sunny portrait painted of those relations in the New Mexico historiography, a close look at all of the evidence reveals that Spanish and Pueblo relations could be both familial-like *and* fraught with fear and suspicion. The character of Spanish-Pueblo relations in the eighteenth century was to some degree context-dependent: in times of raiding, for example, some (but not all) Pueblos and Spaniards formed alliances to protect their communities; but this does not mean that these alliances held across time or erased memories of the prerevolt period or the revolt itself. It is also not difficult to believe that (some, but not all) Pueblos and Spaniards formed close relations, to the point that Spaniards, for example, came to serve as godparents to Pueblo children. But, this does not mean that all Pueblo-Spanish relations, throughout the entire eighteenth century, took on this character. Culture—or that thing that is comprised of what Clifford Geertz described as "webs of significance" in which people are immersed and which they themselves "have spun"[13]—is generated out of the interrelations and interactions of individuals and groups of people. It is not, however, completely shared or internally consistent across a group of people. There can be individuals or groups in a culture which have— to some degree—diametrically opposed beliefs and practices (or "significances"). As I discuss at the end of this chapter, it is completely "normal" to see variations in meaning, beliefs, and practices within a broader "culture." Not all threads of a web of significance are shared by all participants. These variations comprise sub-cultures, and it is these individuals and sub-cultures which account, at least in part, for variations in beliefs and practices like the ones that existed in eighteenth-century New Mexico.

Since familial-like relations and alliances have already been addressed in the historiography, I want to focus on what has not been addressed in that historiography in this chapter. Why is it that some Pueblos and Spaniards got over their fear of one another to form alliances and friendships, but others did not? What was the cause of the lingering suspicions and fears that are apparent in the eighteenth-century documentation? In the following sections of this chapter, I will use theoretical insights from anthropological studies of trauma and state terror combined with ethnohistorical methodology to explain why I think there is evidence of fear and suspicion late into the colonial period in the New Mexican documentation. In doing so, I will paint a more complex portrait of Spanish-Pueblo interculturality than exists in the current historiography.

The term "ethnohistory" was first used by anthropologists to describe research done for the Indian Claims Act of 1946. It originally referred to the study of the pasts of Native North Americans, typically through documentation, ethnographic data or other forms of testimony and evidence.[14] Anthropologists who did historical research on Native North America were, and are, called "ethnohistorians": they are anthropologists who do archival research on (typically) Native North America. Historians obviously also research and write about Native American histories; but, since archival research was not something that most or even a majority of anthropologists did in the 1950s, a special term was devised for those individuals who engaged in such research in the discipline. Methodologically, ethnohistory—no matter who practices it—has much in common with cultural, social and microhistory and, in fact, is probably considered to be a variation of one or more of them by historians.[15] But, for anthropologists like myself, the term has a specific meaning: it describes an anthropologist who does archival research and writes histories (about Native communities, typically in the colonial period or early postcontact period) rather than conducting fieldwork in contemporary communities and producing ethnographies.

Ethnohistorians—no matter their discipline—employ a broad range of methods to reconstruct Native American pasts and histories. It is necessary to do so, because Native people did not typically leave written records behind and/or are difficult to locate in documentation. In other words, ethnohistorians often have very little documentation to work with; and the documentation they do have is typically written by individuals who sought to colonize and subjugate Indian peoples. Ethnohistorians must figure out ways to "read" past those biases and to fill in gaps in documentation. This is where, for me at least, theory comes in to play: by looking at similar case studies, and the theory derived from those studies, ethnohistorians can suggest answers to questions raised (but not answered) by their documentation or offer possible explanations for why individuals and groups behaved in the ways that they did in the past. This is what I do in the rest of this chapter: I offer an explanation for the evidence of trauma I uncovered through close examination of the eighteenth-century documentation by comparing it to other anthropological studies of tragedy, trauma, and terror.

## THE CULTURE OF TRAUMA

The Spanish-Pueblo interculturality after the 1692 reconquest of New Mexico can best be described as a culture of trauma: that is, Spaniards and Pueblos created a shared set of beliefs and practices that, when enacted, perpetuated suspicion and fear in both groups even when such fears do not appear to have been rooted in any sort of reality. This culture of trauma functioned much like the "culture of terror" and "space of death" that Michael Taussig argues existed on the rubber plantations of Colombia at the turn of the twentieth century. In an effort to explain how and why the torture and murder of Indian rubber workers reached epidemic levels, Taussig argues that through their interactions, rubber workers and company employees created a situation where enslavement, torture, and even murder were normalized and made mundane and where terror became "an organized culture with its systematic rules, imagery, procedures and meanings."[16] While it is not known how many Putumayo Indians were tortured and/or murdered, by all accounts, it was a large number. Company officials, it appears, tortured and killed them if they did not bring enough rubber in or simply for sport and enjoyment. One report explained that "to amuse themselves, company officials practice shooting, using Indians as targets, and on special occasions such as Easter Sunday...shoot them down in groups or...douse them in kerosene and set them on fire to enjoy their agony."[17]

Over time, many explanations have been offered for why this genocide was perpetrated: because the Indians would not work or refused to participate in the debt-peonage system used to acquire rubber from them; to beat the "uncivilized" or "savage" out of them; or because company employees feared that they would rebel; or to create solidarity among company employees. While not denying that these were factors which underwrote the behavior, Taussig argues that torture and murder became the aim of rubber production—rather than a means to ensure that production would be carried out.[18] As incomprehensible as this may seem, Taussig argues that the rubber company employees—not just white men, but Indian guards who worked for them—simply came to enjoy torturing and murdering Indians.

The situation in New Mexico in the eighteenth century that I wish to describe differed from the Colombian rubber plantations in the sense that Spaniards did not create a culture of terror in order to rationalize the torture and murder of Pueblo people. It is not that torture or murder of Pueblos did not occur in New Mexico; and it may be that Spaniards rationalized this behavior in similar ways that were found in Colombia. But that was not the point or goal of New Mexico's culture of trauma in the eighteenth century. Rather, I argue there was a culture of trauma in eighteenth-century New Mexico in which both Spaniards and Pueblos forged identities and discourses about themselves and each other and which found their basis in one, shared, fear or threat: that violence, and even death, was always and forever imminent. Both Spaniards and Pueblos were, not surprisingly, traumatized by the revolt of 1680; and because this was so, a culture of trauma in New Mexico emerged which reflected that experience.

This culture of trauma was similar to Taussig's culture of terror in that—as in Colombia—it did not matter in the least that the fears perpetuated through the culture of trauma were not based in any actual threat of Spanish attack or retaliation or Pueblo rebellion; what mattered was that Spaniards and Pueblos *believed* that rebellion and attack were always and forever looming on the horizon. A "web of significance" emerged which found its origin in these shared fears and which engulfed (some) Pueblos and Spaniards. As a result, the Pueblos are depicted in much of the Spanish documentation for the period as always and continually on the verge of revolt. Conversely, in those documents where Pueblos were interviewed or interrogated about their supposed revolt plans (or "secret meetings"), they often voiced concerns that Spaniards were violent aggressors who were on the verge of storming Pueblo towns. As in Colombia, Spaniards and Pueblos held a set of beliefs about each other that, once created, appear to have become a self-sustaining sub-culture which perpetuated itself through time—despite the fact that its existence had little factual basis in reality or that, at certain points in time, alliances and familial relations existed between them. It had a life of its own, beyond the will of any one individual or set of individuals involved in its creation. And, as in Colombia, it had real effects: Spaniards and Pueblos treated each other in ways that they might not have had there been no shared culture of trauma.

These suspicions and fears operated in a tautological manner in New Mexico: they circulated around the province through time, and with no real referent or link to an "on the ground" event, as each successive generation passed on stories—and the message of trauma encoded within them—about the past. There is evidence of the transmission of trauma in the documentation: when explaining to Spanish officials why they revolted in 1680, Don Pedro Nanboa of Alameda declared "that the resentment which all the Indians have in their hearts has been so strong, from the time the kingdom was discovered, because the religious and the Spaniards took away their idols and forbade their sorceries and idolatries; that they have inherited successively from their old men the things pertaining to their ancient customs; and that he has heard this resentment spoken of since he was of an age to understand."[19] These fears and suspicions fed on themselves in the eighteenth century: that is, they were not fueled through time by actual evidence of revolt planning but by intergenerational remembering of a traumatic event (the revolt itself) and/or period of time (the decades leading up to the revolt). As part of this transmission, memories of the past were reconfigured to become the prologue to the traumatic event. The years or even decades preceding the revolt were read in hindsight for indices and foreshadowings of the trouble that lay ahead; and, in doing so, new meanings were attached to that period in time.

Studies of tragedy survivors and "memory work" reveal that such practices commonly follow the experience of a traumatic event. The trauma is set up as the "founding myth" of a people; as such, it plays a crucial role in the creation of group identity over the generations. Descendants of those who survived the traumatic event become "carriers" of traumatic memory, and shape their personal identities around that memory. They become "wounded survivors of a distant past" whose burden it is to carry forth the memory of the trauma that may have occurred a very long time ago. Group identity, too, can be linked to this founding myth: descendants may perceive of themselves as collectively carrying "scars" caused by the trauma. Those who do not carry such scars cannot be members of the group, or are not "authentic" members of the group.[20]

I suspect that, in addition to memory work, the act of creating negative images (or stereotypes) and projecting them onto the Pueblo population helped to perpetuate fears and suspicions evident in the documentation and thus the creation of the culture of trauma following the revolt. In Colombia, Taussig argues that the men who ran the plantation system projected the idea that both the jungle where the plantations were located, and its inhabitants, were "wild" so that they could "reflect back to the colonists the vast and baroque projections of human wildness that [they] needed to establish their reality as civilized people....And it was only because the wild Indians were human that they were able to serve as labor—and as subjects of torture." One of the things that made the Putumayo Indians "wild" was their supposed consumption of human flesh.[21] In reality, the Putumayo Indians were not cannibals, but that, of course, did not matter. What mattered is that company employees believed they ate human flesh; and because they believed they ate human flesh, they were "wild" and "savage" and their torture and murder was justified. The supposed savagery of the Indians was a fantasy; but this fantasy had real effects.

The exact same projections of the "savage" versus the "civilized" were common in colonial Latin America and served to justify in the minds of Spaniards all sorts of behaviors, practices, and beliefs. In other words, this was a common trope throughout the New World, into which beliefs about Indian people were inputted. The reports generated from the earliest expeditions to New Mexico described the Pueblos as cannibals who ate human flesh and kept slaves taken from war.[22] In the eighteenth century, Spanish authorities frequently described the Pueblos living in a state of ignorance and barbarity, and as idolators who frequently reverted to their "bad customs."[23] Such projections surely fueled the suspicions and fears of the Spaniards that are evident in the documentation for this period. Pueblo people most likely created and projected their own cultural constructions and tropes onto Spanish people as well, but because they did not leave written documentation behind, it is difficult to know what they were. The point is that, suspicion and fear were perpetuated through the creation and projection of negative imagery and stereotypes by both Spaniards and Pueblos.

Trauma was not just transmitted in families or by stereotyping; it was also transmitted via the everyday interactions and conversations that occurred between Spaniards and Pueblos. For example, in 1784, the Tewa Indians complained about being labeled rebellious and witches. They complained that the Spaniards living in the area attended church in San Juan armed, presumably because they feared the Pueblos. They reasoned that it was not their fault that they were ignorant of church doctrine since the friars did not teach them anything: in other words, they believed the Spanish feared them because they were unconverted (and therefore lacked a Christian "conscience" to guide their actions).[24] In 1818–1819, friars collected letters of certification concerning their performance of duties in New Mexican missions and churches.[25] The Isleta governor complained about the fact that they were called pagans. He emphasized that "we do not commit the crime of [idolatry]...which we have been charged with."

Such evidence indicates, again, that Spaniards viewed Pueblo people with suspicion and fear until the end of the colonial period. But it also shows that anxiety and mistrust were sustained via the everyday "microaggressions" that occurred between Spaniard and Pueblo in the mundane, routine, interactions between Spaniards and Pueblos at church and in villages.

In his discussion of how torture and murder become normalized and even mundane in Colombia, Taussig writes that it is "in the coils of rumor, gossip, story, and chit-chat," that "ideology and ideas become emotionally powerful and enter into active circulation and meaningful existence."[26] It is difficult to locate evidence of "rumor, gossip, or chit chat" in the eighteenth-century documentation from New Mexico. However, the limited evidence does suggest that, as in Colombia, it was in everyday interactions—in addition to intergenerational remembering and stereotyping—that the culture of trauma was maintained and perpetuated. Thus, there was no need for there to be evidence of revolt or attack planning to sustain the culture of trauma in New Mexico because memory work, stereotyping and "microaggressive" daily interaction were enough to fuel the circulation of fear and suspicion in the province through time.

## IDENTITY FAILURE

What I have been describing, in part, is the role that not just stereotyping, but stigmatization of individuals or groups of individuals, plays in a culture of trauma. Erving Goffman defines a stigmatized person as someone who possesses an attribute that is "deeply discrediting"—someone who, for whatever reason, is "reduced from a whole and usual person to a tainted, discounted one."[27]

Stigmatization played a role in the culture of trauma created after the Pueblo revolt because a negative, "discrediting," identity was foisted upon a group (the Pueblos) without that group's consent. Rubber plantation employees in Colombia believed the Putumayo Indians were cannibals. They believed they possessed a deeply discrediting attribute which reduced them to a tainted sub-class of people upon whom torture and murder were justified. Clearly, and as discussed above, Spaniards in New Mexico stigmatized Pueblo Indians as uncivilized and barbarous from the first moments of contact—as they did throughout the New World. This stigmatization fueled the fears and suspicions of Spaniards throughout the eighteenth century.

But Spanish authorities, too, were stigmatized by the revolt in the sense that, in the eyes of other Spaniards, they failed in their civilizing mission to the degree that their underlings were able to wrest control of the province away from them and drive them from their adopted homeland. In the eyes of Spanish society, their "discrediting attribute" was that they allowed the colonial power structure (Spaniards "on top"; Indians "on the bottom") to be upended due to their own incompetence. They failed colonial Spanish society and they were failures at carrying out the duties of proper Spanish citizens and leaders.

One gets the sense that Spaniards understood that the revolt was a stigmatizing event in the documentation from the period immediately following the revolt. If I had to identify the main emotion of the Spanish authorities after the revolt, it would not be anger (although anger is clearly in evidence in the documentation) but bewilderment. They appear to have been totally taken by surprise by the revolt and are in disbelief that the Pueblos would do such a thing. In numerous declarations, Spanish authorities stress that the revolt happened "in a time of the greatest quiet and tranquility in the kingdom" and of "complete peace." Juan, a Pueblo Indian from Alameda was asked "why they killed religious and Spaniards and burned the church and all the houses, which they did after living so long a time among the Spaniards, protected from enemy Apaches, being Christians and living quietly in their pueblos and under the law of God?"[28] Fray Antonio de Serra complained in a letter written a month after the revolt had occurred that the Pueblos who had done the greatest harm were those who "have been most favored by the religious and who are the most intelligent."[29] While in hindsight the causes of the revolt might seem obvious to us now, Spanish authorities denied that the "ruin" originated due to them forcing the Pueblos to work for them "or of other drudgery which might have aggrieved" them. Governor Otermín (the governor under which the revolt took place) insisted that "in no other time had they been so protected as in mine."[30]

In short, sometimes an individual's or a group's identity is "spoiled" by their having participated in or experienced a traumatic event—not necessarily because of anything they did (although this might be a factor), but because of the way outsiders perceive of their actions. In the wake of the revolt, the Spanish authorities experienced identity failure. In order to mitigate the damage done to their identity (to "manage" it), they argued in the documentation that their superiors would read that there was no way they could have known that a revolt was being planned because the most acculturated Pueblo Indians gained their trust and hid their true intentions from them.

Of course, this version of events was a complete fabrication and fantasy. It is widely recognized that one of the events that precipitated the 1680 revolt was an idolatry campaign carried out in 1675. Governor Juan Francisco Treviño had 47 men who admitted to practicing sorcery arrested, imprisoned, sold into slavery or flogged. Four of the sorcerers were sentenced to death. Three were hung; the fourth committed suicide before the punishment could be carried out. It is the consensus of historians that this idolatry campaign was the last straw for Pueblo people. Popé—the leader of the revolt—began to plan for the 1680 revolt at Taos in late 1675. In fact, Matthew Liebmann writes that there were so many revolts in the seventeenth century as to comprise a "legacy of rebellion."[31] So to say that Pueblo people were living quietly and happily in the period leading up to the revolt was simply a fabrication, designed to save face.

Feeling ridiculed and ashamed seem to have been part of the experience of identity failure: "what grieved us most were the dreadful flames from the church and the scoffing and ridicule which the wretched and miserable Indian rebels made of the sacred things, intoning the alabado and other prayers of the church with jeers." We might ask, why did Spanish authorities make shame and ridicule—something one might "normally" wish to keep to oneself—public in this manner? It seems to me that revealing that the Pueblos ridiculing them might have served an identity management function: by presenting themselves as shamed and ridiculed they perhaps sought to gain sympathy, appease their superiors, "forestall" their anger over or distract attention from their failure to avert the rebellion. In a very different time and context, Andrew Strathern argues that elaborate displays of shame may work as a "social cosmetic"—it "dresses up" or "decorates" what is perceived to be inappropriate behavior in order to avert the anger or judgment of others.[32] Spanish expressions of shame—real or feigned— were used to mitigate the consequences of (in this case) incompetent leadership or behavior and to manage identity failure.

The realization of their identity failure may help to explain why Governor Otermín wanted to return to New Mexico immediately after the rebellion to reassert control over the region and the derision with which he spoke of the Pueblo individuals who carried out the revolt. In September of 1680—one month after the revolt had occurred— Governor Otermín argued it was necessary to return to New Mexico immediately, so that "Christianity may not perish" and "the discord of the devil may not gain control among the natives, with idolatries and superstitions, which is that to which their stupid ignorance predisposes them, for they live blindly in their freedom and stupid vices."

While it very well may have been that Otermín was concerned for the souls of the Pueblo people, I also suspect that he sought to return to New Mexico to bring the Pueblo communities back under the yoke of Spanish rule as quickly as possible in order to prove his competence as governor of the province—or to rectify his failed identity.

As it turned out, Otermín did not return to New Mexico until December of 1681; and his attempted reconquest did nothing to "fix" his failed identity. The first pueblo that he "reduced" was Isleta, which he described as being occupied by "inept and stupid people, full of fear" who might easily obey the "summons of the apostates." Upon leaving New Mexico in early January, being unable to gain control over any other Pueblo community, Otermín complained that some Isletans had run away "returning to apostatize from the holy faith in order to live according to their blind and stupid desires, their natural inclination being toward the devil...."[33]

In trying to explain why the reconquest had failed Otermín complained that instead of finding a province full of individuals sick and tired of Apache and Ute raiding and living under a tyrannical government, Pueblo communities had experienced very little raiding in their absence and they were happy with their government because the ruling elite encouraged the "natural inclinations[of their people] toward obscenities, idolatry and liberty." In addition, his soldiers "spent more time prying into the trapdoors of the pueblos through which they passed in order to steal, than in seeking souls to reduce."[34] As they had done to explain why the 1680 revolt was a surprise, Spanish authorities presented themselves as badly misjudging the Pueblo people in order to explain the failed reconquest. This justification, too, was a fabrication. Although there is not much documentation on the post-revolt period, interrogations of Pueblos captured by people by various Spanish authorities revealed that Po'Pay—the planner and leader of the revolt—was deposed within a year of the revolt being carried out, and before Otermín had even appeared to reconquer the province.[35] If Otermín misjudged anyone, it was his men who appeared to have no commitment to carrying out the reconquest and were instead only interested in enriching themselves through looting.

## THE "CULTURE" IN THE CULTURE OF TRAUMA

In arguing that Spaniards and Pueblos created a shared set of beliefs and practices (or the "intercultural" in the terms of this volume), I do not mean to imply that they consciously agreed on what was to constitute this culture or that there was give and take (a reciprocity) between

Spaniards and Pueblos in creating this culture—ideas that have traditionally been associated with the culture concept in anthropology. In the formative period of the discipline, anthropologists defined "culture" as an orderly and integrated, self-sustaining, whole or totality of shared meanings, beliefs, and practices that are passed down from generation to generation. More recently, this "culture concept" has been thoroughly criticized: anthropologists argue that cultures are not, in fact, bounded wholes—especially in an increasingly globalized world. Nor are they necessarily shared: anthropologists now recognize that what "order"—or (in the classic anthropological sense) integrated set of beliefs and practices—gets defined as representative of some group's culture is a highly politicized process. In any given society, there are powerholders who define what is "normal" or normative; and there are those upon whom such norms are imposed, negotiated, and resisted.[36]

Neither one of these definitions of culture quite describes Spanish-Pueblo interculturality in the post-revolt period. Pueblos and Spaniards never entered into an agreement (tacit or otherwise) about what would constitute accepted beliefs, behaviors, or practices. Even more recent definitions of culture, which acknowledge that not everyone in a society has the power to create norms, do not really describe accurately the culture of trauma that existed in post-revolt New Mexico. Instead, what I am describing is a "sub-culture" that was generated out of groups of individuals experiencing the same set of events (the 1680 revolt, and the events leading up to it). It was, in the words of Akhil Gupta and James Ferguson, a "cultural territorialization" or an "association of place and culture" which was the result of "ongoing historical and political processes."[37] This sub-culture was not generalized to the entire population of New Mexico in eighteenth-century New Mexico (as the term implies). There were other "cultural territorializations" of different scales which functioned alongside of or were interlinked to greater or lesser degrees with the (sub-)culture of trauma. Not all of these associations of people in Spanish and Pueblo villages were even as formalized as the sub-culture of trauma: there were associations that were more "structures of feeling" than full-blown "sub-cultures"—or social experiences that were "emergent" or "in process" and that lacked a certain degree of organization or recognition which the sub-culture of trauma, for example, possessed.[38]

The coverage or extent of the sub-culture of trauma was variable. Some groups or communities may have only fallen under its influence periodically or not at all. Here I am thinking of Pueblo communities

located far from Spanish centers of power in New Mexico during
the colonial period—such as Hopi, Zuni, Acoma, and Laguna. They
may never have been a part of the sub-culture of trauma, or been
influenced by it only periodically, because they had so little contact
with Spaniards in the colonial period. In highlighting post-revolt
relations in the way that I have done, I do not mean to leave the
impression that all Pueblo-Spanish interactions were colored by
memories of the revolt. This was simply not the case. Given the evidence I have presented here, it might be surprising that, in other
contexts (i.e., sub-cultures or structures of feeling), Pueblos adopted
and incorporated into their own societies aspects of Spanish ways
of living, beliefs, and traditions. Pueblos, for example, converted to
Christianity. The opposite was also true: some Spaniards adopted
Pueblo practices and beliefs (such as their curing and healing methods). There *was* "pragmatic accommodation" between Pueblos and
Spaniards. Spaniards, apart from Pueblos, and Pueblos, apart from
Spaniards, also struggled to maintain activities, traditions, and behaviors that they believed were indigenous to their people and made
them "Spanish" or "Pueblo."[39]

One aspect of current theorizations of the culture concept that does
apply to the situation found in eighteenth-century New Mexico is the
emphasis upon the fluidity of culture. Cultures are not sealed, unitary,
entities that are akin to billiard balls moving about on a pool table.[40]
Instead, their borders are porous, sometimes so much so that it can
be difficult to distinguish one culture (or sub-culture) from another.[41]
In the eighteenth century New Mexico appeared at some points, or
in some places, to be a "pigmentocracy" beset with racial and class
divisions which divided Spaniards and Pueblos, while at other points
and places as a largely mestizo society where Spanish and Pueblo had
blended together—much to the disdain of authorities outside of the
province. I have seen colonial New Mexico described both ways in the
historical literature.[42] Just because these descriptions contradict each
other does not mean they are wrong or inaccurate. It means that New
Mexico was a complex place culturally, with numerous associations of
people and groups creating meaning simultaneously. In short, the sub-
culture of trauma existed within a broader social matrix composed of
numerous sub-cultures or less-defined structures of feeling operating
alongside (and sometimes interweaving with) each other. These cultural formations—existing within the same, broader, social matrix—
could both contradict and appear consistent with one another: some
promoted intercultural harmony, while others promoted strict social
separation. If one were to take a bird's eye view of this broader social

matrix of the geographic region called "New Mexico" in the colonial period, one would see a series of overlapping, fragmented, subcultures or less-formalized interrelations and interactions, tenuously hanging together like a poorly made collage held together by a thin veneer of social glue or tape.

Whether Pueblos and Spaniards wanted it or not, the revolt linked them together in ways that they had never experienced either with each other or with other groups of people. The particular experience of the revolt, in short, created an association between them—of culture and place—that was neither agreed upon nor desired but existed nonetheless. Once linked together in this way, Spaniards and Pueblos began to have behavioral expectations of each other. Taussig, in describing the culture of terror in Colombia, argued that—like "culture" more generally—it had rules, imagery, procedures, and meanings. The same was true for New Mexico. Spaniards believed that Pueblos continued to plot their demise based on their previous experience with them, but also in accordance with the expectations of the sub-culture of trauma. Pueblos believed that Spaniards were going to attack them based on the same premises. In other words, once created, the sub-culture of trauma shaped expectations and behaviors (as culture does in any context). It is out of this shared experience of a set of events that the sub-culture of trauma emerged in colonial New Mexico and shaped Spanish-Pueblo interculturality. It was what I would call "culture by default": "culture" sometimes appeared in New Mexico without the conscious effort or will of a group of people, and without any desire for shared meaning-making.

No knotted cords were ever circulated in Pueblo communities after 1701. Nevertheless, the knotted cord worked as a signifier— a mimetic device that called up memories of the 1680 revolt and the war that was waged on Pueblo communities by Spanish colonizers—in the discourses that comprised the culture of trauma in New Mexico. The Pueblo Revolt, symbolized by the knotted cord, was a "horrendous event that [left] indelible marks upon...group consciousness, marking...memories forever and changing...future identity in fundamental and irrevocable ways."[43] Through an analysis that combines historical and anthropological theory and methodology (called ethnohistory when applied to the study of Native America), it is possible to delineate the impacts of the 1680 Pueblo Revolt on Pueblo and Spanish worlds in eighteenth-century New Mexico. "Fear of the knotted cord" hung over New Mexico in the colonial period like a bad nightmare from which it was difficult, if not impossible, to wake.

## Notes

1. Andrew Knaut, *The Pueblo Revolt of 1680: Conquest and Resistance in Seventeenth-Century New Mexico* (Norman: University of Oklahoma Press, 1995), 177. See also: David Weber (ed.), *What Caused the Pueblo Revolt of 1680?* (New York: Bedford/St. Martin's, 1999), 8.
2. Matthew Liebmann, *Revolt: An Archaeological History of Pueblo Resistance and Revitalization in 17th Century New Mexico* (Tucson: University of Arizona Press, 2012), 190; David Weber, *The Spanish Frontier of North America* (New Haven: Yale University Press, 1992), 7.
3. Spanish Archives of New Mexico, Center for Southwest Research at the University of New Mexico, Series II, Provincial Records, reel 3: frame 757 (hereafter cited as SANM reel: frame number).
4. The sources are numerous: Liebmann, *Revolt: An Archaeological History of Pueblo Resistance and Revitalization in 17th Century New Mexico*; Knaut, *The Pueblo Revolt of 1680*; Weber, *What Caused the Pueblo Revolt of 1680*; Michael Wilcox, *The Pueblo Revolt and the Mythology of Conquest: An Indigenous Archaeology of Contact* (Berkeley: University of California Press, 2009).
5. Revolt/"secret meeting" investigations: New Mexico Originals, Bancroft Library at the University of California Berkeley, volumes 1, 6, 10, and 14 (hereafter cited as NMO volume number, document number, where available); SANM 3: 752–762 [1702]; SANM 3: 878–888 [1704]; SANM 3: 927–963 [1704–1705]; SANM 5: 92–114 [1715]; SANM 4: 377–458 [1712]; SANM 5: 986–1004 [1720]. Idolatry and witchcraft investigations: Archivo General de la Nación, Mexico City, Inquisición volume 735 [1706] (hereafter cited as AGN, by volume number, document number: frame number, where available); Ralph Twitchell, *The Spanish Archives of New Mexico*, vol. 2 (Cedar Rapids: Torch Press, 1914), 142–163 [1708]; Archivo General de la Nación, Mexico City, Provincias Internas volume 36, document 3: frames 315–317 [1709] (hereafter cited as AGN PI, volume number, document number: frame number, where available); SANM 4: 841–884 [1713]; Biblioteca Nacional, Mexico City, volume 6, document 3 [1712] (hereafter cited as BN, volume number, document number: frame number, where available); SANM I, #117, NMO 1, 18 [1714]; SANM 5: 165–183 [1715].
6. SANM 3: 869–871.
7. See for example: AGN PI 36, 3.
8. SANM 13: 237–326.
9. SANM 5: 986–1004.
10. SANM 19: 740–771.
11. Knaut, *The Pueblo Revolt of 1680*, 17–88; Liebmann, *Revolt: An Archaeological History of Pueblo Resistance and Revitalization in 17th Century New Mexico*, 29–49.
12. John Kessell, "Spaniards and Pueblos: From Crusading Intolerance to Pragmatic Accommodation," in *Columbian Consequences Volume 1:*

*Archaeological and Historical Perspectives on the Spanish Borderlands West*, ed. David Hurst Thomas (Washington, DC: Smithsonian Institution Press, 1989). On raiding in the province during the eighteenth century see: Elizabeth John, *Storms Brewed in Other Men's Worlds: The Confrontation of the Indians, Spanish and French in the Southwest, 1540–1795* (College Station: Texas A&M Press, 1975). For more general treatments of Pueblo and Spanish interactions in the eighteenth century, see my book *Pueblo Indians and Spanish Colonial Authority in Eighteenth Century New Mexico* (Tucson: University of Arizona Press, 2013); Charles Cutter, *The Protector de Indios in Colonial New Mexico 1659–1821* (Albuquerque: University of New Mexico Press, 1986). Marc Simmons, "History of Pueblo-Spanish Relations to 1821," in *Handbook of North American Indians: Southwest*, ed. Alfonso Ortiz (Washington, DC: Smithsonian Institution, 1979); Edward Spicer, *Cycles of Conquest: The Impact of Spain, Mexico and the United States on the Indians of the Southwest, 1533–1960* (Tucson: University of Arizona Press, 1962).

13. Clifford Geertz, "Thick Description: Toward and Interpretive Theory of Culture," in *The Interpretation of Cultures: Selected Essays* (New York: Basic Books, 1973), 5.
14. Patricia Galloway, *Practicing Ethnohistory: Mining Archives, Hearing Testimony, Constructing Narrative* (Lincoln: University of Nebraska Press, 2006), 3–4.
15. On Microhistory see: James Brooks, Christopher R. N. DeCorse, and John Walton (eds.), *Small Worlds: Method, Meaning and Narrative in Microhistory* (Santa Fe: School for Advanced Research, 2008). Much has been written on the intersection between anthropology and history, and the ways that cultural and social historians have employed anthropological theory in their research and writing. See, for example, Lynn Hunt (ed.), *The New Cultural History* (Berkeley: University of California Press, 1989); Peter Burke, *What Is Cultural History?* (Cambridge: Polity Press, 2004); James Cook, Lawrence Glickman, and Michael O'Malley (eds.), *The Cultural Turn in U.S. History: Past, Present & Future* (Chicago: University of Chicago Press, 2008).
16. Michael Taussig, "Culture of Terror—Space of Death: Roger Casement's Putumayo Report and the Explanation of Terror," *Comparative Studies in Society and History*, 26, 3 (1984): 495.
17. Ibid., 474–476.
18. Ibid., 479–495.
19. Charles Hackett and Charmion Clair Shelby (trans.), *Revolt of the Pueblo Indians of New Mexico and Otermin's Attempted Reconquest 1680–1682* (Albuquerque: University of New Mexico Press, 1942), 61.
20. Carol A. Kidron, "Surviving a Distant Past: A Case Study of the Cultural Construction of Trauma Descendant Identity," *Ethos*, 31, 4 (2003): 513–544.
21. Taussig, "Culture of Terror—Space of Death: Roger Casement's Putumayo Report and the Explanation of Terror," 483–484.

22. George Hammond and Agapito Rey (eds. and trans.), *Narratives of the Coronado Expedition, 1540–1542* (Albuquerque: University of New Mexico Press, 1940), 158.

23. See for example SANM 10: 832–851, SANM 16: 979–983 for comments on the Pueblos' barbarism. The number of documents describing Pueblos as idolatrous are too numerous to list in a footnote. See AGN PI 36, 3: 315–317 for efforts Spanish authorities employed to rid them of their idolatry at the beginning of the century or state of the mission reports such as BN 9, 30 or Archives of the Archdiocese of Santa Fe reel 53: frames 823–836 (hereafter cited as AASF reel number: frame number).

24. AASF 52: 779–780.

25. Spanish Archives of New Mexico, Series I (land records), document number 1365.

26. Taussig, "Culture of Terror—Space of Death: Roger Casement's Putumayo Report and the Explanation of Terror," 464.

27. Erving Goffman, *Stigma: Notes on the Management of Spoiled Identity* (New York: Simon and Schuster, 1963), 3. It strikes me that, defined in this way, "stigma" is very close to "stereotype." The difference is that stereotypes can be positive in nature; stigmas are always, by their very definition, negative and discrediting in the words of Goffman.

28. Hackett and Shelby, *Revolt of the Pueblo Indians of New Mexico and Otermin's Attempted Reconquest 1680–1682*, 181, 206, 345.

29. Ibid., 58.

30. Ibid., 206.

31. Liebmann, *Revolt: An Archaeological History of Pueblo Resistance and Revitalization in 17th Century New Mexico*, 47–49.

32. Andrew Strathern, "Why Is Shame on the Skin?" *Ethnology*, 14, 4 (1975): 355.

33. Hackett and Shelby, *Revolt of the Pueblo Indians of New Mexico and Otermín Attempted Reconquest 1680–1682*, 122, 347, 355.

34. Ibid., 371–372.

35. Jane C. Sanchez, "Spanish-Indian Relations during the Otermín Administration, 1677–1683," *New Mexico Historical Review*, 58, 2 (1983): 133–151; Liebmann, *Revolt: An Archaeological History of Pueblo Resistance and Revitalization in 17th Century New Mexico*, 71–79.

36. The literature on what "culture" is, and how its definition has changed over time is voluminous. For a basic introduction to the debate, see: Ted Lewellen, *The Anthropology of Globalization: Cultural Anthropology Enters the 21st Century* (Westport: Bergin & Garvey, 2002), 29–60.

37. Akhil Gupta and James Ferguson, "Culture, Power, Place: Ethnography at the End of an Era," in *Culture, Power, Place: Explorations in Critical Anthropology*, ed. Akhil Gupta and James Ferguson (Durham, NC: Duke University Press, 2001), 4.

38. Raymond Williams, *Marxism and Literature* (New York: Oxford University Press, 1977).

39. I write at length about Spanish-Pueblo relations more generally in the eighteenth century in my book *Pueblo Indians and Spanish Colonial Authority in Eighteenth Century New Mexico* (Tucson: University of Arizona Press, 2013).

40. William Roseberry, *Anthropologists and Histories: Essays in Culture, History and Political Economy* (New Brunswick: Rutgers University Press, 1989), 85.

41. Gupta and Ferguson, "Culture, Power, Place: Ethnography at the End of an Era," 2–3.

42. For example, compare Knaut's description of colonial New Mexican culture before the revolt (which stresses how much the two populations intermixed) with Ramón Gutiérrez's description of the eighteenth century (which stresses the opposite). Knaut, *The Pueblo Revolt of 1680*; Ramón Gutiérrez, *When Jesus Came, the Corn Mothers Went Away: Marriage, Sexuality, and Power in New Mexico, 1500–1846* (Stanford: Stanford University Press, 1991).

43. Jeffrey C. Alexander, "Toward a Theory of Cultural Trauma," in *Cultural Trauma and Collective Identity*, ed. J. Alexander, R. Eyerman, B. Giesen, N. Smelser, and P. Sztompka (Berkeley: University of California Press, 2004), 1.

# 6

# *BIENVENIDO*, MR. INQUISITOR: ON THE SOCIOCULTURAL DYNAMICS OF INQUISITORIAL VISITS

*William P. Childers*

The title of this essay derives from Luis García Berlanga's satirical film *¡Bienvenido, Mr Marshall!* (1953), in which the inhabitants of a Castilian town, having heard a rumor that George Marshall, of the Marshall Plan, is to pass through on his way to Portugal from France, fantasize about the advantages his aid will bring.[1] Believing the US delegation will expect all Spaniards to behave like the romantic gypsies of Andalusia, they prepare for his anticipated arrival by redecorating the town and dressing up in costumes, transforming even their speech and behavior to resemble the B-movies starring Lola Flores. Berlanga's subtle film is simultaneously a parody of that gypsy/flamenco genre of Franco-era cinema, a denunciation of socioeconomic conditions in rural Spain, a critique of US foreign policy, and a multilayered analysis of the ways the expectations of various agents converge in the representations that shape their perceptions of themselves and reality. These processes become visible through the anticipated presence of an authority figure, whose power enthralls the local population, leading them to perform their identities in a way they never would otherwise. In the sixteenth century, the arrival of the inquisitor on his visit to the towns of his jurisdiction produced a similar effect, which is to say, a vivid dramatization of the disequilibrium in power relations constitutive of intercultural phenomena. Such encounters never take place under conditions of absolute equality among the participants. In the push and pull as what we term "culture" is negotiated, some oppositional meaning may be smuggled in. Intercultural studies might be defined as the study of the consequences of the power differential always present when those of different cultural backgrounds meet.[2]

Though the Spanish Inquisition is now seen primarily as an institution for *repressing* cultural difference, it also proactively *promoted* cultural uniformity by encouraging ordinary citizens to identify with the Counter-Reformation and denounce their neighbors for so-called crimes against the faith. During the visits they made to their districts, inquisitors would read out a list of such crimes, known as the Edict of the Faith, and then remain for several weeks, receiving testimony from anyone who desired to come forward and confess or make accusations.[3] Simply by appearing, these witnesses affirmed their loyalty to Church and Crown, though they often had ulterior motives: to prove themselves right in theological disputes, to settle local scores, or simply to enhance their own status. The records of the testimony they gave provide a fascinating window into intercultural relations in an ethnically diverse society under pressure to assimilate to a single cultural identity. Of course, force and the threat of force were being used to impose religious conformity on Old and New Christians alike, but ordinary citizens were also invited to *collaborate* in constructing the ultra-orthodox Catholic hegemony that served to unify Spain under the Hapsburg monarchs. In effect, this drew a line between the "good" Christians who were by extension loyal Spaniards, and the various groups suspected of heresy: *conversos*, Moriscos, and the odd assortment of doubters, blasphemers, and free thinkers among the Old Christian population.

In the pages that follow, after an introduction to the inquisitorial visits and a general description of the records of them preserved in the Archivo Diocesano de Cuenca (ADC), I will examine particular aspects of the testimony collected on such visits, revealing the double movement whereby those members of the community whose social position was most in line with Counter-Reformation values sought to turn the inquisitor's presence to their own advantage and use it to enhance their status, while others, whose existing identity aligned them more with the pre-Tridentine peasant culture of New Castile, were coerced into conformity. A particular focus will be the impact of the inquisitorial visit on the cultural difference of the Moriscos of Granada who had been brought to live in La Mancha during the War of the Alpujarras (1568–1571). I will conclude with a discussion of some of the methodological and theoretical consequences for intercultural studies of the dynamic at work in the inquisitorial visit.

# I

As standard bearer of the Counter-Reformation, the Inquisition was at the center of a complex cultural dynamic, in which the emergent post-Tridentine order was imposed simultaneously on Old Christians and on more recent converts such as the Moriscos, descendants of those who accepted baptism at the beginning of the sixteenth century. The Crown's decision to incorporate a new series of "crimes against the faith," such as blasphemy, bigotry, concubinage, and fornication, into the purview of the Inquisition gave this institution a key role in the process of *confessionalization*, the imposition of religious conformity as a means of consolidating monarchical power and unifying the state. The use of this term is partly a result of misgivings about "Absolutism," which has been shown to be less absolute than previously thought, at least during the Hapsburg dynasty. Prior to the emergence of the modern secular state, confessionalization was an effective tool for consolidating and centralizing power.[4] In effect, through the Inquisition the monarchy wrested control over the pedagogical project of the Counter-Reformation away from the church hierarchy. Enforcement of these reclassified offenses had previously been overseen by the bishops, who lacked both the resources the inquisitors had at their disposal, and their rapacious zeal. There was significant friction between inquisitors and bishops over these jurisdictional disputes. What comes through strongly in the documentation is the tolerant, almost lackadaisical attitude of the bishops regarding enforcement, when compared with the aggressive, rigorous stance of the Inquisition. It was this institutional *ethos* aimed at transforming society that served the Crown's interests so well.[5] The Supreme Council of the Inquisition, a branch of the monarchy, was now able to set priorities for religious indoctrination and conformity, which made the inquisitorial visit a more confrontational situation, as townspeople scurried to situate themselves in relation to the sudden arrival of someone with so much power over their lives and property. As the examples below will show, local Old Christian communities did not respond uniformly to the expectation that they would at least outwardly conform in their behavior and speech to the new orthodoxy. While some clung to previous attitudes of irreverence or moral autonomy vis-à-vis the Church hierarchy, others saw changing circumstances as an opportunity to consolidate or even enhance their social standing.[6]

Inquisitorial pressure similarly places Moriscos at a crossroads in terms of cultural assimilation. In many towns of New Castile, there was no Morisco presence to speak of prior to the War of the Alpujarras. As a result of this conflict they were removed from Granada and scattered across the territory of the Crown of Castile in 1570. Despite ups and downs, their integration in their new host communities was showing signs of success by the 1590s. As we will see, however, the ongoing process of negotiation of their identities with local religious and civil authorities could be abruptly cut short by an inquisitorial visit. Over the years, practices viewed as too Muslim were abandoned, mainly under the direction of parish priests, while others, considered harmless or even valued for their exotic difference, were retained. The examples we will consider are burial rites on the one hand and wedding celebrations on the other. Under the inquisitorial gaze, however, *all* cultural differences between Moriscos and their old Christian neighbors were made to appear suspect; any divergence, any particularity, became a sign of their failure to fully commit to their adopted faith.

Given such conditions, comparable in their cultural dynamics to those holding sway under colonialism, each cultural practice comes to have at least two meanings: the one it has for its practitioners within their own frame of reference, and the one it has from the point of view of the emerging hegemonic system.[7] Moreover, the double code quickly bifurcates further; once the new, external meaning associating the practice with heresy is understood by the populace, a decision must be made whether to adopt this officially sanctioned point of view or cling to the original, localized understanding. The former path leads to denunciation of one's neighbors, the latter to some form of semi-clandestine persistence in the heretical view, be it tacit or overt, whose meaning has now changed. Through its power to mark specific cultural practices as heretical, the Inquisition reveals in its extreme form a principle that should guide intercultural studies generally, the previously mentioned fact that every intercultural encounter takes place in a power disequilibrium; there is no level playing field. We are always dealing, then, not only with a variety of cultural practices, but also with a multiplicity of significations assigned to *each* practice. The negotiation of cultural difference is concentrated at the "nodal points" where significations accumulate.

The inquisitorial visit was an effective tool for bringing this monarchical agenda for reform of customs and beliefs into contact with local views and behaviors. Each spring, one of the two inquisitors assigned to every tribunal was obliged to take a tour of part of the district. Ideally, the two inquisitors would take turns making this annual trip, and would coordinate their trajectories in such a way that the entire district was visited in a regular cycle, every few years. Though it would later fall into disuse, the practice was maintained fairly strictly throughout the reign of Philip II. The inquisitor would arrive in one of the large towns of the district, where, at a mass that all were obliged to attend, he would read the Edict of the Faith. The inquisitor would remain in town for about a month, sometimes longer, collecting declarations of witnesses from the town and the surrounding area, where local priests were instructed to read the Edict of the Faith as well, encouraging their parishioners to make the short trip to the larger, nearby town where the inquisitor was eagerly waiting to hear their denunciations. Once the visit was concluded, he would be off to another town, until he finally completed his circuit and returned to the tribunal, usually after about three months.[8]

For most inquisitorial visits, the only surviving documentation is the *relación de visita*, which summarizes each accusation, but does not record who the witnesses were or when they gave their testimony. Much more valuable, but also much rarer, are the *libros de testificaciones*, large-format, bound volumes that were carried from town to town during the visit. The inquisitorial scribe transcribed witnesses' declarations into the pages of these books as they were given, almost verbatim—mainly just the pronouns are shifted from first to third person—and in the precise order in which the testimony was given.[9] These books, which generally run to 500 folios or more, covering as much as a decade, are of great value to the historian interested in gauging the impact of the Inquisition, not just on the individuals actually put on trial, but on the entire community of the (ostensibly) faithful, since they contain much information that does not find its way into other records, including among other things the names and personal information of the witnesses, whether they came forward of their own accord or were called to testify, whether they made more than one accusation, and whether or not they could sign their names. Moreover, many of these declarations did *not* lead to trials, so the "cases" would be completely lost were it not for the testimony recorded during the visit. Ultimately, the transcripts of all the declarations given during a month-long stay by the inquisitor constitute a kind of "snapshot" of how the local community responded to his presence.[10]

The following examples all come from visits by the inquisitors of Cuenca to the district of La Mancha during the 1590s. The Tribunal of Cuenca, which included much of La Mancha within its jurisdiction, houses the best-preserved archive concerning inquisitorial visits. The richness of the documentation housed there permits a much fuller reconstruction of the inquisitorial visit than would be possible for any other tribunal. Not only have they preserved the full series of *libros de testificaciones* for the sixteenth and early seventeenth centuries, but they also have an extensive collection of supporting documents not found elsewhere.

For all the tribunals, letters back and forth to the Suprema are conserved in the Archivo Histórico Nacional (AHN) in Madrid. There also may be *relaciones de visita*, such as those that have been painstakingly transcribed by José María García Fuentes for the Granada tribunal.[11] However, the Inquisition archive of the Archivo Diocesano de Cuenca (ADC) preserves a much richer and more complete set of documents regarding visits, including, in addition to the *relaciones de visita, libros de testificaciones,* and letters between the tribunal and the Suprema: hundreds of confessions taken on visits; dozens of letters from local priests attesting to their having read the Edict of the Faith and exhorted their parishioners to go and see the inquisitor; in some cases, additional testimony offered in those towns by witnesses not healthy enough to travel; documents attesting the oath sworn by local officials to respect the inquisitor's authority and aid him as necessary; lists of witnesses with marginal notes used by the inquisitor during his visit; and books used in the seventeenth century by the prosecuting attorney, who consulted the records of the visit to decide who should be put on trial; as well other minor documents, too varied to list here.

Taken together, the *libros de testificaciones* along with other supporting documentation of the visits constitute a snapshot "mapping" inquisitorial power onto conditions on the ground. This amounts to a case study of what Stuart Hall terms *articulation*.[12] As Hall uses the term, this is the moment in which power structures from above are implemented in concrete circumstances. In the seemingly mechanical process of such implementation, a handing off of power occurs, whereby abstract, theoretical directives are concretized in specific instances. There is necessarily a certain leeway here, a margin for interpretation, an opening that can even give rise to a counter-hegemonic response. Hall envisions these moments of articulation as the most precarious in the consolidation of any hegemony, for the very reason, of course, that it is here that power ultimately expresses itself in the everyday lives of ordinary folk. Inspired by Hall's work and the ascendancy of the Birmingham school, *cultural* studies found points of articulation to be an ideal locus for examining the ways apparently passive consumers in postindustrial societies at times refused simply to inhabit the readymade subject positions prepared for them.[13] The work of *inter*cultural studies demands an even greater attentiveness to moments of articulation, as it is precisely here that the nodal points of intercultural contact are worked through. Insofar as interculturality always implies a dominant culture and at least one marginal culture, the concept of articulation can be understood as that moment in which the dominant culture is imposed, but the displaced culture does not necessarily disappear. It may blend with the dominant, the two may coexist in a dynamic of public/clandestine, or it may be more openly espoused as a form of symbolic resistance. All of these possibilities are in play during inquisitorial visits, in which the official religious culture is articulated onto existing sets of practices and beliefs.

## II

A double cultural transformation is taking place, then, in rural Spain at the close of the sixteenth century. On the one hand, Counter-Reformation doctrines that contradict longstanding popular beliefs are being imposed, with the Inquisition serving as an instrument for enforcing this imposition. This means that people are called upon to give up the locally grounded, semi-autonomous system of values and beliefs that still existed in a certain tension with the centralized, official teachings of the Church even at the end of the sixteenth century. At the same time, the ethnoreligious minorities—*conversos* and Moriscos—are subject to intense scrutiny to determine whether or not their everyday customs and behavior correspond with that of the Old Christian majority. Again, the Inquisition was the chief means by which this obligatory cultural assimilation was policed. The examples I want to consider of these two types of cultural change imposed from above will serve to differentiate two kinds of participation by the local population during an inquisitorial visit, and thus two quite different responses to the articulation of Counter-Reformation ideology in rural New Castile.

The post-Tridentine doctrines that most frequently come up in inquisitorial proceedings are known by the shorthand terms "simple fornication" and "error about estates" (*error sobre estados*). Both refer to infractions that only came under inquisitorial jurisdiction after Trent, and both have to do with frequently held, persistent views the Church sought to eradicate. The first concerns a widespread popular opinion, according to which it is not a sin to have extramarital relations with an unmarried woman, to which is usually added the caveat, "as long as you pay her for it." The denial of the sinful nature of coitus takes other forms as well, to be sure, but the most widespread is this notion that turning it into an economic transaction somehow places it in another, nonsinful, category. In *libros de testificaciones,* topic of simple fornication comes up again and again in conversations among men while they are working in agricultural labor, reaping wheat, picking grapes, etc. In these conversations, one individual typically emerges as a "holdout," refusing to give up the popular belief while other members of the group remonstrate with him. When the inquisitor comes to town, the witnesses come forward to denounce their unfortunate comrade.

In late February 1593, Antón López d'Escobar, Felipe de la Torre, and Juan de la Osa, all 30-somethings, were out pruning grapevines. To begin with, Antón got Juan to acknowledge it *is* a sin to have "carnal access" with a married woman; then Antón queried, "well, what about with a *single* woman, then?" to which Juan shot back, "No, that's not a sin." Although Juan later said it just slipped out, and he immediately denied the intention, his coworkers both went to see the inquisitor to denounce him.[14] One is left with the impression that they were deliberately trying to trip him up, just to get him to misspeak himself, so they would have something they could use against him. Similar examples can be found in almost any inquisitorial visit after Trent. Whether or not we suppose a deliberate strategy of entrapment, there is little room for doubt that these vignettes are confrontations between those who still hold to a medieval popular view that extramarital sexual relations under certain circumstances need not be considered sinful, and those who have adopted the Church's official position. It is worth noting that the "holdout" often responds, "Well, *I* do not hold it to be a sin," or words to that effect, clearly staking out a position of resistance. Obviously, we only have records of such conversations when someone present insisted upon the doctrine's being respected, and then took the initiative of reporting it to the Inquisition. Presumably there were occasions when no one objected to the heretical view; in fact, such conversations may have been quite frequent, and could have served to propagate the heretical position in a semi-clandestine manner. If so, the conversations we find today in the *libros de testificaciones* are perhaps only the visible tip of a potentially much larger invisible iceberg, and the practice of declaring that simple fornication is not a sin could be a way of testing others' reactions to find out whether they defend the Church's position or not. We can only surmise what the results might have been on such occasions, and speculate that this relatively mild heresy could have been just the starting point for discussions that ended up challenging other aspects of Counter-Reformation orthodoxy.[15]

The other doctrine being imposed after Trent is the highly unpopular affirmation that God prefers the "religious estate" to that of marriage. In its twenty-fourth session, held in 1563, the Council of Trent enhanced the role of all those who were recognized as having "religious" status by insisting on the superiority of the celibacy over marriage (based on Paul's clear preference in *First Corinthians* 7:1–9).[16] The defense of this doctrine was often taken up by *beatas*, lay women who had taken a vow of celibacy and therefore claimed the enhanced status of the religious, though they were not cloistered nuns. *Beatas* did not usually take any vow other than celibacy and a general commitment to devote themselves to God, and frequently continued to live at home and move about as freely as any other women; thus their status as religious women in a Counter-Reformation context was uncertain. Ecclesiastical authorities sought to resolve the inherent ambiguity in *beatas'* condition, encouraging them to cloister themselves and follow a specific rule, and where possible, aiding the conversion of *beaterios* to convents. In turn, *beatas* tenaciously defended their claim to higher social standing based on the Tridentine doctrine of the superiority of the religious estate, that is, their celibacy. Thus they frequently come forward to denounce those who affirm the equality or superiority of marriage over those who have taken a vow of celibacy. After the Protestant Reformation, the Church made this tenet something of a litmus test of acceptance of ecclesiastical authority. To deny it was to flirt with Lutheranism, but for many married people struggling to raise a family it was hard to accept. Does God not appreciate the effort and sacrifice they make in bringing their children up to be good Christians? Must they accept *beatas'* telling them to their faces that their status within the Church was lower? As the records of inquisitorial visits show, the doctrine was frequently challenged in private conversations. With no superior to obey and no seclusion from worldly matters, *beatas* were seen by their neighbors as having the best of both: freedom from caring for husbands and children, but without the corresponding obligations of nuns.[17]

These *beatas* are the self-styled monitors of religious orthodoxy in general, particularly of acknowledgment of the doctrine of estates, as this justifies their status. They rebuke any denial of the inferiority of marriage made in their presence, but they also make a mental note of who was present and eventually come forward to denounce it to the inquisitor, with a detailed list of corroborating witnesses. Moreover, *beatas* almost always have additional denunciations to make. Everything proceeds as if they had been waiting for the inquisitor to come, storing up accusations, with the expectation that his visit would provide the opportunity for them to assert the primacy of their embracing of the culture of ultra-orthodox Counter-Reformation Catholicism over the more lackadaisical outlook of many of their fellow townspeople. Indeed, the inquisitorial visit was the ideal occasion for a *beata* to shore up her status as a religious woman entitled to public recognition of her superior standing based on the doctrine of estates. She was sure to be among the first to declare, and would stay the longest, denouncing a whole list of offenders against the faith, while perhaps confessing some tiny infraction of her own. Undoubtedly she was aware of the gaze of her neighbors as they watched her approach the place where the inquisitor was holding audience, and she knew they would notice and comment on the duration of her testimony.[18]

Thus it comes out quite dramatically in the visits that those who make a great show of their piety, having staked their status in the community on their willing acceptance of Counter-Reformation Catholicism, sought to turn the inquisitor's presence to their own advantage. They laid rhetorical traps for those they suspected of nonconformity, kept tallies of who said what and before which other witnesses, and generally prepared their testimony, sometimes over a period of years, awaiting the opportunity to report it. In this sense, the lines of a struggle for power and status have long since been drawn, and the arrival of the inquisitor is simply the event that allows one faction—that of the pious—to make a strategic bid for increased influence. Of course, the inquisitor will shortly leave, while they will remain behind. Their final vindication, therefore, depends upon the Inquisition's following through and punishing the individuals they have denounced.

In these two examples, then, simple fornication and celibacy versus marriage, we have seen how the inquisitor's visit revealed and sharpened internal division within the Old Christian majority. A faction emerges that continues to affirm the autonomy of the peasantry to formulate their own outlook and values, implicitly rejecting Counter-Reformation pressure to accept the authority of the Church in defining social norms as well as religious beliefs and practices. Opposed to this faction are those, like many *beatas*, who chose to denounce their neighbors for heresy. They often appear to have elected to stake their claim to higher status on the Inquisition's ability to enforce the prohibition against locally held cultural values. They see power emanating outwards from the central authorities of Crown and Church and choose to associate themselves with it. Now let us turn our attention to an ethnoreligious minority, the Moriscos, who are especially vulnerable to inquisitorial scrutiny, since their ancestors were Muslims and therefore "infidels" by definition. In effect, the inquisitor's presence tended to reinforce the line separating Old Christian and

Morisco populations; whatever blurring of that line had begun to take place through integration of the Moriscos into Castilian society was abruptly reversed as a consequence of the inquisitorial visit.

## III

Denunciations against the Moriscos of Granada who had been sent to live in La Mancha after the Alpujarras War tend to follow quite a different pattern than we have observed within the Old Christian population. What we often see in their case are indications, sometimes subtle, occasionally quite explicit, that the witnesses who come forward to denounce their practices did not necessarily think of them as crimes against the faith until they heard the reading of the Edict during mass. These are distinct Morisco customs, whose relation to Islam is unclear to their neighbors, and even, at times, to the inquisitor himself, as we shall soon see.[19] The two most common are: clothing the dead in new, clean, linen garments for burial, a practice that puzzled Christians who at the time were accustomed to bury the dead in their old clothes, of no further use to the living; and Morisco weddings, which were accompanied with performances of Moorish music from Granada and the famous dance known as the *zambra*.[20] Each of these types of denunciation obeys a distinct chronology of its own. Generally, witnesses who come forward to accuse Moriscos of participating in Muslim burial rites refer to incidents that occurred a decade or more earlier, in the years just after their arrival from Granada. The oldest of the newly arrived Moriscos, who died during those years, are described as turning to face Mecca on their deathbeds, and their spouses are accused of dressing them in fresh linen garments, in accordance with their own custom. In its most extreme form, the desire to "die a Muslim" leads to deathbed confessions of having never been truly Christian, such as that of Miguel, in Quintanar. When the inquisitor came years later he was treated to the same story by multiple witnesses: how he publicly repented of ever having accepted baptism, and how his body, which could not be buried in consecrated ground, was instead dumped on trash heap, where the children threw stones at it, and finally the dogs ate it.[21] These are the "holdouts" among the Moriscos. Subsequent generations appear to have given up traditional burial practices. Of course it is possible that they simply learned to hide them more carefully, though even that would indicate an internalization of Old Christian perceptions of them.

In contrast, denunciations against Moriscos for participating in weddings at which they danced the *zambra* refer to more recent events.

A wedding is a more public event than the death of a member of the family and subsequent preparation of the corpse for burial. Even after Moriscos had either ceased to shroud their dead in accordance with their own traditions or at least had learned to conceal it more carefully, they continued to celebrate their weddings quite openly in the way they had done in Granada, with traditional Hispano-Arabic music and dancing. The point is worth stressing: the *same* Morisco communities that, in the process of assimilating, either surrendered or were more cautious in hiding their burial practices, *maintained* their weddings. Thus Moriscos were negotiating the process of their cultural assimilation into New Castilian society, retaining cultural practices that were accepted or even enjoyed by their Old Christian neighbors, while discarding those that fell under censure.

The attitude toward these weddings revealed during the visits is especially interesting. When the inquisitor Velarde de la Concha arrived in Quintanar de la Orden in September 1590, he read a version of the Edict of the Faith which, among many other things, exhorted hearers to come forward if "anyone has been married in accordance with Moorish rites and customs, and has sung Moorish songs or played *zambras* or *leilas* on prohibited instruments." Having heard this, many townspeople lined up to describe Morisco weddings they had attended, but none of them was aware of any Moorish rites, only the music and dancing. This led Velarde to write the *Suprema* in Madrid, literally inquiring after the meaning of "and" in the text of the edict, where it talks about Moorish rites *and* singing and dancing. Is it a crime against the faith to marry with Moorish song and dance, even if there are no Muslim rites performed?[22] The response from Madrid is just to write down everything the witnesses wish to declare and back in Cuenca they can sort out whether there is any heretical intention of practicing Islam in anything they describe.[23] So Velarde dutifully collects descriptions of Morisco weddings from several people, who obviously never shied away from attending them. Some witnesses acknowledge having attended seven or eight of them during the nearly twenty years since the Moriscos of Granada were first brought to Quintanar, after the War of the Alpujarras. Matías Hernández del Corral, a weaver, even comes forward to "confess" that he plays the guitar at such weddings, and has learned a few songs from the Moriscos. Asked about his own genealogy, he insists that he is Old Christian, he just enjoys the Moorish music.[24]

Here the impact of the inquisitorial visit is quite different from what we saw with errors concerning simple fornication and estates, where an internal struggle was being waged concerning the abandonment of traditional values within the community, and the adoption of a new, officially sanctioned set of values. The Moriscos are newcomers in Quintanar and most other towns within the jurisdiction of the Cuenca tribunal. The townspeople view certain of their customs with ambivalence, combining puzzlement, curiosity, and even, at least in the case of the music and dance, enjoyment. The potential for intercultural dialogue here is strong. One can even find evidence that their cultural difference, far from being an obstacle to their social integration, was facilitating that process.[25] The arrival of the inquisitor, however, and the reading of the Edict of the Faith, drew a bright line between sanctioned, "Christian" cultural practices, and those of the relatively recently arrived exiles from Granada. That people like Matías Hernández del Corral came forward at this point to give testimony against them certainly cannot be taken to indicate a preexisting animosity toward the Moriscos. Rather, it is a direct and immediate consequence of the inquisitor's visit. One can in this case speak of a pedagogy of fear, intended to unite the population against the Moriscos through suspicion of heresy, stigmatizing their cultural practices as inherently un-Christian. To take this reasoning a step further, it is perhaps not too much to say that the encouraging of a suspicious attitude toward anything Moriscos do that deviates from the cultural norms of Old Christians is part of a larger project constituting Moriscos as a distinct "race," and by contrast, establishing the racial superiority of Old Christians. Indeed, in a recent paper, Mercedes García-Arenal has argued that by the end of the sixteenth century, it had become officially sanctioned opinion that religious belief was a congenitally inherited trait—that Moriscos were incapable by birth of becoming sincere Christians. Only its biological terminology distinguishes nineteenth-century racism from this position.[26]

It is worth mentioning that none of the testimony concerning Morisco weddings that Velarde de la Concha collected in Quintanar led to anyone being put on trial for "*Mahometismo*." Nonetheless, his visit clearly altered local residents' perception of Morisco weddings. It marks a definite before and after in the process of negotiating the tension between their cultural identities and their status as members of the community.

## IV

Faced with an institution like the Inquisition, which used force and the threat of force to eradicate unsanctioned cultural practices, there is an understandable tendency to focus on its repressive function and view the accused as its more-or-less passive victims. When we shift our attention, however, to the witnesses, particularly if we study their denunciations in the context of the inquisitorial visit, a more complex picture emerges. Yes, religious authority is being brought to bear on local populations by the centralizing power of the monarchy, and it exercises pressure in the direction of conformity. But people acting locally make decisions on a daily basis about how to respond to that pressure. For some, it is an opportunity to push private agendas, to enhance their own status and punish rivals, enemies, or outsiders viewed with suspicion.[27] For others, it is an opportunity in another sense, to defend local allegiances, consolidate opposition to the Crown, and create more-or-less open, more-or-less concealed networks of inconformity. The Morisco ethnoreligious minority, as relative newcomers in the towns of the jurisdiction of Cuenca, are caught in the middle, and in that sense they offer the widest scope for the expansion of monarchical power through the Inquisition, since factionalism will be weaker in their case. This is not by any means the only instance in which it appears the Crown took advantage of the Morisco situation to extend its power. Indeed, the whole history of Granada after 1492 is a blueprint for the expansion of monarchical power.

Such an understanding of the social dynamics at work during inquisitorial visits implies that early modern state power, while functioning in a spectacular, Baroque modality, was nonetheless not as one-sidedly authoritarian as we often assume, for example when we loosely refer to the Hapsburg monarchy as "Absolutist." As Foucault taught us in numerous texts, the modern state—of which Hapsburg Spain is at least an important precursor if not a precocious exemplar—exercises power in a positive sense to incentivize the development of subjectivities that actively insert themselves into the established order.[28] Even in the absence of a transparent public sphere such as Habermas considers indispensable for modern, democratic societies, another kind of participation in the construction of the emergent order is available to parishioners. Hegemony is achieved through *consent*, though this does not necessarily mean well-informed, freely given consent. When the inquisitor comes to town, the forms of agency that come into play are constrained, of course, by the limitations imposed by monarchical and ecclesiastical authority. Yet they are equally fractured and fragmented by the play between openness and secrecy in the actor's own cautious yet risky game of seeking alliances in a precarious and always untrustworthy situation. The Inquisition demands secrecy of all who depose during the visit, but given the charged atmosphere, rumors inevitably swirl concerning who is declaring and against whom. Rather than the transparency of the public sphere as described by Habermas, then, the visit transpires in an opaque social space in which half-hidden factions jockey for position through ambiguous public performances. Several years ago, I introduced the term "Baroque public sphere" to try and explain the performative nature of power relations in early modern Spain, where the complex play of attitudes hidden and revealed gives rise to the kinds of public staging of status relations and private settling of accounts to which the inquisitorial visit so beautifully lent itself.[29]

Yet within this social space, state and ecclesiastical authority were brought to bear in a particular way in shaping the representation of the Morisco minority. As I have argued, local communities of la Mancha did not have their minds made up in 1571 when the Moriscos of Granada were brought there, nor even, it appears, some 20 years later, when visits like Velarde de la Concha's to Quintanar took place. The active part played by royal institutions in creating and regulating Morisco identity and the image of it among the populace can be usefully viewed through the lens of Michael Omi and Howard Winant's theory of "racial formation."[30] Arguably the Moriscos were being constituted as a "race" in late sixteenth-century Spain. Indeed, in keeping with Omi and Winant's notion of the systemic nature of the racial formations of a given society, they were being incorporated into a larger system of relations between racial groups, whereby *conversos*, Moriscos, and gypsies came to constitute the racial others of Old Christians. It was this racial system that first made "Old Christian" a recognizably separate group, in much the way that the new black/white polarization after Plessy versus Ferguson made "whiteness" a social category capacious enough to include Irish and Italians, who had not previously been identified as belonging to the "same race" as the English and other Northern Europeans.[31] As Américo Castro famously argued, the Old Christian commoners were thereby endowed with a sense of "honor," since they at least were free of the racial "taint" of Jewish or Moorish ancestry.[32] The fact that "purity of blood" thereby became the first model of the Spanish nation led directly to the posing of the Morisco Question, which essentially amounted to asking whether the descendants of Muslims could ever truly belong to the nation. Their "impure blood" was taken to mean they could never become "good Christians," and therefore could never be "good Spaniards," either. Once the issue was framed in this way, the eventual expulsion of the Moriscos began to appear simply a matter of time. Interventions by the Inquisition contributed significantly to this process by implanting suspicion in parishioners' minds. Customs that were initially marked only as *distinct* were made to appear *heretical*, not so much due to any clear link to Islam, but because they were *Morisco* customs. Under such institutional pressure, their otherness came to be perceived as intrinsically threatening. Moriscos indeed found ways to engage with the baroqueness of the public sphere, performing their otherness as a positive cultural feature and even bringing lawsuits in defense of their claims to the status of Old Christians.[33] Yet the inquisitorial visit demonstrates how much the deck was stacked against them. Through the powerful ecclesiastical institution it controlled, the crown sought to foreclose on any possibility of intercultural dialogue, in favor of a more monolithic cultural uniformity, which increasingly stigmatized the ethnic other in racialized terms that had little to do with religious belief.[34]

Insofar as intercultural studies is often bound to focus on cultural misunderstandings, perhaps the most valuable lesson to be learned from studying an extreme form of encounter between cultures like the inquisitorial visit is that such misunderstandings are seldom innocent. Rather, they are the product of a combination of at least three factors: (1) the power disequilibrium existing at the outset, marking each cultural system's position within a hierarchical arrangement; (2) the double code of significations, referring not simply to practices from two or more cultures, but to the plurality of understandings of *each* practice, such that a single cultural *sememe* comes to have at least two meanings; and (3) the strategic choices individual actors make in interpreting one another's behavior, given both the availability of these multiple frames of reference and the power disequilibrium with respect to which they must situate themselves. Naturally these choices are governed by the desire for higher status, with individuals trying, insofar as it is available to them to do so, to associate themselves with people one step higher on the social ladder. Late sixteenth-century New Castile was a site where an emergent hegemonic culture stigmatized certain beliefs and practices as unacceptable, but these beliefs and practices could therefore also signify refusal to conform. In the examples, we can see how distinct factions within the populace responded differently to this pressure in accordance with differences in their access to power and status. Ultimately, though, the Moriscos were available as scapegoats, over and against whom the Old Christian majority came to feel more unified. The result was the creation of a clearly demarcated us/them distinction, leading to a racialized social order based on underlying religious orthodoxy, which succeeded in quelling any oppositional perspective for the next three centuries.

# NOTES

1. This essay is dedicated to Tina Leisner McDermott in grateful acknowledgment of her help in revising the paper I originally read at the intercultural studies conference in St. Louis in 2013.

2. In these formulations, readers familiar with postcolonial theory may recognize echoes of such theoretical notions as "hybridity," as discussed in Homi K. Bhabha, *The Location of Culture* (London and New York: Routledge, 1994), 159–174.

3. Miguel Jiménez Monteserín transcribes instructions for carrying out visits and copies of the Edict of the Faith in his *Introducción a la inquisición española* (Madrid: Editora Nacional, 1980), 291–295, 497–541. I. Villa Calleja describes the procedure of proclaiming the edict and conducting a visit in "Edictos de Fe (siglos XV-XIX)," in *Historia de la Inquisición en España y América*, dir. Bartolomé Escandell Bonet and Joaquín Pérez Villanueva, vol. 2, *Las estructuras del Santo Oficio* (Madrid: Biblioteca de Autores Cristianos and Centro de Estudios Inquisitoriales, 1993), 301–333.

4. See Bartolomé Bennasser, *"Confesionalización" de la monarquía e Inquisición en la época de Felipe II: dos estudios* (Valladolid: Secretariado de Publicaciones e Intercambio Editorial, Universidad de Valladolid, 2009). The role of the Inquisition in confessionalization under Philip II is specifically discussed by José Martínez Millán, *La inquisición española* (Madrid: Alianza, 2007), 121–154.

5. I am currently working on a more comprehensive treatment of inquisitorial visits, which will include a section devoted to this issue.

6. Two of the best studies of how the Spanish Inquisition displaced popular/local belief systems to impose conformity with the Counter-Reformation remain William A. Christian's *Local Religion in Sixteenth-Century Spain* (Princeton, NJ: Princeton University Press, 1981) and Sarah T. Nalle's *God in La Mancha: Religious Reform and the People of Cuenca, 1500–1650* (Baltimore: Johns Hopkins University Press, 1992). See also my own *Transnational Cervantes* (Toronto: University of Toronto Press, 2006), 4–14.

7. Aníbal Quijano theorized this cultural ambivalence under the heading "coloniality of power." "Colonialidad del poder, cultura y conocimiento en América Latina," *Anuario mariateguiano*, 9 (1997): 113–121.

8. Inquisitorial visits have not been much studied as such. In English, a brief introduction to the subject can be found in Henry Kamen, *The Spanish Inquisition. An Historical Revision* (London: Weidenfeld and Nicohlson, 1997), 179–181. Jean-Pierre Dedieu describes the typical inquisitorial visit in *L'administration de la foi. L'Inquisition de Tolède (XVIe-XVIIIe siècle)* (Madrid: Casa de Velázquez, 1992), 183–190. In her recent book, Kimberly Lynn devotes a chapter to the visit, viewed exclusively as an activity of the Inquisitor, with no interest in the agency of those who testify. She briefly mentions the *libros de testificaciones* from

the Toledo tribunal, to which she refers, in keeping with the Inquisitor's perspective, as "visitation books." *Between Court and Confessional. The Politics of Spanish Inquisitors* (Cambridge: Cambridge University Press, 2013), 52–64.

9. Linguists Rolf Eberenz and Mariela Agostinho de la Torre discuss the reliability of inquisitorial transcripts of witness testimony as evidence for sixteenth-century Spanish. They agree that the *libros de testificaciones* come very close to verbatim transcripts, with only the pronouns shifted and a modicum of legal terminology added, such as the frequent use of the adjective *dicho* "(afore)said," to indicate that someone or something has already been mentioned. *Conversaciones estrechamente vigiladas: Interacción coloquial y español oral en las actas inquisitoriales de los siglos XV a XVII* (Zaragoza: Pórtico, 2003), 21–39.

10. To date, the *libros de testificaciones* have been grossly neglected by scholars, though that is beginning to change. The *libros de testificaciones* for the tribunal of the Canary Islands, housed in the Museo Canario, are quite voluminous and have been employed in studies of that tribunal, as Francisco Fajardo Spínola explains in "La actividad procesal del Santo Oficio. Algunas consideraciones sobre su estudio" *Manuscrits*, 17 (1999): 97–117. He describes their value in the following terms: "Mucho podría decirse sobre el valor de los libros de testificaciones como fuente que refleja, mejor que otro tipo de documentos inquisitoriales, la realidad social sobre la que el Santo Oficio actuaba, tanto porque muchas denuncias no daban lugar a un proceso, sino que eran archivadas, cuanto por la inmediatez y frescura de estos documentos; e incluso porque muestran la acción del Santo Oficio en su base, al nivel de los comisarios de los pueblos" (108). A recent publication makes use of *libros de testificaciones* from the Valencia tribunal, some of which are housed in the Archivo Histórico de la Universidad de Valencia: Juan Antonio Barrio Barrio, "Prácticas y procedimientos jurídicos e institucionales de la Inquisición Real de Valencia. Los edictos y las testificaciones a finales del siglo XV," in *En el primer siglo de la Inquisición Española. Fuentes documentales, procedimientos de análisis, experiencias de investigación*, coord. José María Cruselles Gómez (Valencia: Universitat de València, 2013), 145–166. I am currently collaborating with an international group of some half dozen scholars undertaking a large-scale survey of the *libros de testificaciones* and similar inquisitorial documents, such as the *cadernos do promotor* used in the Portuguese and Brazilian tribunals.

11. José María García Fuentes, *Visitas de la Inquisición al Reino de Granada* (Granada: Editorial Universidad de Granada, 2006).

12. Stuart Hall, "Race, Articulation, and Societies Structured in Dominance," in *Black British Cultural Studies. A Reader*, ed. Houston A. Baker, Jr., Manthia Diawara, and Ruth H. Lindeborg (Chicago: University of Chicago Press, 1996), 16–60.

13. The theoretical statement that unlocked this critical doorway was Stuart Hall, "Encoding/Decoding," in *Culture, Media, Language*, ed. Stuart Hall,

Dorothy Hobson, Andrew Lowe, and Paul Willis (London: Hutchinson, 1980), 128–138. Two breakthrough studies in this vein were David Morley, *The 'Nationwide' Audience: Structure and Decoding* (London: British Film Institute, 1980) and Ien Ang, *Watching Dallas: Soap Opera and the Melodramatic Imagination* (London: Methuen, 1985).

14. ADC Inq, libro 326, fols 318r–319r.

15. This is not necessarily to imply that these strategies are deliberate on the part of individual speakers. Consider in this regard Ranajit Guha's description of the spontaneous functioning of rumor: "rumour is 'immediate unpremeditated utterance'...improvised within the rebel community not as a conscious device to rally the people, but spontaneously, without deliberation, that is, by the force of ideology alone." *Elementary Aspects of Peasant Insurgency in Colonial India* (Durham and London: Duke University Press, 1999), 262.

16. *Canons and Decrees of the Council of Trent*, trans. Theodore Alois Buckley (London: Routledge, 1851), Session 24, Canon X, p. 179: "If any one shall say, that the marriage state is to be preferred before a state of virginity, or of celibacy, and that it is not better and more blessed to remain in virginity, or in celibacy, than to be joined in matrimony; let him be anathema."

17. General treatments of *beatas* and their social and religious contexts in early modern Spain can be found in the following studies: Mary Elizabeth Perry, *Gender and Disorder in Early Modern Seville* (Princeton, NJ: Princeton University Press, 1990); Adelina Sarrión Mora, *Beatas y endemoniadas. Mujeres heterodoxas ante la Inquisición. Siglos XVI a XIX* (Madrid: Alianza, 2003); Elizabeth A. Lehfeldt, *Religious Women in Golden Age Spain: The Permeable Cloister* (Aldershot, UK: Ashgate, 2005); Lisa Vollendorf, *The Lives of Women. A New History of Inquisitional Spain* (Nashville: Vanderbilt University Press, 2005); and Alison Weber, "Locating Holiness in Early Modern Spain: Convents, Caves, and Houses," in *Structures and Subjectivities: Attending to Early Modern Women*, ed. Joan Hartman and Adele Seeff (Newark: University of Delaware Press, 2007), 50–74.

18. For detailed discussion of specific examples, see William P. Childers, "Another Side of Beatas: Their Testimony During Inquisitorial Visits," in *Lives and Works of Early Modern Women in Iberia and the Americas: Studies in Law, Society, Art, and Literature in Honor of Anne J. Cruz*, ed. Adrienne L. Martin and María Cristina Quintero (New York: Arte Poético, forthcoming).

19. Of course, the relation between Morisco customs and Islam, especially in the case of the Granada Moriscos, was a fraught question in the late sixteenth century. As is well known, Francisco Núñez Muley, in the face of royal suppression, argued cogently that Moriscos' customs were not intrinsically Islamic in nature, but compatible with Christianity. Francisco Nuñez Muley, *A Memorandum for the President of the Royal Audience and Chancery Court of the City and Kingdom of Granada*,

trans. Vincent Barletta (Chicago: University of Chicago Press, 2007). The leading study of the consequences of this ambiguity between culture and religion for the Inquisition's persecution of Moriscos remains Mercedes García-Arenal, *Inquisition y moriscos. Los procesos del Tribunal de Cuenca* (Madrid: Siglo XXI, 1978). This magisterial work is based entirely on trial records, however, and does not take evidence from the *libros de testificaciones* into account.

20. The customs of shrouding the dead and marriage feasts as practiced by Moriscos are discussed by Pedro Longás, *La vida religiosa de los moriscos*, facsimile edition, preliminary study by Darío Cabanelas Rodríguez (Granada: Universidad de Granada, 1998), 277–283, 287–288.

21. ADC, Inq, libro 326, fols 198, 206, and 211.

22. AHN, Inquisición, legajo 2545, letter of October 18, 1590: "Acerca de lo cual tengo duda si casándose los moriscos en haz de la Iglesia por solo bailar la zambra y cantar a su modo d'ellos y en su lengua se puede proceder por el Santo Oficio contra ellos. Y la razón de dudar me hace la letra del capítulo del edicto cuyo traslado va con esta por la copulativa qu'esta en él que parece presupone que casándose según sus ritos y bailando la zambra se proceda que inquiera d'esta culpa y no por sólo el baile y cantares. V[uestra] S[eñoría] sea servido de mandar lo que en este particular se debe hacer porque sobr'el acuden testificaciones en oyendo el edicto. Dios guarde a V.S. como puede, etc. En el Quitnanar 18 de octubre de 1590." Inside this letter is a half sheet of paper in Velarde's own hand, transcribing from the Edict of Faith: "o si algunos se hayan casado según rito y costumbre de moros, y que hayan cantado cantares de moros o hecho zambras o leilas con instrumentos prohibidos."

23. Another scrap of paper included with the letter of October 18, 1590 gives the gist of this response: "que reciba información d'estas ceremonias y ritos y la envíe al tribunal para que allá lo cualifiquen y hagan justicia."

24. ADC, Inquisición, libro 326, fols 207–208. One of the songs he said he learned from them was "Alhambra hanina," which he says was a song "about certain Moorish captives." This is undoubtedly a version of the lament of the Moriscos of Granada, "Alhambra hanina gualcoçor taphqui," documented by sixteenth-century Sevillian historian and literary scholar Argote de Molina in his *Discurso sobre la poesía castellana* (Madrid, 1575). Argote de Molina's use of this poem is briefly discussed by Leah Middlebrook, *Imperial Lyric: New Poetry and New Subjects in Early Modern Spain* (University Park: Pennsylvania State University Press, 2009), 43n.31.

25. I have published a case study showing how Morisco cultural difference facilitated such integration in practice: "Manazanares, 1600: Moriscos from Granada Organize a Festival of 'Moors and Christians,'" in *The Conversos and Moriscos in Late Medieval Spain and Beyond, Volume One, Departures and Change*, ed. Kevin Ingram (Leiden and Boston: Brill, 2009), 287–311.

26. Mercedes García-Arenal, "Unbelief in Belief: Belief as Inheritance," (paper presented at the annual meeting of the Renaissance Society of America, New York, March 27–29, 2014).

27. Nowhere has this aspect of inquisitorial activity been better documented than in Jaime Contreras, *Sotos contra Riquelmes: regidores, inquisidores y criptojudíos* (Madrid: Anaya and Mario Muchnik, 1992).

28. Examples include "The Subject and Power," the afterword to Hubert L. Dreyfus and Paul Rabinow's *Michel Foucault: Beyond Structuralism and Hermeneutics*, 2nd edn (Chicago: University of Chicago Press, 1982), 208–226; *The History of Sexuality Volume 1: An Introduction* (New York: Vintage, 1990); and *Discipline and Punish* (New York: Vintage, 1979), from which I have chosen this passage in particular: "The individual is no doubt the fictitious atom of an 'ideological' representation of society; but he [*sic*] is also a reality fabricated by this specific technology of power that I have called 'discipline'. We must cease once and for all to describe the effects of power in negative terms: it 'excludes', it 'represses', it 'censors', it 'abstracts', it 'masks', it 'conceals'. In fact, power produces; it produces reality; it produces domains of objects and rituals of truth. The individual and the knowledge that may be gained of him [*sic*] belong to this production" (194). In a similar vein, Anthony J. Cascardi has theorized Spanish baroque culture's generation of subjects desirous of control in "The Subject of Control," afterword to *Culture and Control in Counter-Reformation Spain* (*Hispanic Issues* 7), ed. Anne J. Cruz and Mary Elizabeth Perry (Minneapolis: University of Minnesota Press, 1992), 231–245.

29. William Childers, "The Baroque Public Sphere," in *Reason and Its Others: Italy, Spain and the New World*, ed. David R. Castillo and Massimo Lollini (Nashville: Vanderbilt University Press, 2006), 165–185.

30. Michael Omi and Howard Winant, *Racial Formation in the United States: From the 1960s to the 1990s*, 2nd edn (New York and London: Routledge, 1994).

31. For a recent discussion of the late nineteenth-century establishment of a biracial caste system in the United States through the reduction of multiple categories of race to the binary black/white opposition, see Emily Epstein Landau, *Spectacular Wickedness: Sex, Race, and Memory in Storyville, New Orleans* (Baton Rouge: Louisiana State University Press, 2013), 45–76.

32. See, for example, *De la edad conflictiva*, 3rd edn (Madrid: Taurus, 1972). Equally important for understanding the political significance of this precocious racial ideology are two articles by historian Juan Ignacio Gutiérrez Nieto, "La discriminación de los conversos y la tibetización de Castilla," *Revista de la Universidad Complutense*, 22 (1973): 99–129 and "Limpieza de sangre y antihidalguismo hacia 1600," *Homenaje al Dr. D. Juan Reglà Campistol*, vol. 1 (Valencia: Universidad de Valencia, Facultad de Filosofía y Letras, 1975), 497–514.

33. For Moriscos' cultural contributions, see my previously cited article, "Manzanares, 1600." I have published an initial study of the lawsuits claiming Old Christian status titled "Disappearing Moriscos," in *Cross-Cultural History and the Domestication of Otherness*, ed. Michal Jan Rozbicki and George O. Ndege (New York: Palgrave Macmillan, 2012), 51–64.

34. Though the question of "race" in reference to the Moriscos is complex, not least because a clearly recognizable biologically based theory of race would not emerge for over a century, nonetheless I am convinced that we do indeed witness in early modern Spain a transition from religious to racial categories for defining social groups. I should emphasize that we are speaking here of racial ideology, and there is no reason to believe Moriscos presented a readily distinguishable phenotype. I intend to deal with these issues at greater length in a study to be titled "Moriscos and Race," a preliminary version of which I gave as a lecture which was subsequently posted online. William Childers, "The Moriscos and 'Race'—Exploring the Roots of Modern Racism in Sixteenth-Century Spain" (lecture at Concordia University, November 24, 2011). On YouTube: www.youtube.com/watch?v=oyHRkFA39XE

# Part III

# A Global Stage for Interculturality

# 7

# Interculturality, Cosmopolitanism, and the Role of the Imagination: A Perspective for Communicating as Global Citizens

*Nilanjana Bardhan and Miriam Sobré-Denton*

## Introduction

Interculturality, as an interdisciplinary concept, holds much epistemic value in a world where intercultural spaces, identities, and projects are proliferating at a dizzying pace. Through the aid of this concept, we can develop interdisciplinary lenses for better understanding cultural interconnectedness and transformation within global flux. Globality is the inevitable condition of our times, and we need to think carefully about what kind of a world we want for the future and chart out ways to steer its processes in directions that will do more good than harm.[1] The concept of interculturality holds promise for this endeavor. As intercultural communication scholars, in this chapter we offer some views from within our field, and hope they will be useful to scholars in other disciplines as well.

Communication is action, and it can transform perceptions and bring about change for the sake of social and global justice. Thus it is imperative that we teach ourselves how to better communicate ethically and critically across cultural differences as global citizens. We first describe interculturality from the perspective of our field and argue that bounded notions of group culture, while they remain powerful, are conceptually limited for understanding how people perform and communicate as global citizens in the spaces between cultures—in the spaces of interculturality. We critique the notion of multiculturalism, use cultural cosmopolitanism as an ethical, communicative, and philosophical framework through which we may envision interculturality for a more humane world, and emphasize the critical role of the imagination in this process. The chapter concludes with a brief snapshot of a qualitative study of Hostelling International—Chicago. We describe how one organization is working, through its programming, to educate underprivileged youth in the Chicago area to imagine themselves as global citizens and cosmopolitan communicators in a world characterized by complex connectivity and unequal power relations.

## INTERCULTURALITY AND COMMUNICATION

The term "interculturality" suggests interaction between different cultures. It also urges us to think about the processes and outcomes of interaction between cultures and across differences. This concept obviously holds great significance for any discipline that deals with culture; however, it is of particular importance in disciplines that have culture as their central focus, such as intercultural communication.

Within the field of intercultural communication, which is part of the larger discipline of communication studies, interculturality as a concept has been slow to gain traction. This is mainly because multiculturalism as an approach to cultural difference is deeply ingrained in the fabric of US society, and the bulk of intercultural communication scholarship emerges out of this country. However, the realization exists that some of multiculturalism's assumptions about difference and identity pose obstacles in the way of theorizing cultural change and transformations that occur through various forms of intercultural communication. The heightened mobilities and technologies of contemporary globalization are influencing identities, modes of belonging and the cultural make-up of entire societies. They are generating hybridity and transformations faster than ever before at the intersections of global and local cultural forces, and these are manifested in the communicative relations formed and the new meanings produced at these intersections where differences meet.[2]

### The Drawbacks of Multiculturalism

While multiculturalism's focus on pluralism and valuing of difference must be duly acknowledged, the approach it takes toward difference assumes a natural separateness between cultures. Cultural particularity is highlighted at the expense of interconnectedness. Within the field of intercultural communication, this has meant that scholarship has mostly conceptualized cultures as bounded entities. According to postcolonial communication scholars Raka Shome and Radha Hegde:

> The rhetoric of multiculturalism celebrates the diverse assemblage of cultures in their pristine flavors—colorful yet standing separate in their authenticity…The discrete positioning of cultures without any sense of their interconnected histories reproduces the violence of colonial modernities and fixes difference in a spectacle of otherness.[3]

Giuliana Prato writes that according to multiculturalism, "culture is treated as a 'thing,' an object to be possessed and shared by a strictly defined group of people and which sets the group apart from other groups."[4] The drawback of this approach is that the scope for the emergence of stereotypes and exoticization of the cultural Other is increased, and the scope for imagining change, creativity, and growth that may be possible through intercultural communication and mutual transformation is reduced.[5] When change and intercultural mixture are not considered, then hierarchies and inequities are maintained in favor of the already powerful. Finally, in the name of cultural group identity, the individual is constrained from exploring change at levels that transcend the group.[6] Therefore, a shift is needed from multiculturalism to the dynamic logic of interculturalism which offers better explanatory power for the natural processes of cultural change over time.[7]

## The Need for Interculturality

Interculturality focuses on difference and how we communicatively perform and navigate differences, rather than on the properties (including communicative properties) of culture. In the words of Arjun Appadurai:

> Culture is not usefully regarded as a substance but is better regarded as a dimension of phenomena, a dimension that attends to situated and embodied difference. Stressing the dimensionality of culture rather than its substantiality permits our thinking of culture less as a property of individuals and groups and more as a heuristic device that we can use to talk about difference.[8]

Furthermore, interculturality focuses on the in-between spaces and interfaces of culture where differences interact. This is the constitutive space of intercultural and intersubjective communicative performance.[9] According to the logic of interculturality, cultures are separate yet connected. According to communication scholar Aimee Carrillo Rowe:

> The inter of intercultural communication is a capacious site of unfolding interactions across lines of difference. It gestures towards the unknown and unknowable space between unevenly located subjects…This is to say that the inter marks a process of becoming that is constituted *between* subjects, who, in engaging the inter are, in turn, reconstituted through their exchange…The space of the inter into which we must insert ourselves in order to engage an/other is fraught, frightening, even as it brims with transformative possibilities.[10]

Several established communication scholars have increasingly acknowledged the creative potential of the in-between and intersubjective space of communication where differences intersect, and they emphasize how such intersections could mutually transform meaning and give rise to new ways of seeing, thinking, and being in relation with the cultural Other.[11] This form of communication is driven by the intention to expand our humanity and our worlds "by constantly demanding of us new meanings, new understandings, new experiences, and, ultimately, new modes of being in the world with others."[12]

Interculturality is also conducive to a critical approach to relations between cultures and the need to change oppressive power dynamics. Cultures are unequal because of unequal plays of histories and power over time.[13] The critical acknowledgment of inequities is necessary to move to the subsequent step, the hopeful and emancipatory step— that of interrupting and reconfiguring cultural power hierarchies through communicative performances capable of bringing about mutual change and transformations. Critical intercultural communication scholar Crispin Thurlow is right on point when he writes that "It is in this way, that interculturality comes to be more about material inequalities, power relations, and ideologies of difference, rather than simply skin color, geographical location, passport, clothing, food, nonverbal behavior, or, of course, languages."[14]

From the perspective of critical interculturality, then, culture is an ideological site of constant struggle between unequal groups and is performed through communicative meaning-making practices.[15] This involves change over time, since "culture is subject to continual reformation or it dies; reproduction involves an element of creative practice."[16] Culture, therefore, is not simply an inheritance, but a creative activity that involves change through the process of interculturality. Interculturality is emergent and transformative and produces nonfixed moments, spaces, discourses, and projects marked by the spirit of "interculture."[17] It prioritizes and makes possible intercultural dialogue in the spirit of global citizenship. The idea of global citizenship leads us toward cosmopolitanism.

## INCORPORATING COSMOPOLITANISM

Cosmopolitanism, as a cultural philosophy, is well suited to illuminate the concept of interculturality within intercultural communication. Cosmopolitanism, translated from the Greek roots of the term, means "citizen of the world." A key notion within cosmopolitanism is the transcendence of the negative constraints of nation-state-centric thinking (e.g., divisive nativism) when it comes to cultural identity, social and global justice and communication. The political and moral dimensions of cosmopolitanism have been debated over centuries, but its cultural dimensions are especially crucial given the proliferating intercultural spaces of interaction in our world.[18] According to a more recent description:

> Cosmopolitanism, the concern for the world as if it were one's *polis*, is furthered by such multiple, overlapping allegiances which are sustained across communities of language, ethnicity, religion, and nationality.[19]

Cosmopolitanism advocates an outward and world-oriented focus through which we can recognize the interdependent nature of culturally diverse humans and learn more about ourselves in the process.[20] Sociologist Gerard Delanty writes that cosmopolitanism enables:

> Conceptualization of the social world as an open horizon in which new cultural models take shape. In this approach, which I term critical cosmopolitanism, the cosmopolitan imagination occurs when and wherever new relations between self, other and world develop in moments of openness.[21]

Cosmopolitanism requires an attitude of self-problematization, reflexivity, openness to the world, and the willingness to change.[22] Thus interculturality lies at the heart of cosmopolitanism and when brought into the folds of intercultural communication, it helps us move from multiculturalism toward interculturalism.

## The Critical Turn

The earlier forms of cosmopolitanism, especially the Kantian and Enlightenment versions, are Eurocentric, elitist, and even racist,[23] and they have been rightly critiqued as such. However, the debates over the last two decades, especially in the disciplines of sociology, anthropology, and education, are taking cosmopolitanism in a more critical and postcolonial direction. According to Walter Mignolo:

> Today, silenced and marginalized voices are bringing themselves into the conversation of cosmopolitan projects, rather than waiting to be included…Bringing themselves into the conversation is a transformative project that takes the form of border thinking or border epistemology—that is, the alternative to separatism is border thinking, the recognition and transformation of the hegemonic imaginary from the perspective of people in subaltern positions. Border thinking then becomes a "tool" of the project of critical cosmopolitanism.[24]

Thus, critical cosmopolitanism is being increasingly positioned as an approach for pushing back against the top-down hegemonic, neocolonial, and neoliberal forces of globalization.

To some, cosmopolitanism suggests a form of hegemonic universalism. Recent deliberations on cosmopolitanism, however, are taking a more qualified approach to universalism. Instead of advocating Cosmopolitanism with a capital "C" (Eurocentric or any culturally specific form for cosmopolitanism), we read more about cosmopolitanisms (in the plural) which suggests the need for dialogue between multiple universalisms arising from various cultural viewpoints and locations from around the world. In other words, we need to provincialize universalisms and vigilantly deconstruct the hegemonic varieties in order to promote dialogue. For example, Mignolo[25] has suggested the term "diversality" and Pollock, Bhabha, Breckenridge, and Chakrabarty have used the phrase "diversity of universals" to emphasize this point.[26] Philosopher Kwame Anthony Appiah refutes the charge of hegemonic universalism by noting that those who align with cosmopolitanism "…suppose that all cultures have enough overlap in their vocabulary of values to begin a conversation. But they don't suppose, like some universalists, that we could all come to agreement if only we had the same vocabulary."[27]

Another prominent charge against cosmopolitanism is that nationalism is a strong emotional force and that the "thin" concept of being a "citizen of the world" cannot replace national and local cultural affiliations. Again, recent debates on cosmopolitanism refute such a dichotomy and argue that one can have multiple and overlapping affiliations and being a citizen of the world is one among many.[28] Cosmopolitanism has to be "rooted"[29] and "situated."[30] Furthermore, as Appiah[31] eloquently points out, cosmopolitanism is not some grand accomplishment but an everyday phenomenon that plays out at mundane levels of everyday intercultural communication. This rooted and mundane approach is called vernacular cosmopolitanism. According to anthropologist Pnina Werbner:

> Vernacular cosmopolitanism—an apparent oxymoron that seems to join contradictory notions of local specificity and universal enlightenment—is at the crux of the current debates on cosmopolitanism…ethnic rootedness does not negate openness to cultural differences or the fostering of a universal civic consciousness and a sense of moral responsibility beyond the local…[Vernacular cosmopolitans] first make parochial interpretations of culture, religion and ethnicity in order to transcend them and assert wider cosmopolitan values.[32]

Furthermore, cosmopolitanism is being positioned not as an identity type, but as a process that is dialogic, relational, and performative. It involves living "on friendly terms with paradox."[33] It is not something that resides within people, rather it is something that is produced through specific types of interactions and intercultural communication.

## COSMOPOLITANISM AS A COMMUNICATION PHENOMENON

While the field of intercultural communication has not paid much attention to cosmopolitanism, the inherently communicative nature of cosmopolitanism is obvious. An oft-quoted description of cosmopolitanism comes from sociologist Ulf Hannerz.[34] According to him, cosmopolitanism is "a mode of managing meaning."[35] If we look at the definition of communication, the link becomes clear. According to Martin and Nakayama, "communication occurs whenever someone attributes meaning to another person's words or actions."[36] To take this one step further, intercultural communication occurs when there is a clear perception of difference between communicators in the process of constructing meaning.

Cosmopolitanism is communicative in other ways as well. It is dialogic and involves the ability to hear and see the cultural Other with empathy and respect. These are qualities of ethical communication.

Delanty writes that cosmopolitanism, when conceived of in terms of intercultural communication, is deliberative, reflective, and critically oriented.[37] He further emphasizes that cosmopolitan dialogue, in intercultural terms, cannot occur unless it produces new learning and meanings. According to Sobré-Denton and Bardhan, cosmopolitanism entails the communicative production of a reality that transcends the "I" to produce a mutual sense of intercultural "We."[38] Werbner writes that "cosmopolitanism is itself a product of creativity and communication in the context of diversity; it must be ultimately understood not merely as individual, but as collective, relational, and thus historically located."[39] Thus cosmopolitanism is relational, situated, and communicatively performed by people and groups who desire to produce cosmopolitan meanings, spaces, places, practices, and structures. In other words, cosmopolitan discourse and practices are consequences of world-oriented intercultural communication performances. According to Kendall, Woodward, and Skrbis, "It [cosmopolitanism] is, then, a *disposition performed* in particular contexts and settings as required."[40]

People and groups consciously "do" cosmopolitanism through communicative praxis. Communicating according to the cosmopolitan ethic is a conscious act. Holton writes that "the emphasis on cosmopolitanism as performance...extends to the ways that cosmopolitan life is performed through conversation, song and consumption of goods, sexual preference and interpersonal relationships."[41] Cosmopolitan performances and "doings" can permeate various aspects of our personal and public lives and relationships. Thus the relational, performative, dialogic, and discursive aspects of cosmopolitanism are significant connections to communication. Furthermore, according to the cosmopolitan ethic, we cannot engage in communication that intends to control or coerce the cultural Other. Communication needs to be vulnerable and dialogic and engage the space of the in-between, the "third space" that is produced through the intersection of cultural differences, the space of mutuality and possible intercultural growth.[42] Thus interculturality lies at the heart of cosmopolitanism when conceived in terms of intercultural communication.

While cosmopolitanism has not yet played a significant role in communication or intercultural communication scholarship, some attention has been paid to its value. In the earlier decades of the growth of intercultural communication as a field within communication studies (1950s to 1970s), cosmopolitanism was positioned as an identity type, that is, a cosmopolitan person. The conceptualization of this identity type was West-centric, mostly focusing on the experiences of the privileged white male traversing the world for work or leisure and able to navigate various cultural settings with ease.[43] It was W. Barnett Pearce who first positioned cosmopolitanism within communication studies as a communication process (rather than identity type) and particular orientation toward the self, difference, and cultural Other. According to Pearce, a cosmopolitan communicator does not deny the humanity of Others, attempts to find as much coordination as possible between different forms of reality and is genuinely accepting of many realities and ways of being. S/he treats others as natives and nonnatives (same and different) and is "deeply enmeshed in local culture while being enmeshed in the largest possible system comprised of all local systems…"[44] More recently, Holliday has called for a critical cosmopolitanism approach to study of intercultural communication which positions cosmopolitanism, as does Mignolo, as a form of intercultural communication that privileges perspectives from the margins.[45]

In general, the more recent critical and postcolonial turn in intercultural communication has opened up space for cosmopolitanism by arguing that for too long, the field has simplistically equated the nation-state with culture.[46] This phenomenon, called methodological nationalism,[47] has largely shaped how we study identity markers within intercultural communication, for example, gender, race, religion, sexuality, and so on. Methodological nationalism poses a barrier in the way of clearly seeing historical overlaps, inequities, and continuities across the planet. This does not mean that we should do away with national perspectives—it means that the national perspective should be of the kind that does not foreclose the vision of cosmopolitanism, and it should allow us to understand the complexities of the global in the local and the local in the global and how cultural transformation occurs through interculturality over time.[48]

## Cosmopolitan Communication and Peoplehood

Sobré-Denton and Bardhan have recently put forward a book-length treatment on how to cultivate cosmopolitanism as a vision for intercultural communication and for communicating ethically as global citizens.[49] They offer two normative notions—cosmopolitan communication and cosmopolitan peoplehood, which are co-constitutive. These two notions are offered in the spirit of interculturality and vernacular/critical cosmopolitanism. They chart out how we can conceptualize cosmopolitanism in terms of intercultural communication scholarship and praxis which prioritizes social and global justice in a highly uneven world. According to them:

> Cosmopolitan communication is a world- and Other-oriented practice of engaging in deliberate, dialogic, critical, non-coercive and ethical communication. Through the play of context-specific dialectics, cosmopolitan communication works with and through cultural differences and historical and emerging power inequities to achieve ongoing understanding, intercultural growth, mutuality, collaboration and social and global justice goals through critical self-transformation.[50]

Furthermore, like Pearce, they position cosmopolitanism not as an identity type but a particular ontological orientation toward the world that is separate from yet entwined with the cultural Other. In so doing, they define cosmopolitan peoplehood as:

> an open-ended, Other- and world-oriented and dialogic ("in-between") identity orientation that is morally committed to addressing social and global injustices in their many forms. It is an embodied way of being in the world that engages views from the margins, celebrates the powers of empathy and the imagination to connect the local/national with the global, and sees ambiguity as opportunity for intercultural growth and learning. Through non-violent entanglement between Self and cultural Others (near and far), it entails differential belonging, intercultural bridgework, kindness to strangers, and continuous engagement in critical self-transformation through cosmopolitan communication.[51]

While it is beyond the scope of this chapter to elaborate in detail on the assumptions and arguments that underlie each of these definitions, suffice it to say that together, cosmopolitan communication and peoplehood make each other possible. Overall, they constitute a frame of reference for communicating ethically and critically as global citizens. Such intercultural communication entails being able to intelligently and empathetically connect the local/national and the global, understand where the cultural Other comes from (not just literally), engage difference positively and creatively, value border views and remain open to newness, possibility, and critical self-transformation through enmeshment with the cultural Other. Cosmopolitan communication and peoplehood can be seen as infusing all levels and forms of intercultural communication—from the intra/interpersonal to the macro/global. Such a view makes it possible to imagine how cosmopolitan spaces of praxis may be produced in micro and macro ways—during face-to-face encounters between people from different cultures as well as in discursive forms involving various cultural actors located near and far.

In the more recent discussions of cosmopolitanism and interculturality, the component of the imagination and the ways in which it grapples with the complex realities of an interconnected world plays a pivotal role.[52] This is important from a communication perspective as well. As Papastergiadis writes, the cosmopolitan imagination "can generate an alternative sense of being in the world and intersubjective relations."[53] If we are to orient toward cultural Others and the World in an open and dialogic way, we must be able to engage in a particular labor of the imagination which is capable of producing a world-oriented imaginary which includes numerous possibilities for ways of being, relating, and communicating across cultural differences. The rest of the chapter focuses on the role of the imagination in cultivating interculturality via cosmopolitan communication and peoplehood, including empirical evidence from a study currently being conducted by Sobré-Denton.

## COSMOPOLITAN COMMUNICATION, PEOPLEHOOD, AND THE ROLE OF THE IMAGINATION

To identify and communicate ethically as a "citizen of the world" requires a certain kind of outwardly oriented labor of the imagination. Such labor involves hope and the envisioning of possibilities for new ways of being and becoming in the spirit of peoplehood.[54] This is an intercultural labor that draws from the social imaginaries of the times and projects outward toward a larger world-oriented imaginary.

Cosmopolitanism, when performed through communication, involves a certain mobilization of the imagination through which societies and individuals within them can continuously self-problematize and alter themselves. This work of the imagination entails accepting that cultural groups are not separate but interconnected and overlapping, that the global and local are enmeshed in each other, the need for continuous negotiation of cultural borders and a deep commitment to global justice.[55] "The notion of critical cosmopolitanism sees the category of the world in terms of openness rather than in terms of a universal system. It is this that defines the cosmopolitan imagination."[56] Beck writes that the cosmopolitan orientation opens up possibilities for "dialogical imagination" and helps us develop the "the art of translation and bridge-building," which involves "situating and relativizing one's own form of life within other horizons of possibility" and "the capacity to see oneself from the perspective of cultural others and to give this practical effect in one's own experience through the exercise of boundary-transcending imagination."[57]

In the rest of this section we elaborate on the notions of the social imagination/imaginary, national imaginary and imagined communities, and global imaginary. We argue for a need for a critical global imaginary and discuss how such an imaginary is conducive to and necessary for interculturality via the notions of cosmopolitan communication and peoplehood.

## The Social Imagination/Imaginary

Mills offers us what he terms the social imagination. According to him, the social imagination is a "quality of the mind" which "use[s] information to develop reason in order to achieve lucid summations of what is going on in the world and of what may be happening within themselves."[58] While positioning the faculty of imagination in terms of Cartesian rationalism (akin to Immanuel Kant's writings on the imagination) and a "fruitful" form of "self-consciousness,"[59] he also highlights the relationship between individuals and society: "The sociological imagination helps us to grasp history and biography and the relationship between the two within society…It is a quality of the mind that seems most dramatically to promise an understanding of the intimate realities of ourselves in connection with larger social realities."[60]

The common meaning of imagination is to be able to create, represent, or envision something that does not exist. However, this explanation takes imagination into the realm of fiction or the unreal and does not help us theorize how the imagination/imaginary can play an active role in bringing about change, interculturality and open up new possibilities in our relations with cultural Others and the World. Here, Cornelius Castoriadis's work and the notion of the imaginary are helpful. Castoriadis offers the notions of the social and radical imaginary, which are based in collective and individual labor. According to him, world-image and self-image are related, and their unity is "borne by the definition each society gives of its needs, as this is inscribed in its activity, its actual social doing."[61] The role of the social imaginary is to provide, through social and symbolic significations, some answers to its needs, identity, and desires. Steger writes that the social imaginary is a "prereflexive framework" for our routine daily activities, a tacit backdrop which grants communal and shared cultural practices a sense of legitimacy.[62] According to Papastergiadis, the imaginary is "the zone within which the creative imagination and social habitus occur…"[63] Social imaginaries, explains Castoriadis, work at the level of connotation rather than denotation, and reality and rationality cannot account for it.

The radical imaginary is creative and not about "discovery" but "active constitution" of something new which partially draws from that which is already known and considered to be normal.[64] New relations and ways of being are produced through the radical imaginary which is "…the capacity to see in a thing what it is not, to see it other than it is."[65] According to Castoriadis, the radical imaginary does not spring from a vacuum but draws from those social significations and imaginaries that are already known in order to imaginatively and discursively project toward something different that leads to continuous alteration of the self and society. The imagination, then, is the individual and collective capacity to combine the existing and non-existing through the process of the radical imaginary. The radical imaginary precedes the distinction between the real and the unreal and makes transformation possible. It can rupture orders, ideologies, and entrenched ways of thinking.[66] Of course, the imagination can work in positive as well as harmful ways and therefore, it is necessary to consider the dimension of the ethical or moral when discussing imagination that works in favor of global justice.[67]

## From National to Global Imaginary

A collective imaginary entails the involvement of a very large number of people feeling like they are morally committed to the protection and well-being of one community. Benedict Anderson helps us understand this phenomenon at the level of the national. According to him, the rise of "print capitalism" was a key factor in entrenching the modern idea of nation, and eventually the nation-state, which started gaining strength around the latter half of the eighteenth century in Europe. By reading materials about those who fell within the boundaries of the nation, people were able to feel a sense of patriotic connection with those many others whom they had never met before located in places they were unlikely to visit. This force of the imagination, according to Anderson, went a long way in creating "imagined communities" of anonymity, that is of disparate groups and people unknown to each other who felt somehow bound together as one nation.[68]

Thus the national imaginary unites different layers of the social into a sense of cultural oneness thereby forming a cultural/national imaginary.[69] Each national imaginary is unique because of the style in which it is imagined, and this style comprises the collective cultural practices and representations that are legitimated by the imaginary of the nation. The national imaginary endures over linear time and is marked by a specific physical boundary.[70] However, tectonic shifts in mobilities (of people, information, and images) and technologies after World War II started shifting the workings of the national imaginary in order to account for the increasingly porous boundaries of nation-states and the increasing consciousness of the world as a single space.[71] Hannerz has termed this increasing sense of interconnectedness between people and globalizing processes as the "global ecumene."[72]

Arjun Appadurai builds on Anderson and the notion of the social/national imaginary to offer the notion of the transnational imaginary. In his words, national imaginaries, when caught up in the cultural flows and disjunctures that crisscross nation-states, "direct us to something critical and new in the global cultural processes: *the imagination as a social practice*."[73] This form of imagination is an active form of creative labor and is not an escape, fantasy, pastime, or matter of "mere contemplation."[74] It helps us establish connections between the local and the global and grasp the interrelatedness of social, political, economic, and cultural phenomena in our world. It helps us understand, contextually, how the global enters and alters the local and how the local can move outward and alter the global. In this way, the imagination helps us develop "scripts for possible lives" and connections across national and cultural borders.[75]

More recently, Steger has used the term "global imaginary" to refer to increased consciousness of the global level rise in consumerism and capitalist ideology along with the workings of sub and supranational actors and organizations engaged with issues that transcend nation-state borders. He writes:

> Globalization involves both the macrostructures of community and the microstructures of personhood. It extends deep into the core of the self and its dispositions, facilitating the creation of new identities nurtured by the intensifying relations between the individual and the globe.[76]

Non-nations-state actors and organizations may act from above (e.g., the World Bank and multinational companies mainly based in the global North) and from below, such as the grassroots resistance movements which started emerging from the left in the latter half of the 1990s which Steger calls "justice globalism" or the effort to challenge the inequities of market globalism. Such actions occur through the power of the global imaginary which, by definition, involves interculturality.

## Critical Imagination as a Source of Creative Agency and Peoplehood

The notions of cosmopolitan communication and peoplehood are undergirded by the spirit of interculturality, global and social justice, and entails the need to transcend the "I" in order to build a collective sense of "We," or peoplehood, in how we imagine ourselves and communicate with cultural Others in our World. They require a form of critical and empowering imagination and empathy for marginalized Others in the interconnected landscapes of our planet, and the ability to meaningfully participate in a critical global imaginary.

The role of the imagination in global cultural contexts is increasingly being described in terms of individual and collective agency and critical possibilities. Appadurai writes that the "unleashing of the imagination" is "now central to all forms of agency."[77] According to Delanty, "...human agency can radically transform the present in the image of an imagined future."[78] While globalization is not a new thing, the manner in which the imagination and imaginaries work and have worked during different epochs of globalization are different. Avtar Brah, in calling for a critical form of imagination emphasizes the need, in current times, to reimagine how to steer contemporary globalization in more humane directions with attention to the "common good, equality, and justice."[79] The critical imagination, according to Brah, makes possible cross-border alliances (e.g., the transnational feminist movement) and the recognition of difference without Othering. Latimer and Skeggs position the labor of the imagination as an act of agency, and a "site of resistance and alterity," which can interrupt and transform normative orders and ideologies that are oppressive. Drawing upon Derrida and Foucault, they underscore how the imagination can find "fissures" within stabilized texts and meanings of how things should be in order to create "the possibilities for imagining differently, for a radical politics from 'elsewhere.'"[80]

The imagination, when mobilized to produce critical global imaginaries that do the work of pushing back from the margins, can "form individuals into a seam of a collective narrative."[81] Fazal Rizvi writes that the imagination "denotes a collective sense of a group of people, a community that begins to imagine and feel things together."[82] The idea of peoplehood is evident here. The critical global imaginary is a collective phenomenon which requires us to rise beyond the Cartesian, rational and autonomous "I" to become part of a larger, critically motivated intercultural "We" that can accomplish global justice action through involvement in radical imaginaries.[83] The Battle of Seattle and the more recent Arab Spring are obvious examples that come to mind. Such an imaginary requires hope, empathy, emotion, affect and responsibility, and the ability to envision the interrelatedness between people, cultures, and issues that cross borders of various kinds. It requires us to be advocates of social and global justice, and see borders as socially constructed and always open to reimagination.[84] In this way, there is no dichotomy between the national and the cosmopolitan, and multiple affiliations and loyalties are seen as possible.

Critical imagination makes empathy, for those near and far, possible. In the words of Szerszynski and Urry, this is the cosmopolitan ability to "inhabit the world from afar."[85] Empathy is "a kind of leaping out of yourself" and the ability to get distance from the microcosm of the "I" and propel the imagination toward the macrocosm of the "We" in order to find common ground across differences.[86] This, in turn, is related to the notions of implicature and solidarity. Implicature, according to Dace and McPhail, is one step beyond empathy: "Implicature extends the notion of empathy from the psychological to the physical [embodied] by acknowledging that self and other are never separate and distinct, but are always interdependent and interrelated."[87] Solidarity, working off of the embodied notion of implicature, entails collective action and communication, enabled by the imagination. According to Calhoun:

> We hold in common a world we create in common, in part by the processes through which we imagine it...[Solidarity is] engagement in shared projects of imagining a better future...For nationalism to give way to some postnational organization of social life will not simply be a matter of new formal structures of organization, but of new ways of imagining identity, interests, and solidarity. A key theme will be the importance of configurations of mutual commitment—solidarity—that are more than reinscriptions of preestablished interests or identities."[88]

Thus, hope, solidarity, mutuality, empathy and the genuine appreciation of difference and the possibilities that reside in zones where differences intersect fuel the critical cosmopolitan imagination.

We now offer a brief snapshot of an ongoing intercultural communication study that focuses on the use of the concepts of cosmopolitanism, social/radical/global imaginaries and imagined communities as pedagogical tools to teach students about interculturality and open up spaces for cosmopolitan hope, memory and dialogue.[89]

## HOSTELLING INTERNATIONAL—SNAPSHOT OF AN ONGOING STUDY

This study, being conducted by Sobré-Denton, demonstrates ways in which the work of the imagination and cosmopolitan dialogue are facilitated through classroom curriculum, experiential learning, and reflection in an intercultural location (the Hostelling International youth hostel in downtown Chicago), and how students are encouraged, both corporeally and imaginatively, to cross cultural borders in the spirit of interculturality.

### Site of Study

Hostelling International—USA (HI-USA) is the US American arm of Hostelling International, a federation of over 4,000 hostels in over 80 countries. HI-Chicago has been specifically working with Communities in Schools (CIS) and Chicago Public Schools (CPS) to promote intercultural communication competence and engage students in participating in intercultural experiences in underserved communities within the city. Through didactic (i.e., classroom exercises and lesson plans), experiential, project-based, and service learning approaches,[90] HI-USA creates cosmopolitan pedagogical opportunities for often highly insulated, underserved communities served by the CPS system and its service learning programs.

Three examples of programming were analyzed in this study. The first is Cultural Kitchen (CK); in this program, high school students spend 10 sessions learning about how members of another culture, of similar ages to the students, spend a typical day. After the classroom research, students go to the hostel and cook a meal for hostellers that represent that culture. The second program, Exchange Neighborhoods (ENS), "pairs two high schools to host the other school in an exploration of each other's cultures," and through this, teaches high school students in inner city schools to "build pride around their own culture, while opening their minds to learn about a new neighborhood and culture of their peers."[91] The third program, called Community Walls (CW), asks its participants to create artwork depicting their own neighborhoods and cultural identities for travelers and tourists; this artwork is displayed throughout the cities in which the hostels and students reside.

With this information in mind, the following overarching research question was posed:

RQ1: *How do HI-Chicago's educational programs engage the imagination of their participants to teach them to interact and negotiate with boundaries and across difference?*

## Method

Over a course of nine months, Sobré-Denton and her research assistant immersed themselves in the site and worked with co-participants to create shared meanings through ethnographic methods. They worked with the co-participants after data collection was completed to utilize the results to illuminate existing power structures, including how race, history, and intercultural communication are taught within CPS, as well as how the City of Chicago can work to desegregate its inner-city youth. The research was engaged in from a participatory action framework that involves participants in the entire research process and returns the research to those participants through its conclusions and potential actions arising from the research.

Sobré-Denton and her research assistant observed nine programming events at HI-Chicago: Four Cultural Kitchens (CK), three Exchange Neighborhoods (ENS), and two Community Walls (CW), as well as orientations for the teachers and classroom visits by HI-Chicago programming staff. Each of the programs included an overnight stay at the hostel, and the opportunity for the CPS students to engage and interact with both domestic and international travelers staying there. Fifty-eight interviewed participants ranged in age from 14- to 58-years-old, and embodied multiple and hybrid ethnicities, races, religions, socioeconomic statuses, and life experiences. Roughly 65% of the interviewees (35 participants) were students in CPS, ranging from freshmen to seniors. All of the students identified as belonging to lower socioeconomic classes, with the racial and ethnic make-up (also self-identified) being 45% African American, 45% Latino, 5% Asian, and 5% White (of whom, all were first-generation, generally Polish or Italian immigrants). Fifty-eight students, teachers, volunteers, and programming staff were interviewed. They were asked questions designed to illuminate the impact of the three kinds of educational programming on the students (and staff) who take part in them. Finally, Sobré-Denton and her assistant perused over a 100 reflection exercises generated by the students throughout the programs. Several themes, indicative of cosmopolitan pedagogy and the role of the imagination in producing interculturality within the chosen site emerged from the data, and some of these are described below.

## Imagining Communities of Hope, Memory and Dialogue

All three programs utilize Hansen et al.'s three arts of cosmopolitan learning through engaging the imagination: hope (particularly present in CK), memory (particularly present in CW), and dialogue (particularly present in ENS).[92] For the purposes of this analysis, imagined communities were defined as "groups of people, not immediately tangible and accessible, with whom we connect through the power of imagination."[93] It should be noted here that all three programs engage the imagination across the three arts; however, due to space limitations, we present each art as illustrative of one specific program.

## The Hopeful Imagination in Cultural Kitchen

Hansen et al. define hope as "a turning toward the future within the present."[94] This is neither a utopian hope nor a hope that is optimistic or pessimistic. Rather, it is a hope that seeks to combine attention to the present with knowledge that the future is, by definition, imbued with change and possibility. In short, the art of hope involves learning to embrace the possibility of the present moment and is a notion that guides the trajectory of both the art of memory and the art of dialogue. The CK program, with its emphasis on understanding a specific cultural group through the creation of a "day in the life" of a teenager from a selected culture, creates an imagined world as rooted in everyday life. This conceptualization of similarities and differences existing simultaneously across national and cultural boundaries is designed to increase cultural curiosity, produce culture-specific learning, and open up the imagination for future engagement with people across differences.

Simon writes that "hopeful imagination" informs the "struggle for a better future...constituted in the need to imagine an alternative human world...in a way that enables one to act in the present as if this alternative had already begun to emerge."[95] Cultural Kitchen instills this sense of hopeful imagination in its students in several ways. To begin with, CK opens a window for students to peer into their chosen culture, creating an imaginative space for individuals both just like them and culturally and geographically distant. One participant stated that she was able to feel that her group's chosen culture, Egyptian culture, seemed "much more real when [we] thought about other kids like [us] living there, not just like something from the news or something." Additionally, the ability to imagine different worlds and to imagine empathizing with individuals who inhabit those worlds fits with Hansen et al.'s notion of hope tying the present to the future.

Three separate CK teachers explained why the students focused primarily on learning about the life of a teenager in their chosen country, rather than focusing heavily on the history of that country: it keeps the students' imaginations grounded firmly in the present-tense, increasing their empathy for and understanding of local lives of other young persons, even those living in places far from their own communities. This is a form of imaginatively "inhabiting the world from afar."[96] Finally, the work done during the didactic, experiential and reflective phases of CK serves to spark a hopeful imagination for future possibilities for interculturality in its students through embedding in them a sense of cultural curiosity and by conceptually diminishing the feeling of cultural distance. As one participant in CK stated:

> The ability to place yourself, the ability to understand that what you've felt in the past, somebody else can be feeling also. Not just the sympathy, it's like, I walk in your shoes but we share similar feelings and suddenly I can imagine what your world looks like. And not even imagine it, I want to go there!

Ideally, CK's pedagogy of hopeful imagination aims to increase participants' desires to travel and cross cultural boundaries in a manner that imagines cultural difference as something to be sought out, rather than be avoided and feared. It encourages the work of the radical imaginary and projects outward from the local toward the global in the spirit of interculturality.

### Imagined and Concrete Cultural Ties Through Memory in Community Walls

The art of memory exists in the tension between remembering and forgetting, or "heeding the voice of the past and at times letting it recede."[97] Hansen et al. find that it is often difficult to consider the present without muting the voice of the past; this is not a case of ignoring the past, but rather a question of interpretation and integration. This ultimately is a question of how one values the past as history and as identity, and it has little meaning outside of an individual's interpretation. When students engage the art of memory, the reflective work done positions them so that they are capable of appreciating the ways others question, judge and value their respective pasts. This can be understood through the words of one CW participant, who expressed that she has learned:

> That everyone's community is different. Like we may do some things the same but they mostly just do something different and you learn things about being different and seeing what other people do and you probably get to do what they do and stuff if you going to ever be in their community.

Another participant concurred, stating that "I think I learned that even if you meet people from another community, it's not that hard to relate to them because they are human beings and they live in a community the same as we do. Like, our communities aren't that far apart." The ability to imagine other communities as being similar to participants' own neighborhoods (despite differences) reduces social and cultural differences between the students and the hostellers, and in essence reduces the size of the world in the imagination of the participants. In this manner, they engage in the global imaginary.

The art of memory points to imagined communities in the way that Anderson conceptualizes them, as social ties to the past, to national and ethnic identity ties, and as ties to community membership.[98] When students in CW are asked to represent their communities through artwork, they are both engaging in how to represent their own memories of their selves, social selves, and neighborhoods, and also creating work designed to capture the imaginations of everyone at the hostel who might view their displays. As such, the art of memory interplays with imagination, in a manner that illustrates how "imagined communities expand our range of possible selves."[99] One participant explained how the work of translating his neighborhood from his imagination to the woodblock representation displayed on the hostel wall led him to understand how his memory and place in his neighborhood led him to reconceptualize his own community as well as himself:

> I just like the way it got me thinking about my community. Yeah sometimes you just never think about it. It just never goes into your mind like "oh my community" You know you're just living your life. You never stop and think. Now I think how would [hostellers] see my community? How would they see me?

In this particular case, individual communities are the spaces of imaginative engagement, both in creating the visual images and in explaining them to travelers at the hostel as a means of assisting them in visualizing all of Chicago, rather than just the "touristy" areas.

## Engagement of the Other Through Dialogue in Exchange Neighborhoods

Hansen et al. describe a third art, dialogue, as the means through which hope and memory coalesce to create a shared imaginative experience. In this manner, the art of dialogue creates a liminal imaginative space between the old and the new, the strange and the familiar—a site of possibility. This is similar to Castoriadis' notion of the radical imaginary.[100] Hansen et al. envision the role of dialogue as something that can be learned and cultivated through a sustained and guided pedagogy. Cosmopolitan pedagogy such as that available at HI-Chicago contains activities which encourage students to consciously or unconsciously ask themselves how they and their cultural Others hold and express values, and in the process helps build solidarity premised on the awareness and appreciation of humans as valuing beings.

The creation of shared imagined spaces through the art of dialogue creates bridges across difference; however, it also encourages a social comparison that has the potential to both broaden participants' horizons as well as make them inevitably compare their own neighborhoods and schools with that of cultural Others. This can serve ego-defensive purposes. For instance, one ENS participant stated: "I used to not like my community that much, but now I see that one's a bit worse... that people go through worse than what people in my community go through so I shouldn't judge my community so much." On the other hand, dialogue creates a means through which to combat stereotyping, discrimination and prejudice, that is, careful and mindful facilitation of the imagination through dialogue has the potential to reshape stereotypical and prejudiced imaginations about other cultural communities into hopeful spaces of connection. In terms of visiting a predominantly African American neighborhood from her own predominantly Latina/o and East Asian neighborhood, another ENS participant stated:

> I have learned not to follow generalizations about this culture... I have heard many things but actually hearing it first-hand from people of that culture my ideas have changed. So I know if like someone to say a generalization about their culture... well actually such and such and such is what I learned about this culture.

A bus ride led by local students around their neighborhood, a guided tour of a school, cooking a meal with stranger who is not that different from the participant—whether they are from a few miles or a few oceans away—allows the imagination to simultaneously strain against its preconceived notions and create outwardly directed imaginaries. Another ENS participant expressed this: "As far as I can think about it, my neighborhood it would be the people I go to school with and now it's like ok…now it's the whole city, there are all these other people who have lives." In this manner, ENS encourages cultural curiosity and specific culture learning in a manner similar to CK, as well as celebrates the notion that difference exists both locally and globally.

*The role of the social/radical/global imaginaries in HI-Chicago's educational programming*

Through this snapshot, we have aimed to illustrate the manners through which the cosmopolitan pedagogical arts of hope, memory and dialogue engage the imagination and imaginaries to facilitate cosmopolitan interculturality. The participants in HI-Chicago's programs seem to be embodying the spirit of world-oriented communication and engaging the in-between spaces of interculturality. They seem willing to open their mind to possibilities and the self to transformation as they engage with differences across cultures. Through empathy, and solidarity with those near and far, they seem to be embodying the spirit of cosmopolitan communication and leaning toward cosmopolitan peoplehood.

We note here that these are only the preliminary findings of this study. One potential area to be explored further involves the site of the hostel itself as a space designed to ignite the imagination regarding possibilities outside of the parameters of both one's home and neighborhood (for the student participants) and the City of Chicago beyond tourist attractions (for the travelers who engage with students at the hostel). Additionally, more attention needs to be paid to the relationship between cultural curiosity, desire for travel, and the social/radical/global imaginaries, specifically in longitudinal terms. That is, how does the shifting imagination of participants realistically impact them over time? Are students who participate in these programs more likely to continue to broaden their imagination regarding their own neighborhoods and identities, cultural Others within their own city, and cultural Others in the country and the World? Are they likely to continue broadening their own ability to transcend cultural borders and boundaries in their future lives? What kinds of links exist between the social, radical and global imaginaries and interculturality, and how are these links facilitated through cosmopolitan pedagogy? These questions are currently being considered in further data analysis of this rich research site.

## CONCLUSION

The notion of interculturality lies at the heart of cosmopolitanism, a philosophy that has persisted for centuries. We hope that through this chapter we have been successful in our effort to show how interculturality, via the values of cosmopolitanism and the cosmopolitan imagination, can be conceptualized in terms of intercultural communication. We also hope that we have sufficiently highlighted the promise such a conceptualization holds for how we may mindfully communicate, in the spirit of peoplehood, for the purpose of creating a more humane world. In the words of Chicana scholar Gloria Anzaldúa, "We can transform our world by imagining it differently, dreaming it passionately via all our senses, and willing it into creation."[101]

In closing, we would like to express our gratitude for the opportunity to write this chapter and for participating in the "Perspectives on Interculturality" interdisciplinary conference hosted by St. Louis University. This conference, which preceded this book, was truly an experience in interculturality, and a remarkable opportunity to hear and learn from colleagues in different disciplines, and hailing from different parts of our world, about their take on interculturality. This experience joggled our own imagination and encouraged us to further explore the links between the imagination/imaginary, cosmopolitanism, communication and interculturality. In writing this chapter, we have drawn liberally from disciplines such as sociology, anthropology, philosophy, cultural studies and education to build our ideas and arguments, and we would be truly delighted if what we have produced is useful to scholars in other disciplines in ways that will keep the dialogue and creativity across disciplines alive. That, itself, would be fitting in the larger move toward interculturality.

## NOTES

1. Sankaran Krishna, *Globalization and Postcolonialism: Hegemony and Resistance in the Twenty-first Century* (Lanham, MD: Rowman & Littlefield, 2009), 1–6.
2. Gerard Delanty, "The Cosmopolitan Imagination: Critical Cosmopolitanism and Social Theory," *The British Journal of Sociology*, 57 (2006): 25–47.

3. Raka Shome and Radha Hegde, "Postcolonial Approaches to Communication: Charting the Terrain, Engaging the Intersections," *Communication Theory*, 12 (2002): 261, 262.
4. Giuliana B. Prato, "Introduction—Beyond Multiculturalism: Anthropology at the Intersections between the Local, the National, and the Global," in *Beyond Multiculturalism: Views from Anthropology*, ed. Giuliana B. Prato (Burlington: Ashgate, 2009), 3.
5. For a more detailed critique of the notion of multiculturalism see Miriam Sobré-Denton and Nilanjana Bardhan, *Cultivating Cosmopolitanism for Intercultural Communication: Communicating as Global Citizens* (New York: Routledge, 2013).
6. Prato, *Beyond Multiculturalism*, 1–19.
7. For a discussion of the value of interculturalism over multiculturalism see Nilanjana Bardhan, "Postcolonial Migrant Identities and the Case for Strategic Hybridity: Toward 'Inter'cultural Bridgework," in *Identity Research and Communication: Intercultural Reflections and Future Directions*, ed. Nilanjana Bardhan and Mark P. Orbe (Lanham, MD: Lexington Books, 2012), 149–164.
8. Arjun Appadurai, *Modernity at Large: Cultural Dimensions of Globalization* (Minneapolis: University of Minnesota Press, 1996), 12–13.
9. See Lenore Langsdorf, "The Reasonableness of Bias," in *Communication Ethics: Between Cosmopolitanism and Provinciality*, ed. Kathleen Glenister Roberts and Ronald C. Arnett (New York: Peter Lang, 2008), 241–261.
10. Aimee Carrillo Rowe, "Entering the Inter: Power Lines in Intercultural Communication," in *The Handbook of Critical Intercultural Communication*, ed. Thomas Nakayama and Rona T. Halualani (Malden: Wiley-Blackwell, 2010), 216, 224.
11. For example, see Walter Fisher, "Glimpses of Hope: Rhetorical and Dialogical Discourse Promoting Cosmopolitanism," in *Communication Ethics: Between Cosmopolitanism and Provinciality*, ed. Kathleen Glenister Roberts and Ronald C. Arnett (New York: Peter Lang, 2008), 47–68; Langsdorf, "The Reasonableness of Bias"; John Stewart, "Cosmopolitan Communication Ethics: Understanding and Action," in *Communication Ethics: Between Cosmopolitanism and Provinciality*, ed. Kathleen Glenister Roberts and Ronald C. Arnett (New York: Peter Lang, 2008), 105–119.
12. Amardo Rodriguez, "A Story from Somewhere: Cathedrals, Communication, and the Search for Possibility," in *The Same and Different: Acknowledging the Diversity within and between Cultural Groups, International and Intercultural Communication Annual XXIX*, ed. Mark P. Orbe, Brenda J. Allen, and Lisa A. Flores (Washington, DC: National Communication Association, 2006), 16.
13. For a postcolonial view of this topic see Homi Bhabha, "Culture's In-Between," in *Questions of Cultural Identity*, ed. Stuart Hall and Paul du Gay (London: Sage, 1996), 53–60.

14. Crispin Thurlow, "Speaking of Difference: Language, Inequality and Interculturality," in *The Handbook of Critical Intercultural Communication*, ed. Thomas Nakayama and Rona T. Halualani (Malden: Wiley-Blackwell, 2010), 241.

15. For a critical interrogation of the relations between power, culture, and communication, see Rona T. Halualani and Thomas Nakayama, "Critical Intercultural Communication Studies: At a Crossroads," in *The Handbook of Critical Intercultural Communication*, ed. Thomas Nakayama and Rona T. Halualani (Malden, MA: Wiley-Blackwell, 2010), 1–16.

16. Craig Calhoun, "Imagining Solidarity: Cosmopolitanism, Constitutional Patriotism, and the Public Sphere," *Public Culture*, 14 (2002): 156.

17. Istvan Kecskes, "Interculturality and Intercultural Pragmatics," in *The Routledge Handbook of Language and Intercultural Communication*, ed. Jane Jackson (New York: Routledge, 2012), 67–84.

18. For a description of the notion of "intercultural space" see Aileen Pearson-Evans and Angela Leahy, "Introduction," in *Intercultural Spaces: Language, Culture, Identity*, ed. Aileen Pearson-Evans and Angela Leahy (New York: Peter Lang, 2007), xv–xvi.

19. Seyla Benhabib quoted in Gerard Delanty, *The Cosmopolitan Imagination: The Renewal of Critical Social Theory* (Cambridge: Cambridge University Press, 2009), 127.

20. Philosopher Martha Nussbaum's writings on cosmopolitanism provoked debates in the early 1990s about the relationship between cosmopolitanism and patriotism; see Martha Nussbaum, "Patriotism and Cosmopolitanism," in *For Love of Country: Debating the Limits of Patriotism*, ed. Joshua Cohen (Boston: Beacon Press, 1996), 2–17.

21. Delanty, "The Cosmopolitan Imagination: Critical Cosmopolitanism and Social Theory," 27.

22. Delanty, *The Cosmopolitan Imagination: The Renewal of Critical Social Theory.*

23. For a full treatment of this topic see Emannuel C. Eze, *Achieving our Humanity* (New York: Routledge, 2001).

24. Walter Mignolo, "The Many Faces of Cosmo-polis: Border Thinking and Critical Cosmopolitanism," in *Cosmopolitanism*, ed. Carol Breckenridge, Homi Bhabha, Sheldon Pollock, and Dipesh Chakrabarty (Durham: Duke University Press, 2002), 174.

25. Ibid., 181.

26. Sheldon Pollock, Homi Bhabha, Carol Breckenridge, and Dipesh Chakrabarty, "Cosmopolitanisms," in *Cosmopolitanism*, ed. Carol Breckenridge, Homi Bhabha, Sheldon Pollock, and Dipesh Chakrabarty (Durham: Duke University Press, 2002), 7.

27. Kwame Anthony Appiah, *Cosmopolitanism: Ethics in a World of Strangers* (London: Penguin Books, 2006), 57.

28. For example, see Pheng Cheah, "Introduction Part II: The Cosmopolitical—Today," in *Cosmopolitics: Thinking and Feeling Beyond the Nation*, ed. Pheng Cheah and Bruce Robbins (Minneapolis: University of Minnesota

Press, 1998), 20–41; Pnina Werbner, "Introduction," in *Anthropology and the New Cosmopolitanism: Rooted, Feminist, and Vernacular Perspectives*, ed. Pnina Werbner (New York: Berg, 2008), 1–29.

29. Kwame Anthony Appiah, "Cosmopolitan Patriots," in *For Love of Country: Debating the Limits of Patriotism*, ed. Joshua Cohen (Boston: Beacon Press, 1996), 21–29.

30. Delanty, *The Cosmopolitan Imagination: The Renewal of Critical Social Theory*; Werbner, "Introduction."

31. Appiah, *Cosmopolitanism: Ethics in a World of Strangers*.

32. Werbner, "Introduction," 14, 15, 16.

33. W. Barnett Pearce, *Communication and the Human Condition* (Carbondale: Southern Illinois University Press, 1989), 203.

34. Ulf Hannerz, "Cosmopolitans and Locals in World Culture," *Theory, Culture & Society*, 7 (1990): 237–251.

35. Ibid., 238.

36. Judith Martin and Thomas Nakayama, *Intercultural Communication in Contexts*, 6th edn (New York: McGraw-Hill, 2012), 96.

37. Delanty, *The Cosmopolitan Imagination: The Renewal of Critical Social Theory*.

38. Sobré-Denton and Bardhan, *Cultivating Cosmopolitanism for Intercultural Communication*.

39. Werbner, "Introduction," 2.

40. Gavin Kendall, Ian Woodward, and Zlatko Skrbis, *The Sociology of Cosmopolitanism: Globalization, Identity, Culture and Government* (Hampshire: Palgrave Macmillan, 2009), 107.

41. Robert J. Holton, *Cosmopolitanisms: New Thinking and New Directions* (Hampshire: Palgrave Macmillan, 2009), 15.

42. Homi Bhabha, *The Location of Culture* (New York: Routledge, 1994); Rodriguez, "A Story from Somewhere." Bhabha introduced the notion of the third space through postcolonial theory and Rodriguez has effectively worked with this notion from the perspective of culture and communication.

43. Judith Martin, "Foreword," in *Cultivating Cosmopolitanism for Intercultural Communication: Communicating as Global Citizens*, ed. Miriam Sobré-Denton and Nilanjana Bardhan (New York: Routledge, 2013), ix–xii.

44. Pearce, *Communication and the Human Condition*, 198.

45. Adrian Holliday, *Intercultural Communication and Ideology* (Thousand Oaks: Sage, 2011); Mignolo, "The Many Faces of Cosmo-polis."

46. Rona T. Halualani, S. Lily Mendoza, and Jolanta Drzewiecka, "'Critical' Junctures in Intercultural Communication Studies: A Review," *The Review of Communication*, 9 (2009): 17–35; Kent Ono, "Problematizing 'Nation' in Intercultural Communication Research," in *Communication and Identity Across Cultures, International and Intercultural Communication Annual XXI*, ed. Dolores Tanno and Alberto González (Thousand Oaks: Sage, 1998), 193–202.

47. Ulrich Beck, *The Cosmopolitan Vision* (Cambridge: Polity Press, 2004/2006).

48. For a detailed discussion of this vision see Charles Taylor, "Why Democracy Needs Patriotism," in *For Love of Country: Debating the Limits of Patriotism*, ed. Joshua Cohen (Boston: Beacon Press), 119–121.

49. Sobré-Denton and Bardhan, *Cultivating Cosmopolitanism for Intercultural Communication*.

50. Ibid., 50

51. Ibid., 89.

52. For example, see Delanty, *The Cosmopolitan Imagination: The Renewal of Critical Social Theory*.

53. Nikos Papastergiadis, *Cosmopolitanism and Culture* (Cambridge: Polity Press, 2012), 103–104.

54. Ibid.

55. Delanty, *The Cosmopolitan Imagination: The Renewal of Critical Social Theory*.

56. Delanty, "The Cosmopolitan Imagination: Critical Cosmopolitanism and Social Theory," 38.

57. Beck, *The Cosmopolitan Vision*, 89.

58. C. Wright Mills, *The Sociological Imagination* (New York: Oxford University Press, 1959/2000), 5.

59. Ibid., 8.

60. Ibid., 6, 13.

61. Cornelius Castoriadis, *The Imaginary Institution of Society*, trans. Kathleen Blamey (Cambridge: MIT Press, 1987/1998), 149.

62. Manfred B. Steger, *The Rise of the Global Imaginary* (Oxford: Oxford University Press, 2008), 6.

63. Papastergiadis, *Cosmopolitanism and Culture*, 102.

64. Castoriadis, *The Imaginary Institution of Society*, 133.

65. Ibid., 127.

66. Chiara Bottici and Renoít Challand, "Introduction," in *The Politics of Imagination*, ed. Chiara Bottici and Renoít Challand (London: Birkbeck Law Press, 2011), 1–15; Richard Kearney, *The Wake of Imagination* (New York: Routledge, 1998).

67. Jane Kenway and Johannah Fahey, "Imagining Research Otherwise," in *Globalizing the Research Imagination*, ed. Jane Kenway and Johannah Fahey (New York: Routledge, 2009), 1–40.

68. Benedict Anderson, *Imagined Communities: Reflections on the Origin and Spread of Nationalism* (New York: Verso Books, 1983/2006).

69. Steger, *The Rise of the Global Imaginary*.

70. Anderson, *Imagined Communities*.

71. Roland Robertson, *Globalization: Social Theory and Global Culture* (London: Sage, 1992).

72. Ulf Hannerz, *Transnational Connections: Culture, People, Places* (London: Routledge, 1996).

73. Appadurai, *Modernity at Large*, 31.

74. Ibid., 31.
75. Ibid., 3.
76. Steger, *The Rise of the Global Imaginary*, 12.
77. Appadurai, *Modernity at Large*, 31.
78. Delanty, "The Cosmopolitan Imagination: Critical Cosmopolitanism and Social Theory," 38.
79. Avtar Brah, "Global Mobilities, Local Predicaments: Globalization and the Critical Imagination," *Feminist Review*, 70 (2002): 38.
80. Joanna Latimer and Beverley Skeggs, "The Politics of Imagination: Keeping Open and Critical," *The Sociological Review*, 59 (2011): 404; see also Kearney, *The Wake of Imagination*.
81. Thomas Popkewitz quoted in Yatta Kanu, "Curriculum as Cultural Practice: Postcolonial Imagination," *Journal of the Canadian Association of Curriculum Studies*, 1 (2003): 68.
82. Quoted in Kanu, "Curriculum as Cultural Practice," 68.
83. Castoriadis, *The Imaginary Institution of Society*.
84. Maria Kyriakidou, "Imagining Ourselves Beyond the Nation? Exploring Cosmopolitanism in Relations to Media Coverage of Distant Suffering," *Studies in Ethnicity and Nationalism*, 9 (2009): 481–496.
85. Bronislaw Szerszynski and John Urry, "Visuality, Mobility and the Cosmopolitan: Inhabiting the World from Afar," *British Journal of Sociology*, 57 (2006): 113.
86. Eva Hoffman, "Life in a New Language," in *Foreign Dialogues*, ed. Mary Zournazi (Annandale: Pluto Press, 1998), 25.
87. Karen L. Dace and Mark L. McPhail, "Crossing the Color Line: From Empathy to Implicature in Intercultural Communication," in *Readings in Intercultural Communication: Experiences and Contexts*, 2nd edn, ed. Judith N. Martin, Thomas K. Nakayama, and Lisa A. Flores (New York: McGraw-Hill, 2002), 350.
88. Calhoun, "Imagining Solidarity," 163, 171.
89. David T. Hansen, Stephanie Burdick-Shepherd, Cristina Cammarano, and Gonzalo Obelliero, "Education, Values, and Valuing in Cosmopolitan Perspective," *Curriculum Inquiry*, 39 (2009): 587–612.
90. Kay L. Gibson, Glyn M. Rimmington, and Marjorie Landwher-Brown, "Developing Global Awareness and Responsible World Citizenship with Global Learning," *Roeper Review*, 30 (2008): 11–23.
91. Hostelling-International Chicago, Exchange Neighborhoods, accessed April 4, 2012, http://www.hichicago.org/about-hi-chicago/community-involvement/exchange-neighborhoods/
92. Hansen, Burdick-Shepherd, Cammarano, and Obelliero, "Education, Values, and Valuing in Cosmopolitan Perspective."
93. Yasuko Kanno and Bonny Norton, "Imagined Communities and Educational Possibilities: Introduction," *Journal of Language, Identity, and Education*, 2 (2008): 241.
94. Hansen, Burdick-Shepherd, Cammarano, and Obelliero, "Education, Values, and Valuing in Cosmopolitan Perspective," 594.

95. Quoted in Kanno and Norton, "Imagined Communities and Educational Possibilities: Introduction," 244.
96. Szerszynski and Urry, "Visuality, Mobility and the Cosmopolitan: Inhabiting the World from Afar."
97. Hansen, Burdick-Shepherd, Cammarano, and Obelliero, "Education, Values, and Valuing in Cosmopolitan Perspective," 595.
98. Anderson, *Imagined Communities.*
99. Kanno and Norton, "Imagined Communities and Educational Possibilities: Introduction," 246.
100. Castoriadis, *The Imaginary Institution of Society.*
101. Gloria Anzaldúa, "Let Us Be the Healing of the Wound," in *The Gloria Anzaldúa Reader,* ed. AnaLouise Keating (Durham, NC: Duke University Press, 2009), 312.

# 8

# TOWARD A COSMOPOLITAN SOCIOLOGY: UNDERSTANDING COSMOPOLITANISM IN KOREA

## *Mun-Cho Kim*

In the early 1970s, economic crisis derived from oil shock caused by the October War between Israel and Egypt and the demise of Bretton Woods Agreements swept developed nations. Affected countries opted for reorganization of national systems through technological and social innovations. During the process, neoliberal economic policies permitting free movements of capital across the borders were promoted. As a result, globe-wide economic infrastructure where most of the world operates based on market profit was constituted. Followed by political globalization, this transnational world system characterized by tight international interdependency has been consolidated. But the 2008 global financial crisis originated from Wall Street, the main street of world capitalism, exposing the very limitations of neoliberal globalization strategies. This study seeks to do the following:

(1) Propose a culture-driven theory of globalization where the logical sequence of the existing economy-driven globalization theory is inversed, as an alternative perspective,
(2) Suggest cosmopolitan sociology as the frame of social analysis with the above perspective in mind,
(3) Explore the value of cosmopolitan sociology by examining the past and current status of cosmopolitanism in South Korea.

## TWO FACES OF GLOBALIZATION

Manuel Castells has recently insisted that economic globalization is entering a new phase.[1] The accumulation of capital used to occur

sporadically at various corners of the world. However, in the new
phase, global scale economic activities are taking place simultaneously
in real time. Castells describes the difference between world economy
depicted by world system theorists and global economy he himself
proposed.

> The informational economy is global. A global economy is a historically
> new reality, distinct from a world economy. A world economy, that is
> an economy in which capital accumulation proceeds throughout the
> world, has existed in the West at least since the sixteenth century, as
> Fernand Braudel and Immanuel Wallerstein have taught us. A global
> economy is something different: it is an economy with the capacity
> to work as a unit in real time on a planetary scale. While the capitalist
> mode of production is characterized by its relentless expansion, always
> trying to overcome limits of time and space, it is only in the late twen-
> tieth century that the world economy was able to become truly global
> on the basis of the new infrastructure provided by information and
> communication technologies.[2]

When it comes to economy-driven globalization, positive and negative perspectives have long been contending. As far as the positive
perspectives go, it can be traced back to the pioneering work of Adam
Smith, *The Wealth of Nations*.[3] He viewed discovery of New World
and voyage to the East India by Europeans in early periods of imperi-
alist reign as an epoch-making event that created new world economy.
Though acknowledging the illegitimate power inequality driven by
the colonization process, Smith argued that globalization in the long
run, with geographically distant nations interacting with each other
while satisfying various desires and increasing consumption, will benefit everyone. He deemed the birth of world economy as the most
significant incident in modern history, enabling the entire world to
share the benefits.

Marx and Engels, by contrast, pointed out the negative aspects
of globalization. In *The Communist Manifesto*, they argued that the
shaping of world market would turn the labor force into a mere
abstract form.[4] Consequently, international proletariats whose only
options are either submission or victory were bound to be mobilized.
International proletariats would reorganize themselves as the war-
riors of revolution, yearning and striving for a socialist system devoid
of poverty, inequality, exploitation, and alienated labor. In this light,
according to Marx and Engels, globalization of economy is the seed
of catastrophe, leading the capitalist class and their opponents to a
contested terrain.

After World War II, world market continued to expand as the scale of international trading increased. In 1994 the Uruguay Round attempted to resolve the problems caused by GATT (General Agreement on Tariffs and Trade) system, and WTO (World Trade Organization) was established. WTO, whose main objective is to abolish institutional barriers of international transactions, launched various plans to alleviate the trade barriers. As a result, globalization in trade and consumption began to accelerate.[5] However, the world market expansion was of unequal nature. Under an unequal distribution system, mostly multinational corporations and developed nations benefited. Thus, the gap between not only wealthy and poor nations but also between the rich and the poor magnified.[6]

Accordingly, the rise of global economy in the past half century or so brought the controversy around globalization to the fore once more. Positive perspectives, arguing that the close international system of cooperation gave rise to the emergence of new international world order, and negative perspectives, warning about the possibility of globe-wide economic crisis as the autonomy of independent states weakened, coexist side by side.[7] It may be said that in influencing our everyday lives, globalization incorporates rather conflicting facets of light and shade, and of aspiration and despair. We are bound to ask then, how are we to react and cope with such challenges? Despite the numerous debates and deliberations on the subject up to date, most of the potential resolutions seem to be in a stalemate, exposed to their own self-limitations. We are currently facing an academic threshold, where searching for a new alternative based on the proper understanding on the very predicament at our door step is of utmost urgency.

## Calling for a New Globalization Perspective

The globalization thesis as a prevailing ideology has usually stressed the positive aspects, such as socioeconomic openness, technological innovation, circulation of various products and services, abundant information and culture, and improved quality of life. Its advocates, while neglecting the negative side effects, claim that globalization has been cruising along the proper track.[8] On the other hand, its critics continue to consider globalization as the main culprit responsible for the eradication of domestic industrial infrastructures and cultural traditions, economic and political dependency of poor countries on rich countries, devastation from excess environmental exploitation, and cultural homogenization.

However, globalization is a complex process, spreading out in varying terrains such as economy, politics, culture and etc. simultaneously. Because of its compound nature, neither absolute acceptance nor rejection is sufficient as they are both partial viewpoints. What we need is a multidimensional perspective that enables us to acquire extensive and comprehensive understanding of the globalization phenomena.

Approaching globalization's composite nature, it is necessary to construct a balanced perspective in order to recognize both positive results and negative side effects. Advocates view globalization as a legitimating ideology, and tend to obscure its unsavory aspects. Rejectionists emphasize the opposite. A multidimensional approach to globalization would allow us to reflect upon the problems of our times by limiting these two dogmatic perspectives. Among the dimensions of globalization that should be considered seriously in a comprehensive approach, the cultural component seems to be crucial because it is known to be "the formidable machine producing cultural difference" (une formidable machine à produire de la différence culturelle).[9]

## CULTURAL GLOBALIZATION

Unlike the economy-driven globalization, usually understood as the outcome of utilitarian motivation, cultural globalization is closely related to the problem of values, and is at the center of the most sensitive and controversial realm in the current debates on globalization. Information, commodities and services, images and designs frequently crossing the border seem to signify the advent of a global culture. A global culture would revolutionize collective lifestyles and identities. However, culture as a machine producing differences has either particularism or localism at its core, and these two attributes help societies or groups to differentiate themselves from others. Particularism and localism guide us in distinguishing and understanding what people in given spaces and localities think and how they act. Thus, if global culture shifting toward homogenization or convergence were to proliferate throughout the world, it would collide with diverse indigenous cultures, and make the culturescape of the world more complex than before.

What both neoliberal market economists and Marxist economists—who hastily concluded that globalization would progress in inevitable and irreversible fashion—did not recognize is that both ethnic feelings and nationalisms have been interacting with class hierarchy to intensify racial and regional conflict. From the late 1980s and onward, in the hidden side of globalization process, we witnessed the revival of nationalism, traditionalism, and religious fundamentalism. The rise of deadly tribal confrontation in Africa, regional and religious conflict in the vicinity of USSR, Middle-East or even parts of Asia and Latin America are among the examples. These cases tell us that cultural globalization does not happen unchallenged, or even smoothly, as both the advocates and the critics of globalization anticipated.

Contestation emanating from local sub-cultures opposing the homogenization trend of globalization is quite prominent. Resistance from women, youths, gays, lesbians, blacks, or ethnic minorities who have been in constant struggle with hegemonic and dominant cultures is witnessed throughout the world.[10]

## Globalization, External Versus Internal

Recently, groups of researchers studying culture started to argue that modern way of life is heading toward differentiated discourses and practices. They focus on the local, concrete, particular, and heterogeneous, emphasizing the micro-aspects of everyday life. For example, advocates of poststructuralism, postmodernism, postcolonialism, feminism, and multiculturalism try to look beyond the macroscopic horizons of globalization, and show great interest in differences, otherness, marginality, particularity, and concreteness at the micro level.

In a macroscopic view of globalization, based on the global versus local dichotomy, it is hard to do away with the zero-sum dilemma where choosing one over the other necessarily relates to the negation of the importance of the alternative. Micro-theorists, in noticing such cognitive limitations, emphasize the very process where local communities are affected by the driving force of globalization and get structuralized. Their endeavors involve investigating both how the global and the local assimilate and reproduce themselves, and how the interaction of the global and the local constitutes a new cultural hybrid.

Ulrich Beck describes this kind of new approach to globalization as "cosmopolitanism." Distinguishing between external and internal globalization, Beck argues that external globalization best characterized by the growth in material interconnections across national boundaries is not enough to understand what is happening in our world. Cosmopolitanism corresponds to internal globalization involving not only growing interconnections across national boundaries but transformation of the quality of social life inside the nation-state. Under cosmopolitanism, exaltation of social consciousness conciliating both spaces of the global (cosmos) and the local (polis) becomes crucial.[11] Denying the dichotomy between global and local, internal globalization implies the "globalization of mind," where the local within the global and the global within the local can be realized and bear fruit.

## TYPES AND TRENDS OF COSMOPOLITANISM

Cosmopolitanism comes from a long tradition of scholarly works. It is typically classified into three types; moral cosmopolitanism, social cosmopolitanism, and cultural cosmopolitanism.[12]

Moral cosmopolitanism, more of a classical version, can be traced back to the expansion period under Alexander the Great when the closed world of Polis turned into a vast empire. However, a more direct form of moral cosmopolitanism was first conceptualized by Immanuel Kant. In order to criticize Western imperialism at the end of the eighteenth century, he saw the need of a new perspective where the limitations of narrow nationality-based framework of thought could be overcome. He set out to search for republican political philosophy, and in the midst of these endeavors *A Study on Perpetual Peace* was written.

In the third chapter of this work, while stressing that hospitality is not a virtue of sociability toward aliens but a very basic responsibility of all humankind, Kant argues that in truly republican political philosophy all men should respect human rights by performing moral duty based on humanitarianism.[13] Today, such moral cosmopolitanism is very much reproduced in Jurgen Habermas's discursive ethics, forming the foundation of normative universalism.[14]

Social cosmopolitanism is directly related to social civil rights and can be defined as the outcome of a compromise between personal human rights and civil rights of ethnic minorities. With the foundations for the concept of modern nation established through the Treaty of Westphalia in 1648, the separation of the social and the political soon followed, and moral cosmopolitanism based on the very notion of human rights gave birth to social cosmopolitanism concentrating on the issue of civil rights. Citizenship based on historicity and locality is the salient subject in discussions of social cosmopolitanism. Social cosmopolitanism, directly related to ethnic prejudices or racial conflicts that heat up hand in hand with trans-national migration, concentrates on dealing with the concept of territory as measured by the place of birth in defining citizenship.[15]

However, in contemporary societies, cultural cosmopolitanism, strongly related to the concept of societal pluralization, holds utmost importance. Cultural cosmopolitanism assumes a pluralist value system to be the foundation of our social world, and respects varying ways of life. In short, instead of treating society as a unitary entity, cultural cosmopolitanism considers society to be the cultural medium free to transform according to the logic of global openness. Manuel Castells, John Urry, and Bruno Latour are considered to have made major contributions to the theoretical formation of cultural cosmopolitanism.[16]

Castells's theory of network society stressed open and flexible structures. It may be proper to say that his theory paved the way to cultural cosmopolitanism. In his theory, society exists in the form of networks rather than territorial spaces.[17] Urry viewed mobility as the very ontological condition of contemporary society, and his thought carried logical traces of cultural cosmopolitanism.[18] Hybridity is a concept that emerged at the crossroads of network and mobility. Hybrid associations are essential to fostering cultural cosmopolitanism,[19] because hybridity provides the foundation of new meaning during the process of cultural globalization.

Meanwhile, Zygmunt Bauman proposed the concept of "liquid modernity" to describe contemporary lives—full of ambiguities, uncertainties, embarrassments, and anxieties. He argues that contemporary world contains contending multiple modernities, and is heading toward a new stage of cosmopolitanism where post-universalism is sought after.[20] Since post-universal cosmopolitanism allows lifestyles and life strategies that all individuals, locals, citizens, and simply anyone living on this planet can relish, it goes beyond both moral and social cosmopolitanisms that stress human rights and civil rights respectively. Thus, post-universal cosmopolitanism can be classified under cultural cosmopolitanism.[21]

## A Glimpse of Korean Cosmopolitanism

Transnational migration has been the driving force behind the changes in global ethno-scape over the last century. The number of trans-Atlantic immigrants showed unprecedented increase in the early twentieth century while cross-continental migration from developing countries to developed countries prospered toward the end of the century.[22] After experiencing rapid expansions in both the scale of economy and trade surplus during the last two decades, the influx of foreigners of different backgrounds has been increasing in South Korea as indicated in Figures 8.1–8.4.

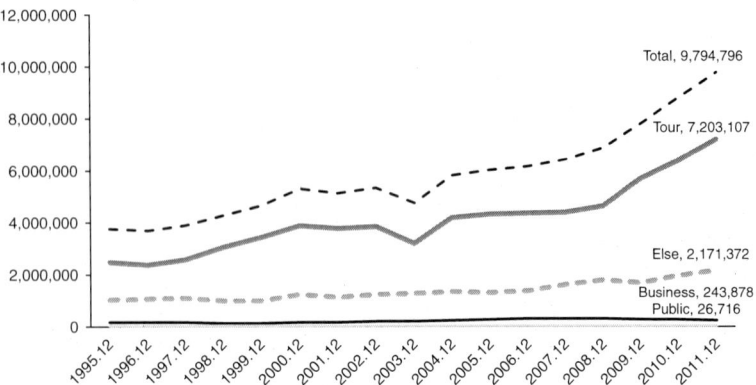

**Figure 8.1** Number of foreign tourists visiting S. Korea.

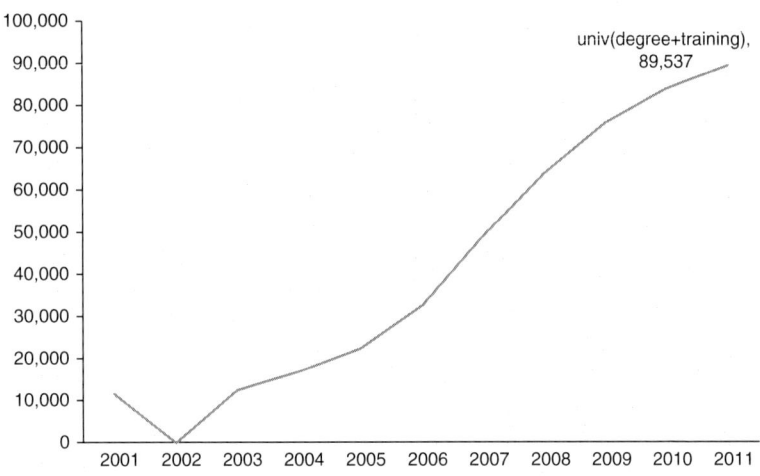

**Figure 8.2** Number of foreign students in S. Korea.

Xenophobia refers to the antipathy toward aliens with different physical appearances, folkways or lifestyles. As the propinquity hypothesis argues, xenophobia can be lifted, resolving the feeling of uneasiness, by repeated exposures to difference.[23] It is undeniable that attitude toward foreigners in South Korea is turning for the better due to the accelerated globalization. The fact that negative stereotypes about black and Korean mixed bloods are being replaced by enthusiasm toward pop-artists and popular athletes from these groups offers support to this observation. However, such a turn in people's attitudes

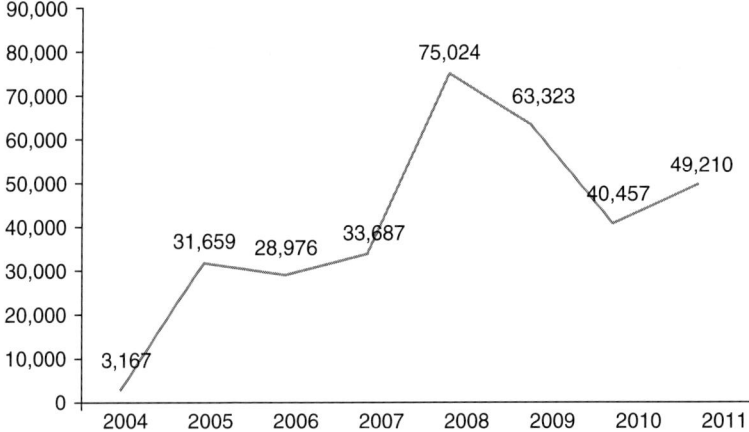

**Figure 8.3** Number of foreign employees in S. Korea.

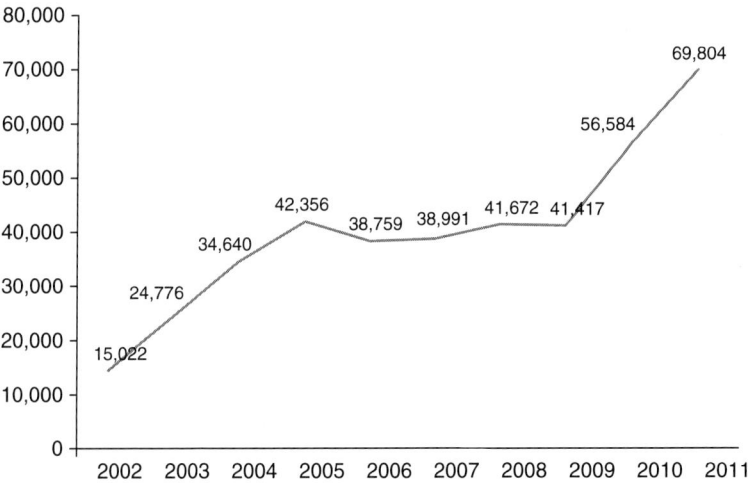

**Figure 8.4** Number of international marriages in S. Korea.

is limited to "special" foreigners who are celebrities. In South Korea, prejudice and feelings of rejection toward "ordinary" foreigners still prevail. The following cases show the existing residues of deeply rooted uneasiness toward people from outside of the national boundaries.

Many Koreans did not recognize the seriousness of the multicultural problems caused by interracial coexistence. The UN CERD Report released in August 2007 said that privileging the "pure-blooded" based on Korea's pride in the nation's ethnic homogeneity has brought about various forms of discrimination against the so-called mixed-bloods in all aspects of life, including employment, marriage, housing, education, and interpersonal relationships.[24]

Evidence indicating the limitations of Koreans' cosmopolitanism can also be found in their attitude toward market opening and foreign cultural products in 2008 East Asian Social Survey (EASS) below. EASS is a biennial social survey project that purports to produce and disseminate academic survey data sets in East Asia. It launched back in 2003, and the data used in this study is from 2008. Countries included in EASS data are China, Japan, South Korea, and Taiwan. 2008 EASS is entitled "Culture and Globalization in East Asia." See Tables 8.1 and 8.2.

The mobility of capital, technology, information, commodities, and human resources is promoted at the global level. National states are too small to react effectively to sprouting global economic, military, informational, sanitary, and ecological problems, and too big to accommodate diverse claims of local communities seeking their own identities. The conception of state based on territoriality is gradually but steadily losing its logical or practical validity. For these reasons, "Think Globally, Act Locally, Live Personally" is an attractive slogan of our time, representing an alternative wisdom of life, and a more cosmopolitan culture, capable of overcoming inner otherness and of shedding lifestyles centered primarily on the self or on the in-groups.

**Table 8.1**   Attitudes toward market opening (EASS 2008)

| Mobility of people and capital is- | CN | JP | KR | TW | F-Value |
|---|---|---|---|---|---|
| -Good or bad for economy | 5.59 | 4.69 | 4.69 | 5.17 | 288.807 |
| -Good or bad for job opportunities for workers† | 5.30 | 4.15 | 4.08 | 4.61 | 384.155 |
| Range | | 7: Strongly good, 6: Good, 5: Somewhat good 4: Neither good or bad 3: Somewhat bad, 2: Bad, 1: Strongly bad | | | |

**Table 8.2**   Exposures to foreign cultural products (EASS 2008)

| | CN | JP | KR | TW | F-Value |
|---|---|---|---|---|---|
| Japan animation | 1.58 | 2.34 | 1.83 | 2.12 | 315.818 |
| Chinese movies | 2.39 | 1.57 | 2.06 | 2.44 | 426.433 |
| Range | 4: Often, 3: Sometimes, 2: Seldom, 1: Not at all | | | | |

# Cosmopolitan Sociology as a Subfield, as an Intellectual Resource or as a Research Paradigm

Sociological research on globalization (especially cultural globalization) based on intersubjective like-mindedness has been led by the scholars of multiculturalism. Cosmopolitan research dealing with human rights, civil rights, and cultural identity of ethnic minorities forms not too much more than a subfield of sociological investigation in general.

However, a few of the subject-oriented researchers did apply or create a number of useful analytical concepts and theories that deal with the problems faced by ethnic minorities. "Theory of otherness," "gender politics" and "study of minority human rights" represent such endeavors to study the subject from a new perspective. Utilizing these concepts and logics, multiculturalist scholars contributed to the extension of relevant intellectual resources by exploring the research space where the once neglected voices of the "ethnic subaltern" can be heard.

The formation of a new perspective, corresponding to the changing world order and going beyond both "cosmopolitan sociology as a subfield of sociological investigation" and "cosmopolitan sociology as an intellectual resource," is not out of our reach, which is why establishing "cosmopolitan sociology as a research paradigm" is very much feasible. Constructing a cosmopolitan social paradigm requires that people-centered social integration (not system integration aiming at functional efficacy) be extrapolated from national to global level. Following are some conceptual requirements needed to realize such a paradigm.

## The Idea of Cultural Creolization

The core of globalization can be viewed through the logics of implosion and openness. As the concept of global village by Marshall McLuhan informs us, globalization is a convergent process where heterogeneous cultural elements are connected and mixed by "border crossing." This convergent process is the mechanism capable of producing the new mode of solidarity based on cultural sympathy, free of closed and exclusive nationalism. In other words, diversified cultural creolization is a basic condition for the construction of a "multicultural politics of otherness," where people with different cultures and various languages live under the shared spirit of egalitarianism, respecting difference and diversity.[25]

## Dynamic Cosmopolitanism Accompanied by Confrontation or Conflict

Cosmopolitanism assumes the hybridization of various cultural elements. It is important for us to recognize that the emergence of such cosmopolitanism involves a dynamic process instead of a smooth transition or simple alteration. The process of confrontation and conflict between heterogeneous elements is inevitable if various historical experiences and cultural conventions are to reach the stage of cultural hybridity. In order to overcome such confrontational situations, adhering to an open social system capable of coordinating value differences or moral discords is a necessary step.[26]

## Accepting Different Modernities

Kwame Appiah emphasizes the importance of staying clear of the errors of relativism while putting heterogeneous cultures and societies under the scope of cosmopolitanism. The relativist perspective supported by numerous social scientists including cultural anthropologists has a certain level of practical value. However, what we need to be cautious about is a danger of "exile of values" obstructing interaction between individuals inherent in said perspective. In short, relativism is capable of setting a path to silence or skepticism by disconnecting the possibilities of mutual communication.[27]

## The Idea of Post-Universal Cosmopolitanism

Universalism contains a risk of inhibiting tolerance or ignoring differences by stressing a single interpretation as an absolute truth. From the pluralist point of view that idealizes a society where a variety of values are realized, universalism is not a goal to yearn for but a target for revision. Ulrich Beck made connections between universalist logic and the logic of closed or exclusive community, hindering the communication between the differences.[28] Examples include exclusive chauvinism which gave rise to Fascism and impermeable nationalisms. We need to supplement the conviction, central to universalism, of promoting a single and only way of existence with cosmopolitanism where not the logic of monologue but the logic of reciprocal dialogue is preferred.

## Pluralist Lifestyle and Pluralist Life Strategy

Individuals have the right to enjoy what they like and need different conditions to do so. Just like it is impossible for all plants to coexist under identical physical environment and climate, individuals cannot grow in an invariable moral environment. Without conditions for diverse lifestyles, individuals cannot pursue their happiness and potential to the fullest.[29] It is not "solidarity organized through identity" but "solidarity built despite differences" that is needed in cosmopolitanism. This is why diversified combinations of pluralist lifestyles and life strategies at the individual, local, national, or even global level are among its pre-requisites.

If "cosmopolitan sociology as a subfield of sociological investigation" is a stream of inquiry about a specific social phenomenon or subject, and if "cosmopolitan sociology as an intellectual resource" reinforces existing sociological study on minorities in general, "cosmopolitan sociology as a research paradigm" can be regarded as an alternate conceptual approach, recasting the current sociological enterprises.

## A Quest for New Cosmopolitan Imagination

The above conditions would have to be satisfied for the new cosmopolitanism as a paradigm to emerge. However, what we also need from sociologists in the academic community is to move beyond simple disenchantment and come up with a new breed of sociological imagination that may be called a "cosmopolitan imagination."

C. W. Mills strongly criticized dominant intellectual trends of 1950s American sociological academic community such as ahistorical empiricism and vague idealism. In doing so, he stressed the importance of sociological imagination: "the insight capable of translating private troubles (individual experiences) into public issues (societal relationships)."[30] Indeed, sociologists sincerely concerned about parochial convention or the pedantry of "*Homo Academicus*," do relate well to Mills's concept of sociological imagination. It can be argued that sociological imagination has today reached a point where a revision should be made to reflect the radical changes sweeping the globe. One should, however, be mindful of Mills's warning that it is easy to get caught up in pitfalls of grand theory when ideas overwhelm facts, and in trivial empiricism when facts override ideas completely. In criticizing both fallacies, he proposed intellectual craftsmanship accompanied by historical consciousness.

Looking back on the actual changes in the realm of sociological imagination of the past, we note that, for classical sociologists, human society as a whole was the object of intellectual inquiry. Going through both World Wars, nations as societies defined and divided borders were heavily researched. However, since the late twentieth century, the range of sociological imagination reached a more global level. These recent changes have been caused mainly by "the intensification of worldwide social relations which link distant localities in such a way that local happenings are shaped by events occurring many miles away and vice versa."[31]

From petty snacks, daily necessities such as clothing and shoes to furniture, automobiles and cell phones, nearly all commodities are jointly produced from assembly lines and disassembly lines scattered around the globe. Also, transnational NGOs or NPOs are organized in order to compensate for the instability of international world order, and are enhancing communications on population problems, poverty, peace, environment, and other themes at the global level. On top of that, cross-civilizational dialogues designed to overcome cultural conflicts and prejudices are fostered. People who suffered the loss of property in the recent financial crisis realized that the "public issue" mentioned by Mills has crossed the national boundaries and become global.

However, cosmopolitan imagination goes beyond the global extension of the cognitive horizon, and suggests a profound ideational transition of conceptual frameworks regarding the relationship between in- and out-groups. The ultimate objective of cosmopolitanism aiming at "globalization within" is to move beyond affirmative concerns about other ethnicities, and to pursue the eventual equalization of "us" and "them." It is for this reason that cosmopolitan imagination can be said to rise above the sociological imagination that mainly stresses intellectual sincerity or empirical relevance.

## USES OF THE COSMOPOLITAN PARADIGM

Due to a certain implosive quality embedded in cosmopolitan sociology, a great amount of time and endeavor is needed if a conceptual framework providing definite explanations or interpretations of the new, complex social reality is to be successfully formulated. Considering the stake that cosmopolitan sociology has in promoting the intellectual status of sociology as a discipline, any such endeavors also need to be carefully monitored with this in mind.

About a century ago, classical sociologist Emile Durkheim wrote about the transition of types of social solidarity from mechanical to organic.[32] Ever since, many researchers have been exploring the subsequent type of social solidarity capable of substituting organic solidarity based on functional interdependence. Despite such efforts, a new form of social solidarity connoting this reality with a single concept is yet to be devised. On that account, the paradigm of cosmopolitan sociology, implying a new mode of solidarity likely to succeed organic solidarity, is worthy of our attention and dedication.

In contemporary life, global events such as the Olympic Games and the World Cup Competition are broadcast world-wide in real time, and can give rise to global sensations. Here, a glimpse of sentimental solidarity stemming from intensive and affective intercourse working behind the organic solidarity can be captured. Eric Fromm once argued that the society has shifted from "the Age of Having" to "the Age of Being."[33] If we acknowledge today's mega-trend of the world going beyond the theme of the old social thought, and entering "the Age of Feeling," based on emotional resonance, it is possible to consider the workings of nonutilitarian social bond called sentimental solidarity as a new source of social integration (Figure 8.5). For instance, indications of it can be identified in such events as the passionate responses to the Three Tenors Concert, and in the crowds of people assembled for the Memorial Ceremony for Mother Theresa.

Research on nonutilitarian solidarity based on emotion is not unprecedented. Marcel Mauss's "Study on Gift,"[34] "Theory of Ritualized Exchange" by Bronislaw Malinowski,[35] and Georges Bataille's "General Economic Theory"[36] are examples. However, sentimental solidarity differs from social solidarity suggested by these nonutilitarian exchange theories. Sentimental solidarity, unlike its predecessors, can affect not only small local communities but also minority group members, national populace, and global citizens. Reciprocal, affective, intercourse-driven, nonutilitarian solidarity does have concrete analytical benefits. It allows us to explore how we can resolve conflicts regarding classes, regions, generations and gender, and offers ways

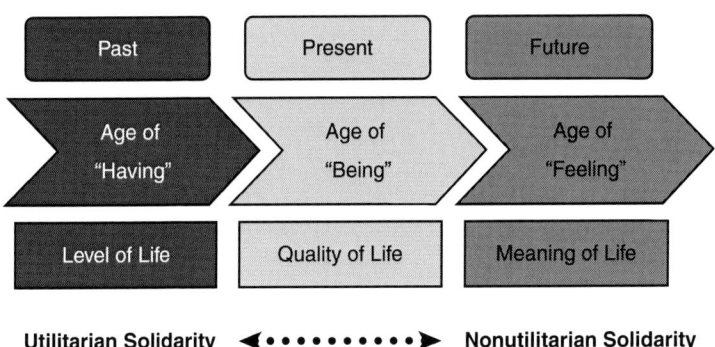

**Figure 8.5**  Transitions in central life-interest.

of examining how to surmount severe racial confrontations and terrorism. These are the potential gifts of the cosmopolitan paradigm, a pattern brought about by the new sociological imagination stemming from an empathetic consideration for the Other.

## CONCLUSION

Sociology was born of social crisis. Its main goal, in the beginning, was to inquire into social order, and it still holds true. Discussions on the formation of what Nicolai Foss describes as "spontaneous social order"[37] may be dichotomized into utilitarian and nonutilitarian perspectives. Traditionally, sociology has long been concentrating on explaining the maintenance of social order realized by nonutilitarian "invisible hands" such as shared values or functional interdependency.

The effectiveness of nonutilitarian solidarity can be appreciated in its three facets: a socioethical aspect that refers to its ability to surmount a society incapable of envisioning people as "species being"; a sociorighteous aspect where justifying public interests is promoted; and a socio-organizational aspect responsible for achieving social unity through collective sentiment. As far as South Korea is concerned, with its low fertility rate and weakening bonds even among relatives, the realization of social unity through amiable solidarity holds utmost importance.

Collective sentiment, with its "emotional reserve army," can be expected to become even more powerful than collective intelligence. Possible outlets for elated collective sentiment can be articulated by means of two ideal types. While the "road to social burning" leads us to the getaway of social segmentation or chaos, the other "road to social building" can usher us into the gateway of a new social order. What we need is intellectual capital that could guide collective sentiment in the right direction, thereby cultivating a society where everyone has a chance to win. Then, an "unbearable heartlessness of being" would be replaced by a "society worth living." Such intellectual potential could be realized by utilizing the cosmopolitan paradigm.

Cosmopolitan imagination stresses the communication between in- and out-groups by surmounting otherness. Also, it implies the possible formation of an alternative social order, fully utilizing the power of reason and sensibility through new-found horizontal solidarity based on amiable bonds. The cosmopolitan paradigm has the potential to move us beyond the logo-centric sociology of the past toward the dawn of a new, "human-centric Sociology 2.0" responding to both scientism and humanism.

# Notes

1. This work was supported by the National Research Foundation of Korea Grant funded by the Korean Government (NRF-2014S1A3A2044729). Manuel Castells, *The Rise of the Network Society* (Malden: Blackwell, 1996).
2. Ibid., 92–93.
3. Adam Smith, *The Wealth of Nations* (LaVergne: Simon & Brown, 2012 [1776]).
4. Karl Marx and Friedrich Engels, "Communist Manifesto," in *The Marx-Engels Reader*, ed. Robert Turker (New York: W.W. Norton, 1978 [1848]).
5. David Korten, *When Corporations Rule the World* (West Hartford: Kumarian Press, 1995).
6. Joseph Stiglitz, *Globalization and Its Discontents* (New York: W.W. Norton, 2002); Hal Sirkin and Jim Hemerling, *Globality: Competing with Everyone from Everywhere for Everything* (New York: Business Plus, 2008).
7. Daniel Cohen, *La Mondialisation Et Ses Ennemis* (Paris: Grasset & Fasquelle, 2004).
8. Tom Palmer, "Globalization Is Grrrreat," *Cato's Letter*, 1, 2 (2002), http://www.cato.org/sites/cato.org/files/pubs/pdf/catosletterv1n2.pdf
9. Jean-Pierre Warnier, *La Mondialisation de la Culture* (Paris: Editions La Decouverte et Syros, 2003 [1999]), 20.
10. Douglas Kellner, *Grand Theft 2000: Media Spectacle and a Stolen Election* (Lanham: Rowman & Littlefield, 2001).
11. Ulrich Beck, "The Cosmopolitan Society and Its Enemies," *Theory, Culture & Society*, 19, 1–2 (2002): 17–44.
12. Gerard Delanty, "The Cosmopolitan Imagination: Critical Cosmopolitanism and Social Theory," *British Journal of Sociology*, 57, 1 (2006): 25–47.
13. Immanuel Kant, "Perpetual Peace: A Philosophical Sketch," in *Kant: Political Writings 2nd and Enlarged Edition* (Cambridge: Cambridge University Press, 1994 [1795]), 93–130.
14. Seyla Benhabib, *The Rights of Others: Aliens, Residents, and Citizens* (Cambridge: Cambridge University Press, 2004).
15. Hannah Arendt, "Zionism Reconsidered," in *The Jew as Parish: Jewish Identity and Politics in the Modern Age* (New York: Grove Press, 1978 [1945]), 131–163.
16. Delanty, "The Cosmopolitan Imagination: Critical Cosmopolitanism and Social Theory."
17. Castells, *The Rise of the Network Society.*
18. John Urry, *Global Complexity* (Oxford: Polity, 2002).
19. Bruno Latour, *Reassembling the Social: An Introduction to Actor-Network Theory* (Oxford: Oxford University Press, 2005).

20. Zygmunt Bauman, *Liquid Modernity* (Cambridge: Polity Press, 2000).
21. Kwame Appiah, *Cosmopolitanism: Ethics in a World of Strangers* (New York: W.W. Norton, 2006).
22. Monde Displomatique, *L'atlas Du Monde Diplomatique* (Paris: Amnand Colin, 2006).
23. Robert Zajonc, "Social Facilitation," *Science* (New Series), 149 (1965): 269–274.
24. UN Committee on Elimination of Racial Discrimination, "Committee on Elimination of Racial Discrimination Considers Report of Republic of Korea," (October 26, 2007), http://www.unhchr.ch/huricane/huricane.nsf/view01
25. Jan Nederveen Pieterse, *Globalization and Culture: Global Melange* (Lanham: Rowman & Littlefield, 2004).
26. Benhabib, *The Rights of Others: Aliens, Residents, and Citizens.*
27. Appiah, *Cosmopolitanism: Ethics in a World of Strangers.*
28. Beck, "The Cosmopolitan Society and Its Enemies."
29. John Stuart Mill, *On Liberty* (Boston: Ticknor and Fields, 1863).
30. C. Wright Mills, *The Sociological Imagination* (Oxford: Oxford University Press, 1959).
31. Anthony Giddens, *The Consequences of Modernity* (Stanford: Stanford University Press, 1990), 64.
32. Emile Durkheim, *The Division of Labor in Society* (New York: Free Press, 1984 [1893]).
33. Erich Fromm, *To Have or to Be?* (New York: Continuum, 2005 [1976]).
34. Marcel Mauss, *The Gift: Forms and Functions of Exchange in Archaic Societies* (New York: W. W. Norton, 2000).
35. Bronislaw Malinowski, *Argonauts of the Western Pacific* (London: Routledge and Kegan Paul, 1922).
36. Georges Bataille, *The Accursed Share Vol. 1: Consumption* (New York: Zone Books, 1991 [1949]).
37. Nicolai Foss, "Spontaneous Social Order: Economics and Schutzian Sociology," *American Journal of Economics and Sociology*, 55 (2006): 73–86.

# 9

# A Netnographic Case Study of Western Expatriates' Attitudes Toward the Chinese in Shanghai

## Henrik Gert Larsen and Leslie Wolowitz

In the past two decades, China has received the lion's share of direct foreign investment and has evolved from an insulated agrarian society into the world's second largest economy. Observers noted that China has recently become increasingly assertive, especially in the aftermath of the global financial crisis.[1] The emergence of a new Chinese super-power is having a profound impact not only on South-East Asia, but also on the role of the United States as the primary arbiter of the post-World War II order—the so-called Pax Americana.[2] History is rich with examples of conflicts between established and emerging powers, and China, as it seeks to assert its national interests, will in all likeli-hood challenge the United States' global leadership.[3] Political scholars often cast international conflict in terms of economic or ideological struggles between powerful nations, but in today's interconnected world, where social media can ignite revolutions, it may be increas-ingly true that "the only remaining superpower is public opinion."[4]

International—or global—psychology is an emerging branch of psychology that focuses on the worldwide enterprise of psychology in terms of communication and networking, cross-cultural comparison, scholarship, practice, and pedagogy. Often, the terms international psychology, global psychology, and cross-cultural psychology are used interchangeably, but their purposes are subtly and importantly differ-ent: global means worldwide, international means across and between nations, cross-cultural means across cultures.[5] Part of understanding intercultural relations within the discipline of International Psychology is locating where pre-constructed stereotypes, not infrequently linked to a social and historical racist system, impact acculturation and propel intergroup conflicts. In this chapter, we present a psychological perspective on potential tensions between the West and China by focusing on conflicting sentiments and attitudes.

## SOCIAL PSYCHOLOGY: CULTURAL BELIEFS AND THREAT THEORY

Contemporary contact theory posits that intergroup contact dismantles stereotypes and reduces prejudice, and from this perspective it could be argued that the expanding economic integration between China and the United States could help defuse potential conflicts.[6] The validity of contact theory is supported by a recent meta-analysis of 515 studies and experiments documenting that European-American (White) test subjects increasingly appreciate Chinese characters or Asian faces proportionally with exposure time.[7] It has been argued, however, that contact studies have only demonstrated a correlation between exposure and positive intergroup attitudes, but not proved any causality. Increased intergroup contact may only accelerate the process of either conflict or coexistence that is already under way.[8] For example, acculturation research has documented that, even after prolonged contact, individuals may fail to appreciate any aspect of the "other" culture, leading to antagonistic acculturation, which manifests as dysfunctional communication, antisocial behavior, self-isolation, and cultural retrogression.[9] Consequently, sociologists have hypothesized that intergroup conflicts might be a function of the amount of contact and the extent of the differences in culture and interests.[10]

> In the impression of the overwhelming majority of Chinese people, Americans are all people who are honest, reliable, and of good moral character. However, once you've live in the country for a while, you'll discover you've been misled.[11]

Despite the ever-increasing contact between the United States and China, recent studies conducted by the Pew Research Center show that the mutual public perceptions are indeed on a negative trajectory.[12] In the United States, a majority now believes that China has overtaken, or will soon overtake, America as the world's leading superpower, with very negative consequences for the United States. Furthermore, people in the entire northern hemisphere perceive China's growing military power as a threat to the Western world, and the US public believes that China constitutes the greatest international threat to the United States, followed by Iran and North Korea.[13] Consequently, 78% of the US public is concerned that the national debt will make America beholden to a China hostile to American interests.[14] Many Americans fear that China's displacement of America as the world's largest economy will swiftly be followed by its rise to the status of military superpower.[15]

From a social psychology perspective, the above-cited studies indicate that the notion of threat is a significant component of the public perception of China. Intergroup threat theory operates with two categories of threats: realistic and symbolic. Realistic threats are fundamentally experiential.[16] However, social identity theory posits that, in the final analysis, all threats have symbolic meaning.[17] Thus, it is hypothesized that events are transformed into symbolic threats by culturally engrained self-understandings, such as superiority, injustice and vulnerability beliefs, distrust and helplessness, and that low-power groups are very susceptible to perceived persecution, whereas high-power groups tend to react more forcefully when challenged.[18]

The perception of China's economic competitiveness has indeed instilled a sense of vulnerability among Western social interest groups, where there is a growing sentiment that China is to blame for a range of unpopular welfare and labor market reforms.[19] It is also argued that China's success is challenging the Western belief that the attributes and institutions of liberal democracy are necessary preconditions for economic development.[20] Thus, observers theorize that the authoritarian development model China has come to symbolize is stimulating deep-rooted distrust of government and fear of authoritarianism.[21] Whether this is true or not, the Pew Research Center found that 68% of the US public believes that China cannot be trusted.[22] Chinese observers, however, contend that, while China is committed to peaceful development, the West is trying to blame China for its own declining influence in world affairs and that the United States has taken a submissive China for granted for too long.[23]

> Experience proves that it is those Asian countries which "draw a tiger with a cat as a model" and mechanically copy the U.S. democratic system which...lag in development.[24]

Scholars argue that the growing perception that American power is in relative decline has facilitated what is referred to as the US military and diplomatic pivot toward Asia, which, from a Chinese point of view, is an obvious attempt to contain China's growing influence.[25] This holds the potential for further tensions, as the Chinese national identity is largely defined by Western humiliations and colonization.[26] Thus, the waning favorability rating of the United States in China[27] may in part be driven by the perception of covert and overt attempts to thwart China's development.[28]

> There are some bored foreigners with full stomachs, who have nothing better to do than try to point fingers at our country. First, China does not export revolution; second, China doesn't export hunger and poverty; third, China doesn't come and cause you any headaches. Just what else do you want?[29]

From a social psychology perspective, it can therefore be argued that current and future US and China relations will be shaped by perceptions of threats infused with symbolic meanings derived from American beliefs of superiority and Chinese beliefs of injustice, as well as shared sentiments of vulnerability. In this connection, intergroup threat theories suggest that realistic threats are likely to trigger anger and fear, whereas symbolic threats may trigger emotions such as disgust, contempt, and rejection.[30] These emotions seem to be reflected both in the above quote by the new Chinese leader, and in the following quote by the former US Secretary of State Hillary Clinton:

> We do have to get tough on China…This country manipulates its currency to our disadvantage, they engage in broad-based intellectual property theft, industrial espionage…What do we get in return from them? Well, we get tainted pet food, we get lead-laced toys, we get polluted pharmaceuticals.[31]

It has been argued that the perception of threat causes dehumanization and infra-humanization of the out-group and, if the US public ends up perceiving the Chinese as cheating, stealing crooks out to poison them, it may inadvertently make open conflict more palatable in the public opinion.[32]

## COGNITIVE PSYCHOLOGY: CONTRADICTIONS AND AMBIGUITY

Although expression of intergroup conflict may at times seem extreme, cognitive theories imply that attitudes are not simply "black" or "white" sentiments, but are composed of several contradicting associations and experiences. The associative-propositional theory (APE) hypothesizes that attitudes are formed by simultaneously occurring emotional and rational processes, which may generate conflicting attitudinal input.[33] The dualism implied by the APE model is, however, rejected by cognitive neuroscientists, who posit that the human evaluative capacity is highly complex, causing attitude formation to be influenced by several integrated and iterative processes.[34] For example, research has demonstrated that the associative processes are highly context dependent, allowing for both positive and negative attitudes toward out-groups to manifest through subtle differences in stimuli.[35] It has been documented that individuals are able to believe prejudiced stereotypes, but at the same time recognize that familiar individuals from the out-group are different.[36] The Pew study also illustrates attitudinal inconsistencies; for example, while 52% of US respondents believe that China poses a major threat to the United States, the same respondents perceive Chinese people as neither aggressive (57%) nor violent (76%).[37] In addition, Chinese people are perceived to be as hard working and inventive as Americans, but at the same time less honest.[38]

Research into "belief complexity" has demonstrated that a complex and nuanced belief structure is positively correlated with moderate views; however, complex beliefs, which are characterized by ambiguity and conflicting notions, may also be a source of attitudinal extremism.[39] Thus, research has demonstrated that when subjects are presented with inconclusive data regarding contentious social issues, the results are attitudinal polarization rather than moderation.[40] It has further been argued that mutual acknowledgment and communication between individuals generate a perception of external norms, which makes it possible to economize mental resources in processing out-group information.[41] Consequently, individuals may also resolve feelings of ambiguity by deferring to perceived group norms, which are inherently prejudiced toward out-group members.[42] It is therefore argued that individuals express prejudice to the extent it is perceived as appropriate within their social context.[43]

In terms of US and China relations, there seems to be plenty of ambiguity. The US foreign policy toward China can best be described as ambiguous, with formal support for a unified China and de facto support for an independent Taiwan, as long as the island's government itself remains ambiguous about its aspirations.[44] From a US perspective, China's policy of noninterference in other countries' domestic affairs is also ambiguous, as it translates into overt and covert support for despotic anti-Western regimes such as North Korea and Sudan.[45] Thus, China is currently perceived as neither

friend nor foe, but perhaps an ambiguous "frenemy" with the potential for serious misperception of intentions and actions.

> China is rising, and it's not going away. They're neither our enemy nor
> our friend. They're competitors. But we have to make sure that we have
> enough military-to-military contact and forge enough of a relationship
> with them that we can stabilize the region.[46]

## NETNOGRAPHIC STUDY OF WESTERN ATTITUDES TOWARD THE CHINESE[47]

Scholars propose that attitudes can be inferred by the empirical observation of cognitive, affective, or behavioral manifestations, although
there is little agreement on exactly how to differentiate between these
in empirical research.[48] To this end, Eagly and Chaiken have proposed
a tripartite attitude construct consisting of: (1) evaluations, (2) attitude
objects, and (3) evaluative tendencies, where the latter is considered
to be the empirical measure of the actual attitude.[49] Consequently, it
is possible to quantify attitudes by applying a frequency distribution
of expressed opinions.[50]

Stangor observed that researchers have measured attitudes using
"whatever technology is most current."[51] Giles suggested that the
social media revolution opens a new realm for social research, where
the researcher can unobtrusively capture the naturally occurring commentary of lived experiences from postings in discussion forums and
subject these to statistical and qualitative analyses.[52] It is estimated
that more than a billion people are engaged in online communities
and social media interaction is fast becoming the most important
peer-to-peer influence channel.[53] Thus "netnography" has become an
emerging form of ethnography.[54]

With the purpose of generating insight into group attitudes toward
emerging China, a recent study by Larsen analyzed the social media
activity of predominantly Western foreigners in Shanghai.[55] Two
online communities were identified, with a combined membership of
around 100,000, and 56,000 discussion topics, more than 700 thematic interest groups, and more than 800,000 postings.[56] Through
a process of open coding and labeling of discussion threads in four
selected discussion forums (two from each community), a category
of 113 dense discussion threads relating to the encounters between
foreigners and the local Chinese population were identified. The subsequent thematic coding of these threads identified the most pervasive
components of this encounter discourse: (1) customs and behaviors of

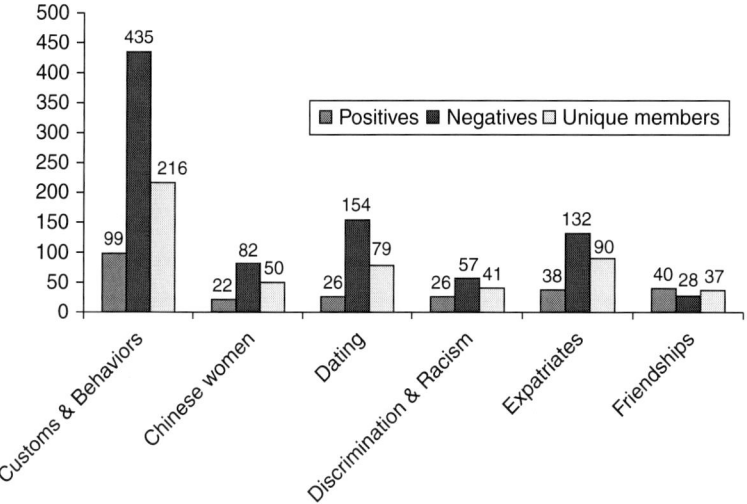

**Figure 9.1** Distribution of negative and positive evaluative statements within thematic categories.

the Chinese population, (2) Chinese women, (3) dating, (4) discrimination and racism, (5) perception of other expatriates encounters with the Chinese, and (6) friendships. The content was analyzed for opinions and evaluative statements relating to these six components, and categorized as either positive or negative. This yielded 251 positive and 888 negative evaluative statements originating for 401 unique community members. Thus, with 78% of the evaluative statements being negative, the results indicate a strong negative attitudinal tendency toward the local Chinese population in Shanghai. Figure 9.1 illustrates the distribution of positive and negative evaluative statements associated with the six identified components, as well as the number of unique community members per component.

This quantitative analysis makes it possible to develop a hypothesis of the attitudinal tendencies' relative strength. For example, dating is perceived relatively worse than the possibility of establishing friendships, and the community is more repulsed by the local customs and behaviors than by examples of discrimination and racism (see Table 9.1).

A 2009 media survey concluded that about 16% of the online population is responsible for around 80% of the influence, and researchers argue these "influentials" act as normative gatekeepers and define what opinions and behaviors are acceptable within the online communities.[57] Consequently, it can be argued that a representation of

**Table 9.1**   Relative strength of the encounter attitudes

| | |
|---|---|
| Dating | Negatives outnumber positives approximately 6:1 |
| Chinese women | Negatives outnumber positives approximately 4:1 |
| Customs and behavior | Negatives outnumber positives approximately 4:1 |
| Expatriates | Negatives outnumber positives approximately 3:1 |
| Discrimination and racism | Negatives outnumber positives approximately 2:1 |
| Friendships | Positives outnumber negatives approximately 2:1 |

influentials in the negative segment of this netnographic study would further support the conclusion that, at the group level, online communities harbor significant negative attitudes toward the Chinese population. By investigating the board status of the members with the largest share of the sampled negative statements, it was possible to document that six of these, constituting less than 0.007% of the largest community, generated around 11% of the content.

## QUALITATIVE ANALYSIS OF NEGATIVE ATTITUDINAL TENDENCY TOWARD CHINESE PEOPLE IN SHANGHAI

The next phase of the analysis consisted of an open coding of the associated meanings of the sampled negative statements, enabling Larsen to identify the actual content of the attitudinal tendencies within each of the six components from Table 9.1.[58] This provides the conclusion of the quantitative analysis with a more immediate insider perspective, characteristic of ethnographic methods. By selecting salient and representative quotes, Larsen's research—through the actual voices of the community members—acquires a degree of ecological validity.[59]

Within the Dating component, there was a clear tendency to judge local women as manipulative and "gold-digging," trading sex for material goods. The local Chinese women were perceived to date Western men for the purpose of securing themselves and their families financially, as illustrated by the following quote:

> I will never get accustomed to the way Chinese girls/women can use sex and money in the same sentence. Culturally, for them, it's ok to do this, but does it mean that if I don't like it that I'm being culturally insensitive? I think it's a disgusting aspect of Chinese culture.[60]

Foreigners who had Chinese wives and girlfriends were often described as naïve, as their relationships were judged as fake due to the perceived materialistic inclinations of these women.

Your wife is just with you because of your money. There are no human qualities you can offer. Apart from being funny when drunk.[61]

It was noted that Chinese men are not very interested in Western women, except for the desire to try sex with a white woman. The lack of interest from Chinese men was considered cultural, as it is assumed that they are looking for potential wives who can be accepted by their families. The community members who could be identified as women expressed that they found Chinese men unattractive, unable to hold a decent conversation, and bad lovers.

> "On average, a lower libido than me. Half of them wouldn't perform oral—"; "Chinese girls don't want that; so you shouldn't either…"; "Give me strength."[62]

The "Chinese women" component is related to the "dating component." This discourse further elaborates on the perceived moral shortcomings as well as the sexuality of Chinese women, where there seems to be a tendency for male community members to see Chinese women primarily as sexual objects.

> I got sick of chinese women, they r ok as sex toys but i wud never treast them as anything else. i despise the chinese people, nobody knows them like they know themselves. thats why any chinese given the chance (ie female) will do anything to marry a non-chinese.[63]

Paradoxically, the foreigners seem to be repulsed when these objectified women are perceived to utilize their sexuality as means to achieve control or benefits, which illustrates a double standard in what appears as the community member's transactional view of the relationship with local women. The tendency of the online communities was to evaluate Chinese women, and especially Shanghainese women, as "gold-diggers" who are willing to "sell" themselves to anyone who is willing to provide for them. From the quote below, it is interesting to note that while the male community member finds it reasonable that the Chinese woman relinquishes her job to serve his needs, she is perceived as a "whore" if she requires more security than just a promise.

> I put up a suggestion that she quit her job to be with me, and I'll provide for her…she said that maybe I could give her security by placing "1–2 years" of her salary with her, so in case anything happens, she have

something to fall back on. Is this not similar to paying a woman long term? (Hated to use the word whore.)[64]

The local Chinese people are in general portrayed as materialistic without the ability or willingness to embrace values appreciated by Westerners:

> Lack of caring about other people's happiness. And lack of caring about being happy. The thing Chinese people care about the least is happiness of others and even themselves. They would rather have money than be happy.[65]

Furthermore, Chinese people are also considered as lacking in moral fiber, lying, and cheating honest Westerners without shame.

> If you expect any of the local players here to be honest business people, you are either a fool, or extremely naive. The only thing they have learned here is how to screw people over.[66]

From time to time, the online community members blamed the Chinese culture and especially Confucianism for instilling morals norms absent of community spirit and empathy:

> the selfishness and lack of empathy that foreigners all seem to agree is a feature of modern Chinese society…I perceive it as being a deep-seated feature of the Confucian mindset.[67]

Consequently, many community members considered the Western societies to be more evolved due to specific cultural and religious values.

> In my humble opinion, as an observer of the Chinese "society" for many years, I do not think that a civil society will develop here unless there emerges a generation who have been completely exposed to Western ideas of society, particularly with emphasis upon the ideas of morality, duty and charity that underpins our societies, and which many of us try, and sometimes fail, to live up to. Although I'm not formally religious…I think that the answer to China's woes may be more Chinese becoming Christians—the ones that I know who are converts are certainly nicer human beings, charitable, caring and empathetic precisely because of their faith.[68]

It was recognized that some local people are "civilized" and that the manners of the younger generations are "better." However, the overwhelming perception seems to be that Chinese people's manners are repulsive:

> Too many dirty habits to discuss, globally they are the worst, even saw signs in Paris only in Chinese telling them not to spit. No English or French sign.[69]

This, in turn, let some community members to consider that the reason for China's perceived backwardness was not only cultural, but also racial.

> After five years in Shanghai, so many things still wind me up. I visit so many countries and find it is only the Chinese that are significantly "different." They are human, but surely a different type of human from the rest of the world...and they know it.[70]

The perceived lack of civility, prevalent dishonesty, an inferior culture, and a crude population motivated some community members to express that Western colonization was the reason why "other" developing countries possess a seemingly higher level of civility than China:

> if Shanghai had remained under British-dominated control until the 1990s, the society here would be similar to that in HK and Singapore. No one can deny that the fundamental reason for HK and Singapore's successful society is largely because of the influence of the former colonial power.[71]

This sentiment led others to express nostalgia for the past colonial order:

> I hate to say it, but we really need the Japanese to come back and slap some heads around. A week or so would do the trick. The Shanghainese would suddenly be nice people again after that experience.[72]

The community members express that there is no significant discrimination of foreigners when engaging governmental or public service institutions. There is, however, a strongly expressed perception of racism in everyday encounters. The Chinese are perceived to classify people based on the tone of their skin:

> the whole chinese [sic] culture revolves around with skin color. eveyrone [sic] is trying to get as white as possible and the darker you are, the worse ur treated.[73]

There is a perception that the local Chinese pander to foreigners and harbor the stereotypical views that a real Westerner is white and blonde. Consequently, community members expressed that it was difficult for nonwhites to find English language teaching positions.

> even if the black man gets rejected for teaching, it is nothing personal...to explain to all parents why the teacher is black is very time consuming.[74]

There are, however, paradoxes and ambiguities. On the one hand, the local Chinese are perceived as pandering to white people; on the other hand, many whites feel discriminated against and taken advantage of:

> I've heard people say in Shanghainese, "This guy is white...lets see how much we can get out of him." This is a racist country. I can barely walk into any shop without paying a 30% "white tax."[75]

Again, China's perceived backwardness was often used as an explanation for this phenomenon.

> I am a white guy and get treated like a dancing monkey all the time by the locals. That's China. Chinese people are very backward when it comes to dealing with people from outside their country.[76]

In terms of other foreigners, the community seems to perceive privileged expatriates to be as arrogant and entitled as the local Shanghainese with a propensity to similar xenophobic attitudes.

> Expats here are unbelievably jerkish. I can't quite pinpoint it. In every other countries I have been to expats seemed to give a **** about the country they lived in and learned the local language but in China they just isolate themselves in expat groups and try to learn as little as possible about China...They also have a hilarious sense of entitlement which I find fascinating.[77]

The community in general proposes two explanations for the negative behaviors of "other" foreigners. Some community members consider the inability to adjust to Chinese culture and especially the lack of language skills as the cause of antisocial behaviors:

> Fo [sic] sure you don't like China, because it's hard to be in a place for 9 ears [sic] and still not understand the basic language. That's why

you have 0 Chinese friends...You're frustrated so all you have is your keyboard to release all your anger.[78]

However, most are inclined to explain bad behaviors as a negative psychological reaction to the Chinese, who are depicted as less evolved than Westerners.

It's not expats [sic] fault they find China and Chinese people offensive to the senses. China and Chinese people ARE offensive to the senses. That's what makes China and it's people Chinese. As far as all the spitting, littering, pissing/defecating in the streets, inconsiderate behavior, lying, cheating etc. go...who cares? Let them do whatever the hell they want. It IS their country after-all. If they want to treat their nation as one giant toilette [sic], garbage dump, and/or monkey cage, then let them...if anything, Chinese and their behavior should make you feel proud not to be from China![79]

Consequently, most expatriates seem to prefer establishing friendships with someone from their own cultural background and, with so many foreigners in Shanghai, it is not necessary to make the effort with the local Chinese:

A point I made earlier is the majority of ex-pats in Shanghai and China in general do not mix with local Mainland Chinese rather they seek out other ex-pat friends.[80]

Several expatriates express that they have good and loyal Chinese friends, but the predominant view is that most foreigners have no interest in establishing friendships with locals, as they are only in China for work and not as immigrants. Thus positive constructions of Chinese individuals seem to function as an exception to the rule rather than as a challenge to existing stereotypes in the narrative conversation of the blog.

They came from UK or the States to do a job for a few years. They are determined only to mix with other expats, and keep their lives as close as possible to their western standards and customs.[81]

## Conceptualization

Grounded theory moves toward conceptualization through axial coding of thematic sub-categories generated from open coding of content. To this end, the authors applied here the central theoretical paradigm in which the sub-categories were classified as: (1) casual conditions, (2) phenomenon, (3) context, (4) intervening conditions, (5) actions/interactions, and (6) consequences (see Figure 9.2).[82]

The purpose of grounded theory is not to prove or disprove theories, but to develop hypotheses. The grounded analysis (Figure 9.2) indicates that the community members' perception of Chinese people

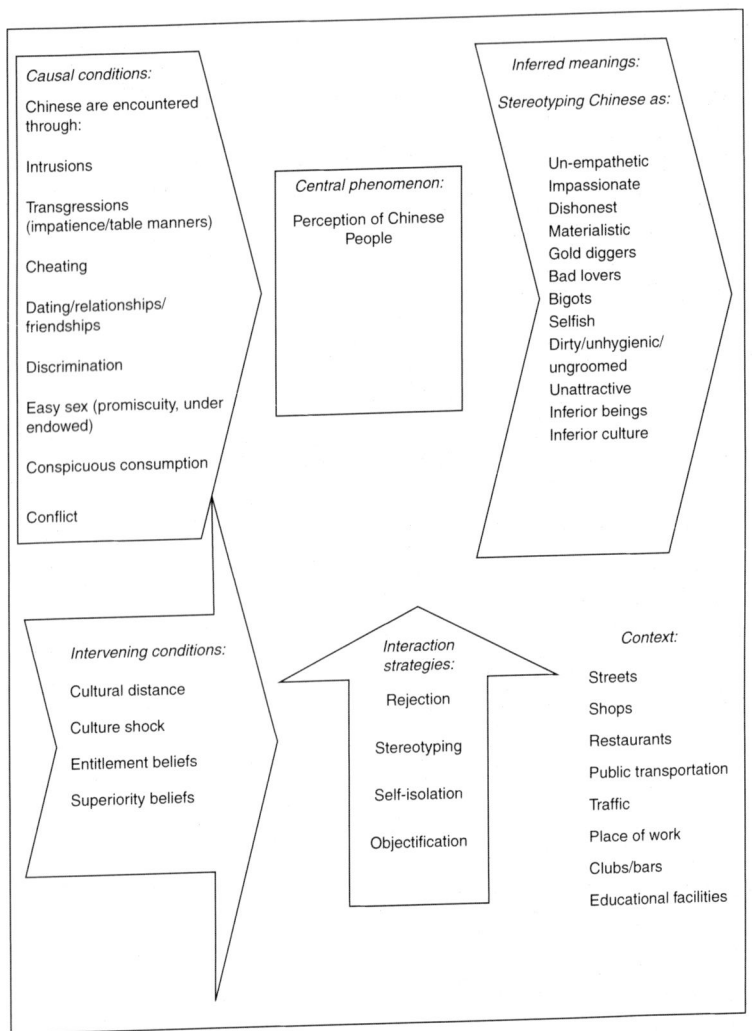

**Figure 9.2** Grounded theory conceptualization of foreigners' perception of the Chinese population in Shanghai.

is shaped by negative encounters. These are mediated by entitlement and superiority beliefs, as well as cultural distance, which give rise to negative interaction strategies, such as stereotyping, rejection, and self-isolation, leading to the formation and articulation of prejudiced and racist attitudes. For example, the experience of having been cheated by a Chinese person may be mediated by cultural distance and beliefs in one's own moral superiority, leading the group member to stereotype Chinese people as inherently dishonest. Other group members with similar experiences add their narratives to the thread and, as the thread grows, it appears that this sentiment is an acceptable group norm. Similarly, the experience of Chinese girls wanting material benefits out of their relationships with foreigners may be mediated by cultural distance and entitlement beliefs, leading community members to reject this behavior as prostitution. The more members who concur or have similar experiences, the more the group perspective constructs the attitude that Chinese girls, in general, are materialistic gold-diggers or prostitutes. These stereotypes appear to solidify if influentials, through their postings, demonstrate approval, and if eloquent community members manage to provide an elaborate cultural and racial explanation for why these stereotypes are true and, thereby, elevate the prejudice from a group norm to what may be perceived as an empirically proven fact.

## Discussion

Contact theory hypothesizes that intergroup contact would dismantle stereotypes. Therefore, individuals with experience such as the China-based expatriates should be less prejudiced than, for example, the US-based respondents of the earlier cited studies conducted by the Pew Research Center.[83] Although most contact studies demonstrate positive effects regardless of the conditions, researchers have concluded that certain intermediate variables increase the likelihood of a positive outcome from intergroup contacts.[84] For example, positive outcomes can occur given equality, common goals, and a common language when the contact is voluntary and when the preexisting out-group perceptions are not overtly negative.[85] Thus research has documented that for example Chinese language skills and cultural competencies are predictive of China-based expatriates' positive psychosocial adjustment.[86]

However the above conceptualization does not support the hypothesis that contact reduces prejudice in out-group attitudes.[87] Our study demonstrates how embedded negative attitudes and perceptions may impact intercultural contact, both reinforcing and creating psychological conflict and distance. We show how the absence of the above mentioned intermediate variables, as well as interpersonal and individual conflict and acculturative stress, then magnifies these negative stereotypes, thus diminishing the potential for constructive intercultural contact.

Several community members noted in their posts that the professional expatriates are typically not interested in learning anything about China, due to their arrogance and/or the temporary nature of their stay.[88] Consistent with this notion, many of the sampled statements made by expatriates on the discussion boards project an identity, which could be characterized as "urban villagers" in an online ethnic enclave, rallying behind pre-contact cultural values and an antagonistic acculturation paradigm.[89] Thus research has indicated that a key factor in the psychosocial well-being of Westerners in China is the size of the social network with people from their own culture, where no positive impact can be measured from relationships with local Chinese.[90] In this connection, research has documented that Western expatriates who congregate in cultural homogeneous communities have a tendency to readily assume group-norms.[91] It can be argued that an online community amplifies this de-individuation phenomenon, as perceived anonymity allows the community members to discount the "social desirability" factor and display antisocial attitudes without inhibitions.[92]

Perhaps as a consequence of the expatriates' career-mitigated migration, the encounters with the local Chinese become "transactional" rather than based on equality and common goals. As most expatriates are in China to perform a job or conclude a project, these individuals may perceive the role of the local Chinese as facilitators of their "mission" in China and, consequently, they end up serving as a repository for all that is usurious in these transactional relationships. In this connection, some scholars posit that globalization is in some ways a continuation of colonialism, and that Westerners in Shanghai represent a clear "linguistic, cultural and ethnic" linkage to the colonial settlers of the nineteenth and twentieth centuries.[93] They argue that the settlement of Western expatriates within the former concession areas of Shanghai induces a colonial nostalgia, a "longing" for colonial rule that was identified by Larsen.[94] The outcome could be described a neocolonial culture of domination and racism toward the Chinese in Shanghai, reflecting stereotypes that have been part of the Western cultural lexicon for centuries, as was the case with the Anti-Chinese movement in the United States during the nineteenth century. For example, the inference by some of the online community members that the local Chinese in Shanghai are inferior, dishonest, materialistic, selfish and that the women are gold-diggers echoes an 1876 comment in the *Mariner Journal* about the Chinese immigrants to California: "That his sister is a prostitute from instinct...That American men, women and children cannot be what free people should be and compete with such degraded creatures in the labor market...they defy the law and keep up the manners and customs of China and utterly disregard all the laws of health, decency and morality." Similarly, Richard Seddon, Prime Minister of New Zealand (1893–1906) argued that Chinese immigrants should not be allowed into the British Empire due to their "unsanitary character."[95] The "other" becomes the embodiment in all that is rejected in the "self." Thus the Western sojourner's quest for material goods and success is often projected into the preexisting perception of Chinese character traits, rather than evaluated in a context of mutual transaction or cultural misunderstanding.

Expatriate community members often postulated that the Chinese are incapable of the same nuanced emotional responses as Westerners, such as empathy, real love, and happiness.[96] These examples of infrahumanization indicate that not only do the online community members' attitudes rest upon preexisting racial attitudes, but also that these attitudes might be facilitated by a sense of symbolic threat to ingrained white superiority beliefs caused by the rapid economic ascension of China.[97] In this connection, research has documented that white people feel more threatened and express more prejudice when other ethnic groups are perceived to have similar job-related competencies.[98] This development is illustrated by the changing fortunes of many expatriates in Shanghai, who now struggle to compete with the local workforce and uphold a standard of living consistent with their neocolonial identity.[99]

Due to the unique historical circumstances of Shanghai, the city's Western expatriates are ambiguously positioned in a simultaneously postcolonial and postsocialist reality, where the first implies privilege and dominance, and the latter liberalization and equality.[100] These contradicting realities seem to infuse the lived experiences with a degree of ambivalence, where Westerners express a desire to discover China, but at the same time reject and ridicule cultural practices when they contradict commonly held Western beliefs.[101] Similarly, Larsen identified that many expatriate men are attracted to, and in relationships with, Chinese women, but at the same time readily label them as gold-diggers.[102] These men look down on the conspicuous consumption of the Chinese, but at the same time recognize that the rapid economic development is the basis of their livelihoods and careers in Shanghai. In this connection, cognitive theories suggest that white people's conflicting associations regarding other ethnicities threaten their self-concept, causing them to resolve this ambivalence by amplifying either positive or negative aspects of their out-group attitudes.[103] Furthermore, with prejudiced group norms firmly entrenched, individual attitudes may only change positively if an out-group member's behavior is strongly inconsistent with the group norms, and when he or she is perceived as a typical representative of the out-group.[104] However, we find that this is not happening among the expatriates in Shanghai.[105] Although community members often stated that they had trusted loyal Chinese friends, girlfriends, or wives, the general sentiment was that these were exceptions and most Chinese conformed to the general stereotypes.

Acculturation research has demonstrated that Western expatriates experience confusion and ambiguity in China, and local psychologists point out that whatever the intermediate psychological mechanism may be, this quite often manifests as anger, anxiety, frustration,

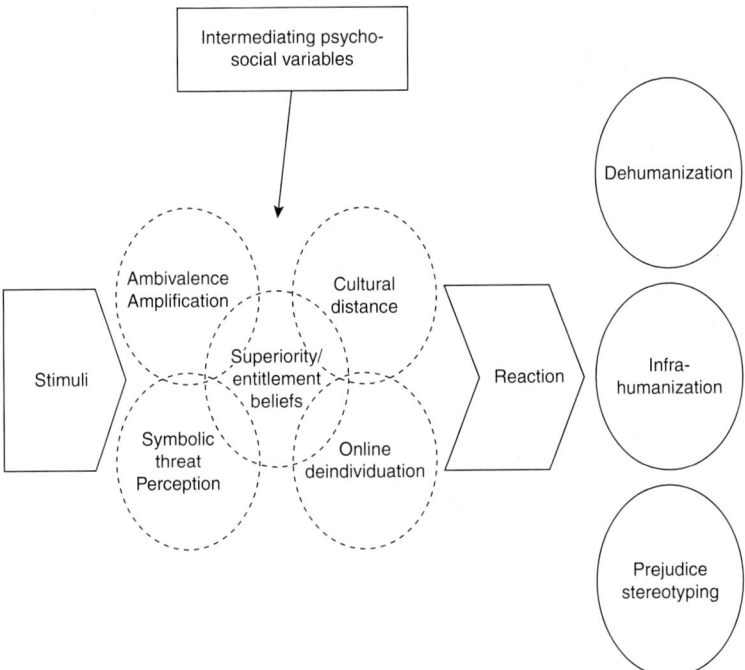

**Figure 9.3** Hypothesis of psychological mechanisms facilitating prejudice among foreigners in Shanghai.

criticism, prejudice, and withdrawal, causing 30–50% of expatriates to leave China earlier than planned.[106] Figure 9.3 illustrates how the discussed psychosocial mechanisms might be facilitating the manifestation of the prejudiced attitudes documented by Larsen.[107]

## CONCLUSION

Applying theories from social and cognitive psychology to a netnographic study of online communities catering to foreigners in Shanghai has provided what may appear as a somewhat surprising perspective on intergroup attitudes. The study[108] identified strong prejudices against Chinese people and China within a culturally immersed population of predominantly Western expatriates and visitors. The authors believe that traditional qualitative and experimental research methods would have been less likely to produce similar insights for the following reasons: (a) most people are aware of the social stigma associated with being identified as, for example, a bigot or a racist and traditional research subjects would avoid revealing controversial thoughts and feelings, and (b) experimental studies relying on deception as a means of soliciting prejudice responses arguably suffer from a lack of ecological validity, due to the use of that deception. It could be argued that traditional ethnographic approaches could yield similar insights. However, this method relies to a certain degree on creating a social relationship between the researcher and the researched community and the question remains whether a traditional ethnographic researcher can ever assume a neutral social position and truly account for the effects of his or her presence. In contrast, the unobtrusive netnographic approach provides a new method for gaining insights into the more controversial aspects of intergroup perceptions with a high degree of ecological validity as the researchers study the naturally occurring exchanges between community members without having to rely on deception or the establishment of social relations, which may act as confounding variables.

The analysis of the sampled discussion threads indicates that the prejudiced attitudes may have strengthened due to everyday transactional contact between the Western online community members and the local Chinese population in Shanghai. This goes against the grain of some of the earlier referenced intercultural contact and exposure theories, but this outcome can be explained by the effect of the intermediate psychosocial variables illustrated in Figure 9.3, and perhaps by the notion that individuals are more inclined to express what is truly on their minds when offered the anonymity of the Internet and a receptive community. It is therefore possible to hypothesize that, for many, China may have come to represent a symbolic threat to Western superiority and entitlement beliefs, which may give rise to or stimulate preexisting prejudice and negative attitudes among Westerners experiencing the rapid development of China first hand.

## NOTES

1. Michael D. Swaine, "Perceptions of an Assertive China," *China Leadership Monitor*, 32 (2010), http://www.hoover.org/publications/china-leadership-monitor/article/5297
2. Ronald Steel, *Pax Americana* (New York: Viking Press, 1970).
3. Aaron L. Friedberg, "The Future of U.S.-China Relations: Is Conflict Inevitable?" *International Security*, 76, 2 (2005): 7–45.
4. Anne Alexander, "Internet Role in Egypt's Protests," *BBC News*, February 9, 2011, http://www.bbc.co.uk/news/world-middle-east-12400319; Simon Anholt, "Explained," http://www.simonanholt.com/Explained/explained-introduction.aspx
5. Michael J. Stevens and Uwe P. Gielen (eds.), *Toward a Global Psychology: Theory, Research, Intervention, and Pedagogy* (Mahwah, NJ: Lawrence Erlbaum Associates, 2007).
6. Hugh D. Forbes, *Ethnic Conflict: Commerce, Culture and the Contact Hypothesis* (New Haven, CT: Yale University Press, 1997), 73; Friedberg, "The Future of U.S.-China Relations."
7. Thomas F. Pettigrew and Linda R. Tropp, "A Meta-Analytic Test of Intergroup Contact Theory," *Journal of Personality and Social Psychology*, 90, 5 (2006): 751–783, doi:10.1037/0022–3514.90.5.751; Robert B. Zajonc, "Attitudinal Effects of Mere Exposure," *Journal of Personality and Social Psychology*, 9, 2 (1968): 1–27, doi:10.1037/h0025848; Leslie A. Zebrowitz, Benjamin White, and Kristin Wieneke, "Mere Exposure and Racial Prejudice: Exposure to Other-Race Faces Increases Liking for Strangers of That Race," *Social Cognition*, 26, 3 (2008): 259–275, doi:10.1521/soco.2008.26.3.259.
8. Forbes, *Ethnic Conflict*, 74.
9. Riki Takeuchi et al., "A Model of Expatriate Withdrawal-Related Outcomes: Decision Making from a Dualistic Adjustment Perspective," *Human Resource Management Review*, 15, 2 (2001): 119–138, doi:10.1016/j.hrmr.2005.04.002.; Hirano Kenichiro, "Acculturation for Resistance," *Journal of Cultural Interaction in East Asia*, 1 (2010): 27–56, http://www.sciea.org/data-j01/04_Articles2_Hirano.pdf; David Matsumoto, Seung Hee Yoo, and Jeffrey A. LeRoux, "Emotion and Intercultural Communication," in *Handbook of Intercultural Communication*, ed. Helga Kotthoff and Helen Spencer-Oatey (Berlin: Mouton de Gruyter Publishers, 2009), 77–97; Over emphasis on pre-contact cultural elements; Kenichiro, "Acculturation for Resistance."
10. Forbes, *Ethnic Conflict*, 82.

11. "The Americans You Don't Know," *People's Daily*, May 22, 2013.
12. Pew Research Center, *U. S. Public, Experts Differ on China Policies. Public Deeply Concerned About China's Economic Power*, September 18, 2012, http://www.pewglobal.org/2012/09/18/u-s-public-experts-differ-on-china-policies/
13. Pew Research Center, *China Seen Overtaking U.S. as Global Superpower U.S. Favorability Ratings Remain Positive*, July 13, 2011, http://www.pewglobal.org/2011/07/13/china-seen-overtaking-us-as-global-superpower/; Pew Research Center, *China's Economic Power*.
14. Pew Research Center, *How Americans and Chinese View Each Other*, November 1, 2012, http://www.pewglobal.org/2012/11/01/how-americans-and-chinese-view-each-other/
15. "America and China. The Summit," *The Economist*, June 3, 2013, http://www.economist.com/news/leaders/21579003-barack-obama-and-xi-jinping-have-chance-recast-centurys-most-important-bilateral
16. Walter G. Stephan, Oscar Ybarra, and Kimberly Rios Morrison, "Intergroup Threat Theory," in *Handbook of Prejudice, Stereotyping and Discrimination*, ed. Todd D. Nelson (New York: Psychology Press, 2009), 44.
17. Kenneth Liberthal and William Davidson, "American Perceptions of China." Annual Lecture in Honor of A. Doak Barnett and Michel Oksenberg, Shanghai, March 1, 2006, http://www.ncuscr.org/files/2006-B-O_lecture.pdf
18. Roy J. Eidelson and Judy I. Eidelson, "Dangerous Ideas: Five Beliefs that Propel Groups Towards Conflict," *American Psychologist*, 58, 3 (2003): 182–192, doi:10.1037/0003–066X.58.3.182.
19. Liberthal and Davidson, "American Perceptions of China."
20. Ibid.
21. Swaine, "Perceptions of an Assertive China"; Peter Hayes Gries, "Problems of Misperception in U.S.-China Relations," *Orbis*, 53, 2 (2009): 220–232.
22. Pew Research Center, *China's Economic Power*.
23. Swaine, "Perceptions of an Assertive China."
24. *People's Daily*, July 11, 2012.
25. Justin Logan, "China, America, and the Pivot to Asia," *Policy Analysis*, 717 (2013): 1–28, http://www.cato.org/sites/cato.org/files/pubs/pdf/pa717.pdf
26. Gries, "Problems of Misperception."
27. Pew Research Center, *How Americans and Chinese View Each Other*.
28. Pew Research Center, *How Americans and Chinese View Each Other*; Bonnie S. Glaser, "Pivot to Asia: Prepare for Unintended Consequences," in *2012 Global Forecast Risk, Opportunity, and the Next Administration*, ed. Craig Cohen and Josiane Gabel (Washington, DC: Center for Strategic and International Studies, 2012), 22–24.
29. Xi Jinping (Mexico, 2009), quoted in "Xi Head Man of China's Future," *Euronews*, November 14, 2011, http://m.euronews.com/index.php?lang=en&article=1556462
30. Stephan, Ybarra, and Morrison, "Intergroup Threat Theory," 51.

31. Hillary Clinton, May 2008, quoted in The USC U.S.-China Institute, "Talking Points: January 14–28, 2009," http://www.china.usc.edu /ShowArticle.aspx?articleID=1318

32. Infrahumanization refers to the perception that the out-group members are only able to experience some basic animalistic emotions, such as anger and pleasure, and not the subtle emotions felt by in-group members such as guilt or empathy; Stephan, Ybarra, and Morrison, "Intergroup Threat Theory," 51.

33. Bertram Gawronski, "Unraveling the Processes Underlying Evaluation: Attitudes from the Perspective of the APE Model," *Social Cognition*, 25, 5 (2007): 687–717, doi:10.1521/soco.2007.25.5.687.

34. Associative propositional evaluation model; Jay J. Van Bavel, Y. Jenny Xiao, and William A. Cunningham, "Evaluation is a Dynamic Process: Moving Beyond Dual System Models," *Social and Personality Psychology Compass*, 6, 6 (2012): 438–454, doi:10.1111/j.1751–9004.2012.00438.x

35. Bertram Gawronski and Galen V. Bodenhausen, "Associative and Propositional Processes in Evaluation: An Integrative Review of Implicit and Explicit Attitude Change," *Psychological Bulletin*, 132, 5 (2006): 692–731, doi:10.1037/0033–2909.132.5.692.

36. J. S. Osland, "The Hero's Adventure: The Overseas Experience of Expatriate Business People." Doctoral Diss., Case Western Reserve University, Psychology, Cleveland, Ohio, 1990.

37. Pew Research Center, *How Americans and Chinese View Each Other*.

38. Ibid.

39. Alice H. Eagly and Shelly Chaiken, "The Advantages of an Inclusive Definition of Attitude," *Social Cognition*, 25, 5 (2007): 582–602, doi:10.1521/soco.2007.25.5.582.

40. Charles G. Lord, Lee Ross, and Mark R. Lepper, "Biased Assimilation and Attitude Polarization. The Effects of Prior Theories on Subsequently Considered Evidence," *Journal of Personality and Social Psychology*, 37, 11 (1979): 2098–2109, doi:10.1037//0022–3514.37.11.2098.

41. Charles Stangor, *Social Groups in Action and Interaction* (New York: Psychology Press, 2004); R. Boyd and Peter J. Richerson, "Gene–Culture Coevolution and the Evolution of Social Institutions," in *Better Than Conscious? Decision Making, the Human Mind, and Implications for Institutions, Strungmann Forum Reports*, ed. Cristoph Engel and Wolf Singer (Cambridge, MA: MIT Press, 2008), 305–324.

42. Samuel Bowles, Jung-Kyoo Choi, and Astrid Hofensitz, "The Co-evolution of Individual Behaviors and Social Institutions," *Journal of Theoretical Biology*, 223, 2 (2003): 135–147, doi:10.1016/ S0022–5193(03)00060–2.

43. Charles Stangor, "The Study of Stereotyping, Prejudice, and Discrimination within Social Psychology. A Quick History of Theory and Research," in *Handbook of Prejudice, Stereotyping and Discrimination*, ed. Todd Nelson (New York: Psychology Press, 2009), 5.

44. Pan Zhongqi, "US Taiwan Policy of Strategic Ambiguity: A Dilemma of Deterrence," *Journal of Contemporary China*, 12, 35 (2003): 387–407, doi:10.1080/1067056022000054678.

45. Daniel Large, "China and the Contradictions of Non-Interference' in Sudan," *Review of African Political Economy*, 35, 115 (2008): 93–106, doi:10.1080/03056240802011568.

46. Barack Obama (2007), *2008 Democratic Primary Presidential Debate Hosted by MSNBC*, transcription available on *The New York Times*, http://www.nytimes.com/2007/04/27/us/politics/27debate_transcript.html?pagewanted=1&_r=2

47. Netnography is essentially the ethnographic study of online communities with the application of both quantitative and qualitative methods.

48. Russell H. Fazio and Richard E. Pettey, "Conceptualizing Attitudes," in *Attitudes, Their Structure, Function and Consequences*, ed. Russell H. Fazio and Richard E. Pettey (New York: Psychology Press, 2008), 1–5; Anthony R. Pratkanis, Steven J. Breckler, and Anthony G. Greenwald, *Attitude Structure and Function* (Hillsdale, NJ: Laurence Erlbaum Associates Publishers, 1989).

49. Alice H. Eagly and Shelly Chaiken, *The Psychology of Attitudes* (Fort Worth, TX: Harcourt Brace Jovanovich College Publishers, 1993), 10–12; Eagly and Chaiken, "The Advantages of an Inclusive Definition of Attitude."

50. Russell H. Fazio and Richard E. Pettey, "Measurement of Attitudes," in *Attitudes, Their Structure, Function and Consequences*, Russell H. Fazio and Richard E. Pettey, eds. (New York, NY: Psychology Press, 2008), 33–38.

51. Stangor, "Study of Stereotyping," 5.

52. Martin Giles, "A Special Report on Social Networking: A World of Connections," *Social Commerce Today* (2010), http://www.socialcommercetoday.com/downloads/Economist_Social_Networking_Special_Report.pdf

53. Robert V. Kozinets, *Netnography. Doing Ethnographic Research Online* (London: Sage Publications, 2010); Deloitte, *A New Breed of Brand Advocates: Social Networking Redefines Consumer Engagement*, 2009, https://www.deloitte.com/assets/Dcom-UnitedStates/Local%20Assets/Documents/Consumer%20Business/US_CP_BrandAdvocates Study_020910.pdf

54. Robert V. Kozinets, "On Netnography: Initial Reflections on Consumer Research Investigations of Cyberculture," *Advances in Consumer Research*, 25 (1998): 366–371, http://www.acrwebsite.org/volumes/display.asp?id=8180

55. Henrik G. Larsen, "Shanghai—'Better City Better Life?' A Netnographic Study of Expatriate Attitudes." Doctoral Diss., The Chicago School of Professional Psychology, Chicago, 2012.

56. Shanghaiexpat.com and shanghaistuff.com

57. Jacques Booghin, Jonathan Doogan, and Ole Jørgen Vetvik, "A New Way to Measure Word-of-Mouth Marketing," *McKinsey Quarterly* (2010), http://www.mckinseyquarterly.com/A_new_way_to_measure_word -of-mouth_marketing_2567; Zuberance Report, *Brand Advocate Data & Insights*, 2011, http://www.zuberance.com/ downloads/brand AdvocateInsights.pdf; Scott A. Golder and Judith Donath, *Social Roles in Electronic Communities*, Association of Internet Researchers (AoIR), Conference Internet Research 5.0. Brighton, UK, 2004, http://web .media.mit.edu/~golder/projects/roles/golder2004.pdf

58. Larsen, *Netnographic Study*, 78–165.

59. Ibid.; The National Science Foundation recommends that data gathered from secondary sources should be de-identified. The user names of the quoted community members are known to the author, but not their actual identities. Source: http://www.nsf.gov/bfa/dias/policy /hsfaqs.jsp#secondarynly the pseudonyms; Ecological validity means that the methods, materials, and setting of a study must approximate the real world conditions that are being examined.

60. Blogger 1.

61. Blogger 2.

62. Blogger 3.

63. Blogger 4.

64. Blogger 5.

65. Blogger 6.

66. Blogger 7.

67. Blogger 8.

68. Blogger 9.

69. Blogger 10.

70. Blogger 11.

71. Blogger 9.

72. Blogger 12.

73. Blogger 13.

74. Blogger 2.

75. Blogger 14.

76. Blogger 15.

77. Blogger 16.

78. Blogger 2.

79. Blogger 17.

80. Blogger 18.

81. Blogger 19.

82. Larsen, *Netnographic Study*; Anselm Strauss and Juliet Corbin, *Basics of Qualitative Research: Grounded Theory Procedures and Techniques* (Newbury Park, CA: Sage Publications, 1990), 96–99; The phenomenon is defined as the central idea or concept toward which certain actions or interactions are directed. Causal conditions are the variables that give rise to the phenomenon. The context refers to the location of the phenomenon and the setting in which actions are taken. Intervening

conditions refer to the conditions that may limit or facilitate the actions. Action or interaction is defined as the set of strategies to manage or respond to the phenomenon. Consequence is the result of the interaction between the phenomenon and action or interaction.

83. Larsen, *Netnographic Study.*

84. Thomas F. Pettigrew, "Intergroup Contact Theory," *Annual Review of Psychology*, 49 (1998): 65–85, doi:10.1146/annurev.psych.49.1.65.

85. Ibid.; Ulrich Wagner and Uwe Machleit, "'Gastarbeiter' in the Federal Republic of Germany: Contacts between Germans and Migrant Population," in *Contact and Conflict in Intergroup Encounters*, ed. Miles Hewstone and Rupert Brown (Oxford: Blackwell, 1986), 59–78; Rachel Ben-Ari and Yehuda Amir, "Contact between Arab and Jewish Youth in Israel: Reality and Potential," in *Contact and Conflict in Intergroup Encounters*, ed. Miles Hewstone and Rupert Brown (Oxford: Blackwell, 1986), 45–58.

86. Sylvia Xiaohua Chen, Verónica Benet-Martinez, and Michael Harris Bonds, "Bicultural Identity, Bilingualism, and Psychological Adjustment in Multicultural Societies: Immigration-Based and Globalization-Based Acculturation," *Journal of Personality*, 76, 4 (2008): 803–838, doi:10.1111/j.1467–6494.2008.00505.x; Jan Selmer, "To Train or Not to Train? European Expatriate Managers in China," *Cross Cultural Management*, 2, 1 (2002): 137–151, doi:10.1 177/1470595802002001087.

87. Larsen, *Netnographic Study.*

88. Ibid.

89. Ibid; James Farrer, "'New Shanghailanders' or 'New Shanghainese': Western Expatriates' Narratives of Emplacement in Shanghai," *Journal of Ethnic and Migration Studies*, 36, 8 (2010): 1211–1228, doi:10.1080/13691831003687675; Kenichiro, "Acculturation for Resistance."

90. Saskia Sassen, *Territory-Authority-Rights: From Medieval to Global Assemblages* (Princeton, NJ: Princeton University Press, 2006), 300; Xiaoyun Wang and Rabindra N. Kanungo, "Nationality, Social Network and Psychological Well-Being: Expatriates in China," *International Journal of Human Resource Management*, 15, 4 (2004): 775–779, doi:1 0.1080/0958519042000192942; Xiangyang Liu, "An Investigation of Expatriate Adjustment and Performance: A Social Capital Perspective," *International Journal of Cross-Cultural Management*, 5, 3 (2004): 235–254, doi:10.1177/1470595805058411.

91. Gail Cort Ambuske, "A Narrative Analysis of the Subjective Experience of US Expatriate Managers." Doctoral Diss., Case Western Reserve University, The Weatherhead School of Management, 1990.

92. A process where the spread of emotions and perceived anonymity induces individuals to behave without their normal restraints; The awareness that prejudiced attitudes are no longer socially acceptable and, therefore, should be suppressed in public settings; Stangor, *Social Groups in Action,*

9–10; Galen V. Bodenhausen, Andrew R. Todd, and Jennifer A. Richeson, "Controlling Prejudice and Stereotyping. Antecedents, Mechanisms and Contexts," in *Handbook of Prejudice, Stereotyping and Discrimination*, ed. Todd D. Nelson (New York: Psychology Press, 2009), 115.

93. Ingrid Huygens, "From Colonization to Globalization: Continuities in Colonial 'common sense,'" in *Critical Psychology. An Introduction*, ed. Dennis Fox, Isaac Prilleltensky, and Stephanie Austin (London: Sage Publications, 2009), 269; Farrer, "Western Expatriates' Narratives."

94. The concession areas of Shanghai were ceded to foreign colonial powers from 1842, at the end of the First Opium War, until 1946; Farrer, "Western Expatriates' Narratives"; Larsen, *Netnographic Study*.

95. Elmer Clarence Sandmeyer and Roger Daniels, *The Anti-Chinese Movement in California* (Urbana: University of Illinois Press, 1991), 25; Jeremy Martens, "Richard Seddon and Popular Opposition in New Zealand to the Introduction of Chinese Labour into the Transvaal, 1903–1904," *New Zealand Journal of History*, 42, 2 (2008): 176–195.

96. Larsen, *Netnographic Study*.

97. Stephan, Ybarra, and Morrison, "Intergroup Threat Theory," 51; Joel Kovel, *White Racism: A Psychohistory* (New York: Pantheon Books, 1984), 4.

98. Michael A. Zarate, Berenice Garcia, Azenett A. Garza, and Robert T. Hitlan, "Cultural Threat and Perceived Realist Group Conflicts as Dual Predictors of Prejudice," *Journal of Experimental Social Psychology*, 40, 1 (2004): 99–105, doi:10.1016/S0022–1031(03)00067–2.

99. Farrer, "Western Expatriates' Narratives."

100. Ibid.

101. Qi Tang, "Foreigners' Archive—Contemporary China in the Blogs of American Expatriates." Doctoral Diss., Bowling Green State University, 2008.

102. Larsen, *Netnographic Study*.

103. Eagly and Chaiken, *The Psychology of Attitudes*, 125.

104. Myron Rothbart and Oliver P. John, "Social Categorization and Behavioral Episodes: A Cognitive Analysis of the Effects of Intergroup Contact," *Journal of Social Issues*, 41, 3 (1985): 81–104, doi:10.1111/j.1540–4560.1985.tb01130.x.

105. Larsen, *Netnographic Study*.

106. Keith Goodall and Malcolm Warner, "Expatriate Managers in China: The Influence of Chinese Culture on Cross-Cultural Management," *Journal of General Management*, 32, 2 (2007): 57–77; Thomas McKinley, "It's All the Rage," *Global Times*, November 8, 2011, http://www .globaltimes.cn/shanghai/community/2011–01/618009.html; Lara Farrar, "50% of New Expats Leave China Early," *China Daily (Beijing)*, November 5, 2009, http://news.asiaone.com/News/Latest+News /Asia/Story/A1Story20091105–178042.html

107. Larsen, *Netnographic Study*.

108. Ibid.

# Part IV

# THE PRACTICE OF
# INTERCULTURALITY

# 10

# Theorizing Interculturality in Healthcare: A Case from a Rural Indigenous Hospital in Mexico

*Jennifer Hale-Gallardo*

## Introduction

The first time I met a Nahua healer in Mexico was inside a public hospital. A woman came to the hospital's traditional medicine clinic asking anxiously whether someone could cure her child of *susto* (Spanish: "fright").[1] Known as *nemouhtil* in Nahuatl, the lingua franca of the Aztec Empire[2] and the language of approximately 1.4 million people in Mexico today, *susto* is considered a potentially deadly illness in which an animating component of the life force has been separated from the body.[3] While people in Mexico have long sought healing for this illness—which afflicts most often children but also men and women of all ages—many physicians consider this malady a cultural fiction. At this hospital however, the staff member understood the woman's request and sent her immediately to a healer who could attend to the child.

In recent decades, Latin American governments have promoted interculturality in healthcare by attempting to bridge indigenous medicine and biomedicine in a complementary manner.[4] While scholars have raised many questions over the years about the promises and pitfalls of linking indigenous medicine and biomedicine,[5] the idea of intercultural health continues to reemerge as part of conversations on the democratization of health and indigenous rights.[6] The Inter-American Development Bank and the Pan American Health Organization have defined best practices in intercultural health as a dialogue that "…involve(s) reconfiguring our perspectives and understandings of the world."[7] This definition emphasizes "…mutual respect, equal recognition of knowledge, willingness to interact, and flexibility to change as a result of these interactions."[8]

This essay is based on ethnographic research I conducted on efforts to incorporate indigenous healers into public healthcare in a rural hospital in Mexico. In my larger research project on which this discussion is based, I studied how indigenous healers negotiated their healing practices with biomedical staff in the midst of renewed federal and state recognition of traditional medicine. In this piece, I argue that biomedicine's cultural authority to define and treat illnesses obfuscates how interculturality can be put into practice in a way that meets the ideals of mutual respect, valorization of indigenous knowledge, and adaptation. I suggest that theorizing interculturality in healthcare requires a great deal of epistemological flexibility in order to accommodate different histories and meaning-making practices of different medical systems.

## A Brief History of Indigenous Medicine and Interculturality in Mexico

In a country in crisis like ours [Mexico], where the majority lacks the economic possibilities to be seen by a private physician... we are obliged to get to know our resources... especially the knowledge of traditional medicine... The efficacy of this knowledge has awakened the interest of contemporary doctors and scientists, who expect to recuperate the valid elements of traditional medicine in an effort that academic medicine be humanized.[9]

Using herbal and animal remedies, minerals, massages, punctures, hot and cold temperature variations, incantations, prayers and rituals,[10] indigenous healers have treated ailments of Mesoamericans since long before the Spanish Conquest. In the earliest years after colonization, many Spaniards recognized the expertise of Native healers and were eager to learn from the "doctores indios" (Indian doctors) they encountered in the land they called New Spain.[11] Franciscan missionary Toribio de Benevente Motolinía, one of the first 12 clerics to arrive in the colonized territory, wrote that he met very experienced Indian doctors who "cured many old and serious infirmities" for which Spaniards had "suffered many days without finding a remedy."[12] Native healers were recognized as "doctors in the complete sense of the term" and "specialists who solved the health problems of their people,"[13] so much so that Franciscan orders established hospitals in the sixteenth and seventeenth centuries where both Spanish and Indian doctors attended to patients.[14]

As the colonial mission grew, the perspective on Native healers changed. The Nahuatl *ticitl*, the Huastec *ilalix*, the Tzeltal *h'ilojel*, the Mayan *h-men*, and healers from hundreds of other indigenous ethnicities were demoted in status and lumped together into a single Spanish category, homogenizing their diversity and their specialties.[15] Calling them collectively *curanderos*, a term that still connotes witchcraft and charlatanism, religious orders mandated the "extirpation of idolatries" and made efforts to destroy local health systems, dismantling medical knowledge that had accumulated over centuries.[16] Nonetheless, healers devalued as medical specialists continued to develop and flourish despite colonial efforts to repress them, hybridizing Spanish and African healing practices together with indigenous modalities and epistemologies.[17]

In 1810, the creole elite founded a regime based on social, economic, and political relationships inherited from Spanish colonialism.[18] The newly independent government presented a continuity of the former social structure, domesticated to fit the reality of the nation-state's racially and culturally mixed citizens. Based on the previous "colonial culture of hierarchy" that had "powerfully shape(d) the clinical encounter,"[19] the government privileged positivist science and reproduced models from France and the United States of curative care and specialty hospitals.[20]

A century later, the Mexican Revolution (1910–1920) consolidated this model with the establishment of the public health care sector and the official exclusion of any healing modality deviating from scientific medicine.[21] In the Revolution's aftermath, debates ensued about how *indios* ("Indians") could best be integrated into the nation-state.[22] Government leaders considered the therapeutic transformation of indigenous people into healthy and productive workers a risky but necessary endeavor.[23] Celebrating indigenous difference as a cultural formation located in the past but working toward its dissolution in the present, the government instituted a new policy called *indigenismo*.[24] The goal was to reform the Indian into a modernist, mestizo citizen: someone who went to school, worked for wages, abandoned subsistence and communal lifestyles and saw the doctor.[25] During the heyday of this policy, the government practiced a "politics of neutralization," and from the 1940s to the 1970s, "disqualified, demonized, and persecuted indigenous healers."[26]

At the same time that indigenous healers were subject to persecution throughout the country, the concept of interculturality in health emerged in Mexican anthropology. In the decades following the Revolution, government agents became concerned with what they perceived as the vulnerable health status of indigenous Mexicans.[27] At the first Indigenist Interamerican Congress in 1940, physicians and *indigenistas*—government officials espousing *indigenismo*—promoted "respect and tolerance towards the ideas and practices used by traditional doctors."[28] An architect of *indigenismo*, physician and anthropologist Gonzalo Aguirre Beltran, was among the first to promote the idea of the intercultural in relation to indigenous health.[29] Well before the current concept evolved, his concept of "intercultural health" was used in a limited sense to suggest that the government should foster complementarity between the two health systems (called institutional and traditional).[30] To do this, he argued that the government should valorize what in his estimation were the positive elements of indigenous healers' practices.[31]

When the World Health Organization declared in 1978 that traditional practitioners could help meet primary health care goals, the Mexican government further pursued Aguirre Beltran's vision of intercultural indigenous health that he proposed decades earlier.[32] Realizing that academic medicine would be unable to reach all of Mexico's population, especially in rural areas, intellectuals working at the National Indigenist Institute (INI) envisioned indigenous people supplementing their own health needs through healers in their communities.[33] Replacing the notion of assimilative *indigenismo* with participatory *indigenismo*,[34] during this period the public health sector and the National Indigenous Institute (INI) collaborated in some of the largest campaigns attempting to link allopathic and popular medicine.[35] Constructing 2,000 rural health clinics and launching formal research projects on traditional herbal remedies, these programs aimed to use intercultural health as a development tool.[36]

While demands of indigenous movements had converged with new efforts to valorize indigenous knowledge, many intercultural health initiatives resulted in only a "partial acceptance of an intercultural orientation."[37] Government officials selectively valorized components of "tradition" they considered worthy of recognition and "traditional indigenous medicines were reduced to medicinal herbs, stripping all ideological elements that accompanied them."[38] Similar to a phenomenon that occurred in other parts of the world, attempts to formalize indigenous medicines promised to transform them:

> From culturally-specific methods for identifying, naming and treating illness to repositories of herbal concoctions where assumptions of efficacy rest(ed) in scientific understanding of biochemistry rather than in native epistemologies of the body and its relationship to family, kinship group, society and cosmos.[39]

Intercultural indigenous health in these contexts meant legitimizing local healing systems in ways that subjugated values and meanings to biomedicine while rendering other kinds of efficacies invisible or illegitimate.[40]

## Inside the Hospital

(We) respect and recognize those traditional doctors, who with their skills more humanist than technical, have resolved the majority of their people's medical problems for many years.[41]

In the early 1990s, the Mexican National Indigenous Institute introduced "mixed hospitals" in indigenous regions. Inviting healers to move their work inside official buildings, these spaces brought the practice of "traditional indigenous medicine" and biomedicine under the same roof.[42] When I conducted my research at a hospital with a long history of intercultural medicine in Cuetzalan, Puebla (2004–2007) the state government had recently renewed its traditional medicine project by employing local healers and building five other hospitals featuring traditional medicine clinics. The federal government also amended the Constitution with language that required government officials to meet health needs by "taking proper advantage of traditional medicine,"[43] and had created the Department of Traditional Medicine and Intercultural Development, shifting official discourse from "assimilation" to one of "absolute respect of culture" through the "participation of the traditional doctor in the health of the communities."[44]

At the hospital, Nahua healers prepared herbal remedies, attended childbirths, and reset dislocated bones. They provided therapeutic massages (*sobadas*) and therapeutic saunas (*temazcales*), and performed many other interventions to restore patients' physical, emotional, spiritual, and social well-being. On occasion, patients would talk to me about their improvements after having gone to see a healer on staff. The healers at the hospital had a good reputation in the many surrounding communities, attesting to their efficacy and expertise.

Despite this local acclaim, many physicians at the hospital held deep skepticism of indigenous healers in general. None of the healers had earned medical degrees, and many were illiterate. The majority of the healers were speakers of a language that members of the dominant culture considered inferior to Spanish, and not really a language at all[45]; monolingual Spanish-speaking physicians often teased me about learning Nahuatl, even though they themselves had lived years among the Nahua, Totonaco, and Otomi-speaking people whom they treated. In contrast to the well-heeled physicians, some healers did not wear shoes as a custom, finding it easier to traverse the hilly, often muddy landscape with bare feet; this of course was not seen well by persons who associated shoes with desired forms of modernity and eschewed markers of indigenous difference. Most significantly, physicians often expressed incredulousness about the contributions of healers to the health of their patients.

The supervisor of the traditional medicine project at the hospital played an important role in advocating for the value of indigenous healers. From time to time, I overheard clinic staff reminding other employees that the hospital was "one not two" in response to the opinion held by some staff that indigenous healers didn't belong in the hospital. Even the most open-minded physicians at the hospital did not hesitate to confess their disapproval of the healers, dismissively characterizing indigenous medicine as just "passing an egg over the body" (a common form of both diagnosis and treatment) or little more than "a bunch of herbs."[46] Midwives at the clinic were sometimes granted more credibility as indigenous practitioners because of the idea that they were "doing something real," they were "catching a real child."[47]

While clinic administrators worked hard to promote the positive contributions of healers, they also struggled to understand the role of indigenous medicine. In their attempts to legitimize the traditional medicine clinic, they were sometimes at a loss to explain what exactly healers were doing. For example, on one occasion the clinic supervisor told international reporters who were visiting the hospital that healers were not "really" healing *bilis* (bile), a well-known local affliction, which healers often treated through massages[48]:

They say "it's *bilis*", but when [the patient] starts to tell them that [they] got angry for this or for the other thing, it's not that [the healer] "gathered up the *bilis*," but it was something that you had to get out of you emotionally. And they massaged you, and they calmed you…because if you come and say I have *bilis* and this, yes it's true, but they [the hospital] will give you an injection, but they won't have listened to you, they won't have calmed you, and here is the part that is true [about the medicine].[49]

As a way to justify the role of healers, clinic administrators often emphasized the palliative aspects of indigenous medicine, downplaying the meaning that healers and patients gave to illnesses and their treatments. For instance, while the clinic supervisor acknowledged that *bilis* existed, from the clinic's perspective it was an ailment resolved through social and psychological effects, and not through the physiological mechanisms that healers attributed to their own medicine. In the perspective of the clinic supervisor, healers offered therapies that were important primarily because of their social and emotional efficacy.

Traditional healers thus provided a kind of affective labor that was bound up with their traditional practices.[50] Healers were praised for their humanism and the trust they were perceived to inspire in their community members. At the same time, they were reminded to "know their limits" and not intrude into the realm of the physicians, considered the realm of physiological efficacy. For example, in the following narrative, the clinic supervisor explained to me the difference between biomedical and indigenous healers:

> I've always said that what happens in traditional medicine, is that they are treating the soul, they are not healing your physical body, and these are the two qualities that should be appreciated: [physicians] cure the physical and [indigenous healers] cure the spiritual.[51]

While this perspective affirmed a role for healers, at the same time it served to reinscribe a nature/culture dichotomy between what was "technically real" (i.e., therapies that operate directly on "nature") versus what was socially meaningful (i.e., therapies that act "culturally" or in this case spiritually). This delimitation of efficacies, and the exclusivity afforded to biomedicine of access to the physiological, is what I will argue for the rest of the essay makes theorizing interculturality in healthcare especially challenging.

## THEORIZING INTERCULTURALITY IN INDIGENOUS HEALTH

After World War II, biomedicine's therapeutic worth converged with ideas of social progress, capitalism, and development, becoming "the gold standard against which other types of medical practice are measured."[52] Medical anthropologist Eduardo Menendez described this hegemonic model as one that focuses on curing disease technocratically and relies on professionalization to obscure its hierarchies and relations of power, such as that between patient versus doctor, researcher versus research subject, biomedicine versus non-biomedical systems, and physician versus popular healer.[53] Under the influence of this model, in everyday parlance a dichotomy is reinforced between such concepts such as scientific medicine versus nonscientific medicine and the objective versus the subjective.

The challenge for theorizing interculturality in this context is that the "majority of social scientists have tended to uphold these boundaries," viewing medicine not as culture, "but as an objective body of scientific knowledge external to culture."[54] While anthropologists have approached biomedicine as an ethnomedicine akin to any other medical system,[55] biomedicine is often considered "the culture of no culture."[56] These dichotomies are buoyed by an analytical distinction made between disease and illness in which physicians treat diseases (the objective pathology) while patients suffer symptoms (their subjective experience).[57] This division of labor is of particular significance to theorizing intercultural medicine, as it rests on assumptions that undermine a substantive intercultural dialogue. If interculturality is characterized by "mutual respect, equal recognition of knowledge, willingness to interact, and flexibility to change,"[58] then biomedicine's exclusive claim on the reality of nature makes theorizing interculturality in healthcare especially difficult in contexts of indigenous alterity.

Anthropologists drawing on social studies of science and technology have much to contribute to this discussion. One of the most fruitful interventions in unpacking the exceptionalism of scientific claims, or the way positivist claims are taken-for-granted as fact, has been made by scholars who emphasize that distinctions between mind/body and illness/disease are never just natural or neutral, but instead are historically and politically produced and contingently embodied.[59] Positing that medical truths are never self-evident, these scholars have emphasized that knowledge is not only shaped by power relations but is also interdependent with the process of creating reality itself.[60] As medical ethnographer Annemarie Mol writes:

> Ontologies are brought into being, sustained, or allowed to wither away in common day-to-day sociomaterial practices, medical practices among them.../Ontologies inform and are informed by our bodies, the organization of health care systems, the rhythm and pains of our diseases, and the shape of our technologies.[61]

In a medically pluralistic context, understanding how truth claims about reality and efficacy in medicine are established is important for deciphering what kinds of intercultural dialogues are conceivable. The work of medical anthropologist Stacey Langwick is instructive here. In a preview of her book on medical pluralism in Tanzania,[62] Langwick engaged an important aperture provided by another medical anthropologist, Byron Good, who wrote:

> Healing activities shape the objects of therapy—whether some aspect of the medicalized body, hungry spirits, or bad fate—and seek to transform those objects through therapeutic activities.[63]

Langwick followed up on this assertion with the compelling question, what if we were to take his gesture seriously? In other words, what if we were to seriously consider biomedical bodies and endangering spirits on par?[64] In her research, she studied how both nurses and healers generated the objects of their intervention through processes of objectification. She argued that "the boundaries and distinctions that constitute objects of therapeutic practices," whether devilish entities or biomedical bodies, are "not self-evident or universal," and entail more than just "different cultural shapes to humans' interactions with physical selves."[65] By seriously considering the ways in which therapies—whether biomedical, folk, or traditional—affected and shaped bodies, she suggested that both biomedical and nonbiomedical therapies objectified the illnesses in which they intervened in consequential ways.

Langwick's example provides a provocative example for theorizing interculturality in healthcare. In the case of the hospital that is the focus of this chapter, claims of social efficacies deemed traditional indigenous medicine complementary, but ultimately incommensurable with biomedicine. Healers were not considered to affect the same realms as physicians. Moreover, the very possibility of imagining a linkage between "biomedical" and "traditional" healing systems was constrained by an episteme that reproduced a division of labor assigning healers to the realm of affect.[66]

These bifurcated claims of efficacy revolved around not only biomedicine's exceptionalism, but also healers' positionality as indigenous subjects. Translations and interpretations of indigenous popular medicine, intrinsic to the Mexican government's recognition of indigenous medicine, take place at the powered boundaries of culture, race, class, and language. As political anthropologist Faye V. Harrison wrote regarding the challenges of truly integrating diversity:

> (The) inequality of positioning by race, gender, class, and their intersections with national or transnational status places concrete limits on how diversity can be managed and integrated.[67]

While Harrison wrote this to describe another institutional setting, a university, it could be easily applied to the hospital where I conducted my study. In Mexico, historical inequities and power differentials between the dominant culture and indigenous people continue to be salient. As these inequalities of positioning intersect with the cultural authority of biomedicine, they result in particularly limited forms of interculturality, which foreclose other, perhaps more substantive, possibilities of what intercultural healthcare could look like.

## CONCLUSION

In Mexico, government recognition of indigenous medicine provokes questions about what intercultural healthcare is and could be for the nation-state. While intercultural medicine projects are considered attempts to democratize healthcare, asymmetrical relations continue to shape the production of truth claims pertaining to the definition of illness and healing. Nowhere perhaps is this asymmetry more apparent than in the relationship between biomedical and indigenous healers.

In this essay, I have suggested that approaching interculturality in healthcare in indigenous contexts requires acknowledgment of the different ontological statuses attributed to illnesses and their treatments. If we assume that intercultural health is the ability to move evenly in a balanced way between knowledge, beliefs, and cultural practices related to health and disease, and the biological, social, and relational body,[68] then a question of ontologies, and the politics associated with these, must be close at hand. Theorizing interculturality in healthcare demands a consideration of how we can seriously account for the different therapeutic subjects and objects involved in the intercultural encounter. An approach that goes beyond just the "social side" of things (for instance, how medicine mediates social relationships) can help reveal how ontologically privileged claims to nature (or to science) are produced and mapped onto bodies, spaces, and practices, shaping the contours of intercultural dialogues in healthcare within a framework of biomedical hegemony.

Anthropologist Patricia Junge wrote that "the call towards a democratization of health comprises a profound political and ethical question."[69] What medical or healing techniques come to be articulated together and what objects of intervention count (i.e., supernatural agents vs. standardized biomedical bodies) become key questions for tracing the kinds of politics at work in the formalization of medical systems. If we hope to achieve an interchange and enrichment among different models of knowledge and skills that are put to the service of the patient,[70] an important first step is to attend to how different frameworks of meaning and ontological realities are negotiated, especially under conditions of social and political inequality.

## NOTES

1. *Susto* is associated with fatigue, headaches, difficulty sleeping, sadness, swelling, and digestive disorders. It can be provoked by sudden fright, for instance after seeing or being attacked by an animal or exposure to "airs" at night, especially those with malignant properties like those released by corpses or near cemeteries. Sometimes with *susto* part of the animating entity of the person becomes trapped in a place, for instance a body of water or land where an accident occurred. Common treatments for this ailment include a *limpia* (Spanish: cleansing), *llamada* (Spanish: a "calling" or a prayerful way of retrieving the lost part of the soul), and *pelotillas* (Spanish: herbal suppositories).

2. Also known as the Mexica Triple Alliance.

3. Italo Signorini, "Patterns of Fright: Multiple Concepts of Susto in a Nahua-Ladino Community of the Sierra de Puebla (Mexico)," *Ethnology*, 21, 4 (1982): 313–323.

4. Javier Mignone et al., "Best Practices in Intercultural Health: Five Case Studies in Latin America," *Journal of Ethnobiology and Ethnomedicine*, 3, 31, published online September 5, 2007, doi: 10.1186/1746-4269-3-31

5. Roberto Campos-Navarro, "Curanderismo, Medicina Indígena y Proceso de Legalización," *Nueva Antropología. Revista de Ciencias Sociales*, 52–53 (1997): 67–87; Craig Janes, "The Health Transition, Global Modernity and the Crisis of Traditional Medicine: The Tibetan Case," *Social Science & Medicine*, 48, 12 (1999): 1803–1820; B. L. K. Pilsbury, "Policy and Evaluation Perspectives on Traditional Health Practitioners in National Health Care Systems," *Social Science and Medicine*, 16, 21 (1982): 1825–1834; Steven Feierman, "Struggles for Control: The Social Roots of Health and Healing in Modern Africa," *African Studies Review*, 28, 2/3 (1985): 73–147; Jaime Tomás Page Pliego, *Política Sanitaria Dirigida a los Pueblos Indígenas de México y Chiapas, 1857–1995* (Tuxtla Gutierrez, San Cristobal de las Casas, Mexico City: PROIMMSE-IIA-UNAM/ Instituto de Estudios Indigenas, 2002); Stacy Leigh Pigg, "Authority in Translation: Finding, Knowing, Naming and Training 'Traditional Birth Attendants' in Nepal," in *Childbirth and Authoritative Knowledge: Cross-cultural Perspectives*, ed. Robbie E. Davis-Floyd and Carolyn Sargent (Berkeley and Los Angeles: University of California Press, 1997); Maria Eugenia Modena, *Madres, Médicos y Curanderos: Diferencia Cultural e Identidad Ideológica* (México: Ediciones de la Casa Chata, CIESAS, 1990); Eduardo Menendez, "La Enfermedad y La Curación? Que Es Medicina Tradicional?" *Alteridades*, 4, 7 (1994): 71–83.

6. Susana Ramírez Hita, "Políticas de Salud Basadas En El Concepto de Interculturalidad: Los Centros de Salud Intercultural En El Altiplano Boliviano," *Avá*, 14 (July 2009).

7. *Investing in Cultural Diversity and Intercultural Dialogue Executive Summary* (Paris: United Nations Educational, Cultural and Scientific Organization, 2009), 9.

218        JENNIFER HALE-GALLARDO

8. John O'Neil et al., *Best Practices in Intercultural Health Executive Summary Prepared for the Inter-American Development Bank and the Pan American Health Organization* (Winnipeg: Centre for Aboriginal Health Research, 2005), 3.

9. Noemi Quezada, *Enfermedad y maleficio: el curandero en el México colonial* (México: Universidad Nacional Autonoma de México, 1989), 122. Author's translation and emphasis.

10. Carlos Zolla, "Medicina Tradicional y Sistemas de Atencion a La Salud," in *El Futuro de La Medicina Tradicional En La Atencion a La Salud de Los Paises Latinoamericanos* (México City: CIESAS, 1987), 72–74. Author's translation.

11. Carlos Viesca Trevino, "Curanderismo in Mexico and Guatemala: Its Historical Evolution from the Sixteenth to the Nineteenth Century," in *Mesoamerican Healers*, ed. Brad Huber (Austin: University of Texas, 2001); Simon Varey, Rafael Chabrán, and Dora B. Weiner, *Searching for the Secrets of Nature: The Life and Works of Dr. Francisco Hernández* (Redwood City: Stanford University Press, 2001).

12. Motolinía quoted in Joie Davidow, *Infusions of Healing; A Treasury of Mexican-American Herbal Remedies* (New York: Simon and Schuster, 1999), 31.

13. Viesca Trevino, "Curanderismo in Mexico and Guatemala: Its Historical Evolution from the Sixteenth to the Nineteenth Century," 48.

14. Roberto Campos-Navarro and Adriana Ruiz-Llanos, "Adecuaciones Interculturales en los Hospitales para Indios en la Nueva España," *Historia y Filosofia de la Medicina*, 137, 6 (2001): 595–608.

15. Viesca Trevino, "Curanderismo in Mexico and Guatemala: Its Historical Evolution from the Sixteenth to the Nineteenth Century."

16. Oswaldo Salaverry, "Interculturalidad En Salud," *Rev. Perú. Med. Exp. Salud Publica*, 27, 1 (2010): 82.

17. Gabriela Coronado, "Competing Health Models in Mexico: An Ideological Dialogue between Indian and Hegemonic Views," *Anthropology & Medicine*, 12, 2 (2005): 165–177; Salaverry, "Interculturalidad En Salud."

18. Page Pliego, *Política sanitaria dirigida a los pueblos indígenas de México y Chiapas, 1857–1995*.

19. Margaret Lock and Vinh-Kim Nguyen, *An Anthropology of Biomedicine* (Hoboken: Wiley-Blackwell, 2010), 174.

20. Viesca Trevino, "Curanderismo in Mexico and Guatemala: Its Historical Evolution from the Sixteenth to the Nineteenth Century.".

21. Campos-Navarro, "Curanderismo, Medicina Indígena y Proceso de Legalización."

22. Heather McCrea, *Diseased Relations: Epidemics, Public Health, and State Formation in Nineteenth-Century Yucatán* (Stonybrook: University of New York, 2002).

23. Ibid.

24. María Josefina Saldaña-Portillo, "Reading a Silence: The 'Indian' in the Era of Zapatismo," *Nepantla: Views from the South*, 3, 2 (2002): 287–314.

25. Ariadna Acevedo Rodrigo, *Paying for Progress: Politics, Ethnicity and Schools in a Mexican Sierra, 1875–1930* (Warwick: University of Warwick, 2004); Stephen E. Lewis, "Mexico's National Indigenist Institute and the Negotiation of Applied Anthropology in Highland Chiapas, 1951–1954," *Ethnohistory*, 55, 4 (2008): 609–632.

26. Page Pliego, *Política sanitaria dirigida a los pueblos indígenas de México y Chiapas, 1857–1995*, 28.

27. Sergio Lerin Piñon, "Antropologia y Salud Intercultural: Desafios De Una Propuesta," *Desacatos*, 15–16 (otoño-invierno 2004): 111–125.

28. Ibid., 119.

29. Gonzalo Aguirre Beltrán, *Programas de Salud en la Situación Intercultural* (Xalapa: Universidad Veracruzana, 1994).

30. Ibid.

31. Ibid.

32. The World Health Organization made this declaration at the International Conference on Primary Health Care at Alma-Atta in the USSR in 1978.

33. Page Pliego, *Política Sanitaria Dirigida a los Pueblos Indígenas de México y Chiapas, 1857–1995*.

34. Ibid.

35. Graciela Freyermuth Enciso, *Medicos Tradicionales y Medicos Alopatas: Un Encuentro Dificil En Los Altos De Chiapas* (Tuxtla Gutiérrez: Gobierno del Estado de Chiapas, 1993); Piñon, "Antropologia y Salud Intercultural: Desafios De Una Propuesta."

36. Piñon, "Antropologia y Salud Intercultural: Desafios De Una Propuesta"; Carlos Zolla and Xavier Lozoya Legorreta, *La Medicina Invisible: Introducción al Estudio de la Medicina Tradicional de México* (Mexico City: Folios Ediciones, 1983).

37. Ibid.

38. Roberto Campos-Navarro, *Legitimidad Social y Proceso De Legalizacion De La Medicina Indigena En America Latina: Estudios de Mexico y Bolivia* (Mexico City: FFL-IIA-UNAM, 1996), 171.

39. Janes, "The Health Transition, Global Modernity and the Crisis of Traditional Medicine: The Tibetan Case," 1804.

40. Ibid.

41. Dr. Salomón García Jiménez, quoted in José Alejandro Almaguer González et al., *Fortalecimiento y Desarrollo de la Medicina Tradicional Mexicana y Su Relación Intercultural con la Medicina Institucional* (Mexico City: Ministry of Health, 2001), 6.

42. Maria Beatriz Duarte-Gómez, Viviane Brachet-Márquez, Roberto Campos-Navarro, and Gustavo Nigenda, "Políticas Nacionales de Salud y Decisiones Locales En México: El Caso Del Hospital Mixto de Cuetzalan, Puebla," *Salud Pública de México*, 46, 5 (October 2004): 388–398.

43. The General Health Law of Mexico currently has a reference to traditional medicine in Article 93: The Secretary of Public Education in Coordination with the Ministry of Health will... "respect and promote the development of indigenous traditional medicine. Programs providing primary healthcare developed in indigenous communities must adapt to the (local) social and administrative structure and the concept of health and the patient's relationship with the doctor, respecting always their human rights." The Constitution reads that governmental officials will "preserve all the elements that give them their cultural identity and to make effective use of traditional medicine" (Federal Legislation, The Constitution of the United Mexican States, November 30, 2005).

44. Almaguer González et al., *Fortalecimiento y Desarrollo de la Medicina Tradicional Mexicana y Su Relación Intercultural con la Medicina Institucional*, 3.

45. Indigenous languages in Mexico are most often referred to as *dialectos* (dialects) and it is not common knowledge to many citizens that indigenous languages are actually real languages in and of themselves.

46. Personal communication.

47. Personal communication.

48. *Bilis* is a malady well-known to many indigenous Mexicans where excess bile spreads throughout the body due to emotional states that produce physical and physiological changes in the body. Usually, the illness is attributed to repressed anger. These altered emotional states were understood to also make a person vulnerable to being attacked by malevolent forces, such as *aires* (or airs), which can in turn, produce emanations that negatively affect others. Biblioteca Digital de la Medicina Tradicional Mexicana (Mexico City: UNAM, 2009).

49. Personal communication.

50. Personal communication; "Affective labor...is labor that produces or manipulates affects such as a feeling of ease, well-being, satisfaction, excitement, or passion." Michael Hardt and Antonio Negri, *Multitude: War and Democracy in the Age of Empire* (New York: Penguin Books, 2005).

51. Personal communication (from interview with clinic supervisor).

52. Margaret Lock and Nancy Scheper-Hughes, "A Critical-Interpretive Approach in Medical Anthropology," in *Medical Anthropology: A Handbook of Theory and Method*, ed. Thomas M. Johnson and Carolyn Sargent (New York: Greenwood Press, 1990); Margaret Lock, "Medical Knowledge and Body Politics," in *Exotic No More: Anthropology on the Front Lines*, ed. Jeremy MacClancy (Chicago: University of Chicago Press, 2002), 191.

53. Menendez described the following structural characteristics in a hegemonic model of medicine: "ahistoricity, asociality, individualism, pragmatic efficacy, commodification of health, asymmetrical relations between physician-patient, subordinate position of 'consumers' of healthcare, exclusion of patient from medical knowledge, legal and academic legitimatization against other healing practices, professionalization, ideological

identification with scientific rationality to exclusion of other models, medicalization, social and ideological control, tendency towards promoting medical consumerism, perspective of quantity over quality, (and) a split between theory and practice." Eduardo Menendez, "Modelo Médico Hegemónico, Modelo Alternativo Subordinado, Modelo de Autoatención," *Cuadernos de la Casa Chata*, 86 (1976, 1983), 102.

54. Deborah Lupton, *Medicine as Culture: Illness, Disease and the Body* (Los Angeles: Sage, 2012), 19.

55. Robert Hahn and Atwood D. Gaines, *Physicians of Western Medicine: Anthropological Approaches to Theory and Practice* (Dordrecht: D. Reidel, 1985).

56. Sharon Traweek, *Beamtimes and Lifetimes* (Cambridge: Harvard University Press, 1992).

57. Arthur Kleinman, *The Illness Narratives: Suffering, Healing, and the Human Condition* (New York: Basic Books, 1988).

58. John O'Neil et al., *Best Practices in Intercultural Health Executive Summary Prepared for the Inter-American Development Bank and the Pan American Health Organization* (Victoria: University of Victoria: Centre for Aboriginal Health Research, 2005), 3.

59. Judith Farquhar, *Knowing Practice: The Clinical Encounter of Chinese Medicine* (Boulder: Westview Press, 1996); Jean Langford, *Fluent Bodies: Ayurvedic Remedies for Postcolonial Imbalance* (Durham: Duke University Press Books, 2002); Stacey Langwick, *Bodies, Politics, and African Healing: The Matter of Maladies in Tanzania* (Bloomington: Indiana University Press, 2011); Margaret Lock, *Twice Dead: Organ Transplants and the Reinvention of Death* (Berkeley, Los Angeles, and London: University of California Press, 2001); Volker Scheid, *Chinese Medicine in Contemporary China: Plurality and Synthesis* (Durham: Duke University Press Books, 2002); Pigg, "Authority in Translation: Finding, Knowing, Naming and Training 'Traditional Birth Attendants' in Nepal."

60. While not questioning the veracity of a disease or illness, truth claims about disease and illness are amenable to being analyzed culturally and socially because they are interpretations that are negotiated and renegotiated as scientific practice develops (albeit not in a teleological or unilinear way). Deborah Lupton, *Medicine as Culture: Illness, Disease and the Body* (Los Angeles: Sage, 2003), 19.

61. Annemarie Mol, *The Body Multiple: Ontology in Medical Practice* (Durham: Duke University Press, 2002), 6–7.

62. Langwick, *Bodies, Politics, and African Healing: The Matter of Maladies in Tanzania*.

63. Byron Good, *Medicine, Rationality and Experience: An Anthropological Perspective* (Cambridge: Cambridge University Press, 1993), 69.

64. Stacey Langwick, "Alternative Materialities: The Making of Therapeutic Objects in Southeastern Tanzania," Paper given at the University of Florida African and African Diaspora Studies Seminar (2004).

65. Langwick, *Bodies, Politics, and African Healing: The Matter of Maladies in Tanzania*, 159.

66. Arguably, this myopic approach to the work that healers do could be particularly problematic in obscuring the physiological effects of indigenous medicine. Although not confined to indigenous medicine, iatrogenic effects have been reported in the past due to a lack of understanding about how multiple medicines might be working together.

67. Faye Venetia Harrison, *Outsider Within: Reworking Anthropology in the Global Age* (Urbana: University of Illinois Press, 2008), 273.

68. Jaime Ibacache Burgos, *El Salud, El Desarrollo y La Equidad en Un Contexto Intercultural* (Temuco: Ministry of Health of Araucanía Sur Chile, 1997).

69. Patricia Junge, "Nuevos Paradigmas en la Antropología Médica." Paper given at *Cuarto Congreso Chileno de Antropología*, 19 al 23 de noviembre de 2001, 2; Author's translation.

70. Almaguer González et al., *Fortalecimiento y Desarrollo de la Medicina Tradicional Mexicana y Su Relación Intercultural con la Medicina Institucional*; Author's translation.

# 11

# Tourist Destination Marketing and Interculturality: The Polish City of Kraków in the British Press

## *Irmina Wawrzyczek*

Cultural studies has always been a "parasitic" cross-discipline creatively borrowing ideas, concepts, and methodologies from more narrowly focused disciplines in order to best elucidate specific problems in question. The chapter that follows situates itself in this tradition as it proposes a methodological apparatus constructed at the intersection of tourism studies and critical media studies in order to investigate interculturality in the context of international leisure tourism and consumer travel. An attempt is made to apply the concept of destination marketing, an area of inquiry within tourism studies that emerged a few decades ago, to the data obtained by means of discourse analysis, a method long employed in print media studies, in order to evaluate whether the newspaper texts promoting foreign tourist destinations are conducive to intercultural engagement. The proposed analytical approach can easily be adapted for similar interpretations of other types and genres of promotion materials produced by the cultural brokers of modern tourism. It can also be applied for comparing the strategies of promoting the same destinations at different points of time in order to diagnose the progress of intercultural awareness.

The proposition of examining interculturality through the compound lens of tourism, media and cultural studies derives additional validity from the characterization of the twenty-first century by the Council of Europe as the epoch in which "cultural diversity is an essential condition of human society, brought about by cross-border migration, the claim of national and other minorities to a distinct cultural identity, the cultural effects of globalization, the growing interdependence between all world regions and the advances of information and communication media."[1] The special type of "migration" considered in this essay is tourism, defined as "a social, cultural and economic phenomenon which entails the movement of people to countries or places outside their usual environment for personal or business/professional purposes. These people are called visitors (which may be either tourists or excursionists; residents or nonresidents), and tourism has to do with their activities, some of which imply tourism expenditure."[2]

The commercial success of tourism industry worldwide strongly depends on the effective promotion of its "product," which involves communicating attractive messages about particular places. Variously called destination marketing or image formation, the activities of promoting tourist destinations constitute nowadays a highly specialized industry in itself, coordinated by several professional bodies, the largest one being the Destination Marketing Association International (DMAI).[3] In 2008, the DMAI endorsed the definition of destination marketing as "a proactive, strategic, visitor-centered approach to the economic and cultural development of a location, which balances and integrates the interests of visitors, service providers, and the community."[4] The recognition of the cultural dimension in destination marketing operations makes the definition a useful reference in the present study.

Central to the concept of interculturality, analyzed by cultural critics, politicians, educators, and frequently debated by bloggers, is the assumption that it means not just bringing members of different cultures together, but involves a degree of interaction between individuals, groups, and organizations resulting in a heightened awareness of the other and seeing one's own culture in a different perspective. Intercultural engagement is "penetration of the other's system: getting out of oneself to see things from the Other's perspective. It is an attitude of opening up, a personal effort of inquiry."[5] The process of such engagement is often referred to as cultural dialogue, a dialogue facilitated by certain "enabling factors." One of them, relevant to the present argument, is "a minimum degree of knowledge about the distinguishing features of one's own and the 'other' culture."[6] According to the theory of image formation process, it constitutes the cognitive image component, that is the intellectual beliefs and attitudes toward a destination formed from the available information.[7]

The present essay is an empirical case study of the cultural knowledge offered to the potential British visitors to the Polish historic city of Kraków based upon 374 newspaper articles and article fragments dealing with that place in the British national daily and Sunday press in the years 2002–2007.[8] These texts are approached here as instances of travel journalism, as more or less open forms of destination marketing. According to the typology of image formation agents proposed by William C. Gartner, they belong to the categories of "Covert Induced II" and "Autonomous," both of medium/high credibility and market penetration.[9] When categorized in terms of the stages of the touristic process, they are either pre-trip or post-trip texts.[10] While nowadays the battle for the customer attention in tourism is shifting toward the Internet, many societies and social groups are still susceptible and responsive to print sources. The press still remains particularly appropriate for promoting tourist destinations due to frequency of publication, defined target readers, low cost, local market penetration, timeliness, relative cheapness for the promotion of small-scale enterprises, and flexibility.[11] The newspaper readership statistics for the United Kingdom in the 2010s, as well as the availability of most national newspapers in the electronic form justify the choice of the British press as viable research material.[12]

While destination marketing and its strategies have been widely discussed from the perspective of economy, politics, business management, public relations, social psychology, consumer behavior, and linguistics,[13] the role of tourism in contemporary culture has been tackled infrequently,[14] and even less so from the perspective of interculturality. What follows is an empirical case study of the British print media destination image of Kraków and its evaluation as an "enabling factor" in a British-Polish intercultural dialogue. The evaluation will be performed by contrasting the foreign press discourses of Kraków with the dominant native discourses of the city.

Discourse analysis adopted here for the investigation of the newspaper texts is by now a well-established and diversified approach to the study of language use and communication that emerged in its modern form at the turn of the 1960s and 1970s.[15] Its affinity to cultural studies is the sensitivity to the contextual circumstances of linguistic communication acts. Applied to the press, discourse analysis aims at showing "how social or political structures are also manifest in the meaning and organization of news reports, and how such news reports may in turn contribute to the formation or change of social cognitions of the readers…"[16] Thus, discourse contributes to the construction of knowledge and meaning.[17]

Of the wide range of DA tools, topical analysis was selected as particularly useful for the purpose of this study. Teun A. Van Dijk claims that topics "represent what news-makers construe to be the most important information about a news event,"[18] and that they "not only suggest what information is most important in the text, but also what is most important 'in the world'."[19] What's more, topics influence the construction of cognitive knowledge structures—or models—by readers about specific events and situations. Topics may be articulated as thematic paragraphs, sentences, or clauses. Topical analysis of the news articles as proposed by Van Dijk was extended in the present study onto all the destination image-building texts concerning Kraków in the study sample to obtain textual evidence about the cognitive models of the city as a place worth visiting offered by the British press. Since topics in newspaper texts tend to occur in clusters and to overlap, the identification of the most prominent themes in the coverage of Kraków required their analytical isolation for the sake of clarity.

The headline of Duncan Lee's article in the mid-market *Daily Mail* "All roads lead to Krakow" (December 10, 2005) accurately reflects the unique position occupied by the city on the British map of Polish tourist destinations. While references to Warsaw, the capital of Poland and the locus of important domestic and international political event, naturally prevailed in the study sample (493 references), Kraków came second (374 references) as a "must see" for anyone traveling to Poland for pleasure and for business. The examination of the coded newspaper material revealed several highly prominent topics related to Kraków. They are presented below in the order of estimated frequency and followed by illustrative examples.[20]

## KRAKÓW AS POLAND'S HISTORIC CITY

The topic appeared most typically as descriptions of the "authentic" Old City (in contrast to the old towns in Warsaw and Gdańsk reconstructed after World War II destruction), the Market Place, St. Mary's Church, numerous historical buildings dating back to the Middle Ages, especially the splendid royal Wawel Castle with its Renaissance Chapel.

> This combination of old and new is typical of Krakow (pronounced Crack-off), the original capital. Spared from major destruction in the Second World War, it has more intact historical buildings, monuments and works of art than any other city in Poland. Most places of interest are located in its compact centre. Wawel Hill is a good place to start,

overlooking the Vistula river which dissects Poland almost from top to bottom. Here you find the imposing castle and a gothic cathedral, where kings and heroes of battle are interred. This, the equivalent of our Westminster Abbey, is the spiritual shrine of the Polish people.[21]

## Kraków as a Lucrative Property Market

This business topic featured prominently in the references to the city's architectural beauty and conveyed the message that buying an apartment in Kraków for rent was good business. Often separate paragraphs were inserted into longer articles about the city that read like concise property advertisements.

> Current prices in the desirable city centre start from £60,000 for a one-bedroom apartment in need of complete renovation, going up to £110,000 or so for a newly-renovated, highly-rentable, two-bed apartment. Meanwhile, £650,000 will buy you the most expensive apartment currently on the market: a three-bed luxury pad smack on the main square. You can pick up a one-bed property, just a half-hour walk from the centre, for just over £30,000.[22]

Information of this kind would often be followed by expert opinion on quick return and profit guaranteed by the presence of foreign companies looking for employee accommodation, a big, native and foreign, student population, easy mortgage procedures for foreigners, no tax when selling after five years, and the constant growth of local property prices.

## Kraków as a Cheap, Short-Term Tourist Destination

This topic revolved around the attractions of the city as a perfect place for a weekend trip for lower-budget visitors due to its good tourist infrastructure available at competitive prices: access by cheap airlines, local transport, hotels, tour operators, and other attractions.

> GETTING THERE: Two nights B&B at the 3* Hotel Senacki in Krakow's Old Town costs from £104 per person based on two sharing. Eurobreak offers a booking service for Ryanair flights from Stansted to Krakow and accommodation.
>
> GETTING AROUND: Tours pre-bookable through Eurobreaks include half-day tours to Auschwitz-Birkenau and the Wieliczka Salt Mines. All cost £22. The Krakow Card offers bus and tram travel plus

discounts for attractions, restaurants, shops and tours. A two-day card costs 50 zloty (£9).²³

## KRAKÓW AS A PLACE OF FUN

This topic serves selling the image of Kraków as a place of entertainment narrowed to excessive consumption of good food and even better cheap drink, and frequenting vibrant local nightclubs.

> With sub-zero temperatures until spring, Krakow is never going to be the new Ibiza but it's still a mecca for night owls. Pasja, a two-storey club with warm pink walls on Szewska Street, is one of the best. Like most places there's no entry fee and half litres of beer cost GBP 1 and vodkas, GBP 1.30. Across the road is Moliere where, perched on stools at the circular bar we drank Polish flag (vodka and grenadine) and Tatanka (bison grass vodka and apple juice) for GBP 3. For something more "underground," try Roentgen club on Szczepanska Street where visiting DJs spin discs and flash strobe lights... It's possible to eat a filling, two course meal for GBP 3 in one of the cafes. Polish staples are bigos (sausage and sauerkraut stew), pierogi, (dumplings with meat or cheese fillings) and barszcz (beetroot soup) as well as wild boar and pig knuckle. A must dine adventure is Chlopskie Jadlo—literally "Peasants' Kitchen". As well as tables, diners can eat perched on a sledge, a cart and a double bed (the "mattress" is actually a table so you don't spill your food). A two-course meal with beers costs around GBP 5 per head. At the ostentatious Wierzynek with its mural-clad walls and formal waiters, a three course meal with wine was GBP 25 per head. Most of that was on wine as bottles start at GBP 15.²⁴

## KRAKÓW AS A CENTER OF JEWISH HISTORY AND CULTURE

This topic involves the historical and ethnic attractions of the former Jewish quarter Kazimierz, the annual summer Jewish Festival, the vicinity of the Auschwitz museum, and Spielberg's *Schindler's List* that was partly filmed in the area.

> South of Wawel Hill lies the Jewish Quarter—Kazimierz—which has enjoyed enormous popularity since featuring in the Spielberg film *Schindler's List*. Until 1943, when virtually the entire population of this ghetto perished in the nearby Auschwitz-Birkenau death camps, this was one of the great Jewish centers of Europe. Some synagogues remain and can still be visited and there are some excellent Jewish restaurants with live music in the evenings. The Ariel Cafe at Szeroka 17 is well worth a dinner.²⁵

## KRAKÓW AS THE CITY OF JOHN PAUL II

The topic peaked in the spring of 2005, the time of the terminal illness and death of Pope John Paul II. Several texts emphasized the pontiff's close links with Kraków, as that in *The Guardian*:

> Krakow, the castled central European city where the Pope spent most of his life, wants to have his heart. Officials and church leaders are quietly campaigning to have the heart removed from his corpse—which is to be buried in the Vatican on Friday—and placed in the city's Wawel Cathedral, the burial place of the kings and saints of Polish history.[26]

## KRAKÓW—THE HOME OF THE WISŁA FOOTBALL CLUB

This less frequent topic was of particular interest to many British newspaper readers at the time as the FC Wisła-Krakow was the mother-club of "Magic" Maciej Żurawski, the then star Polish footballer of Celtic Glasgow. Indeed, Żurawski's £5 million transfer to Celtic Glasgow in 2005 generated more references to Kraków in the study sample than any other event that year. The fact that the Wisła stadium was considered as a possible place of some elimination matches in the 2012 UEFA European Football Championship could enhance the value of Kraków as a tourist destination among British football fans.

> CELTIC star Maciej Zurawski signed from Wisla Krakow and the Hoops went there last summer for a friendly. Has a population of 757,430 and the Wisla Stadium, which will host group matches in EURO 2012, can take 33,000 fans.[27]

These and several less prominent Kraków topics identified in the British national press between 2002 and 2007 marketed the city as a walkable area of about 2,2 square miles consisting of the Old Town with its unique 10 acres Market Square and the Wawel Hill with the Royal Castle complex. It was reported to have precious architectural sights, museums, and art galleries. Conveniently accessible by cheap airlines, it offers quality accommodation at stylish yet relatively inexpensive hotels, plenty of tasty food and surprisingly cheap drink, entertainment at numerous night-clubs and excellent shopping opportunities for local handicraft and art objects. Other cultural attractions consist of the former Jewish district, recently revitalized as a historic urban theme park, and of a possibility of making a day trip to the Auschwitz Museum. Another attraction involves following in the footsteps of the celebrities who once visited or frequented the city. In addition to its leisure potential, Kraków offers business opportunities of profitable property investment in buy-to-lets. Significant from the point of view of interculturality are the omissions of local people from the city's destination image, except when mentioned in the service roles of hotel staff, waiters, flower vendors, English-speaking property lawyers and consultants. Its student population is registered as a colorful and cheerful addition to the local bars and night-clubs, and as potential tenants of the apartments for rent.

## KRAKÓW'S UNIQUE PLACE IN POLISH NATIONAL CULTURE

Kraków, the number one tourist destination in Poland according to the British Press, features prominently in the Polish culturescape. It constitutes a Geertzian "multiplicity of complex conceptual structures, many of them superimposed upon or knotted into one another, which are at once strange, irregular, and inexplicit," a perfect object for anthropological "thick description."[28] A remarkable attempt at grasping and rendering those structures of meaning was made by sociologist Paweł Kubicki in his study entitled *Miasto w sieci znaczeń. Kraków i jego tożsamość*.[29] Adopting the proposition of the influential American pioneer urban sociologist Robert E. Park that "the city is a state of mind," he identified and characterized several mythical narratives of Kraków well rooted in Polish cultural imagination. A selection of the most persistent ones, from Kubicki's much longer, more refined and historically nuanced list, is outlined below to subsequently serve as a checklist in estimating the compatibility of the British Press image of Kraków as a tourist destination with the city's image in Polish culture.

## KRAKÓW'S FOUNDING MYTH

It tells the story of Kraków as the founding place of the Polish nation and state. At its core is the legendary heroic King Krak fighting the dragon and defeating it with the help of a resourceful shoemaker. Like in many similar Indo-European founding myths, the hero's victory over the evil demon made his city eternal, exceptional, and invincible. An important part of the myth is the city's archetypal topology, its location on and around a hill, on the biggest Polish river. This mythical meaning of Kraków is revived in the times of national distress and insecurity as a symbolic narrative of an archaic order and integrity.[30]

## KRAKÓW AS THE AXIS MUNDI

Related to the founding myth, it refers to the symbolic image of Kraków as a spot where earth and sky come closest on the Wawel Hill, physically dominating over the rest of the city, with its monumental royal castle and the Cathedral. The presence of the tombs of many Polish kings, queens, and national heroes in the chapels and vaults of the Cathedral made the shrine a national pantheon embodying the sacred spiritual and secular national values.[31] The axis mundi symbolism od Kraków has been reinforced by the new urban legend of the Wawel Chakra, a belief that a certain place on the Wawel Hill emanates powerful spiritual energy and is one of the few strongest places of power on the Earth.

## THE MYTH OF THE GOLDEN AGE KRAKÓW

This mythical narrative of Kraków incorporates a whole range of events, ceremonies, and rituals—coronations, royal parades, and funerals—taking place in the city's glorious period when it functioned as the seat of the Polish Kingdom between 1320 and 1596. It became a vibrant center of economic prosperity, of politics, learning, literature and arts, and the many places of the saints' cult drawing pilgrimages to venerate their relics earned Kraków the reputation of "the Polish Rome." Long after the city stopped being the capital, its mythologized glorious past made it the most appropriate place for rituals of greatest national significance such as the ceremonial funeral of Tadeusz Kościuszko in 1818 and the Nobel Prize winning poet Czesław Miłosz in 2004.[32]

## THE MYTH OF ANTICOMMUNIST KRAKÓW

This narrative emerged in the postwar decades under Poland's Communist leadership, the time when Kraków was out of favor with the new regime due to its royal roots, the landed gentry ethos, intellectual and Catholic pretensions, the cultural prestige of the conservative middle class, and the alleged marginalization of the working class, who were themselves slow to embrace communism. After the collapse of the communist rule, followed by the radical socioeconomic processes of globalization and European integration, the anticommunist reputation of the city has been sinking into oblivion, yet up to the end of the twentieth century it added to Kraków's reputation as an island of true Polishness.[33]

Kubicki also observes the nearly total absence of the Jewish quarter Kazimierz from the symbolic space of Krakow. Although the Jews constituted about 25–30% of the city's population before World War II, and Kazimierz is one of the city's oldest administrative districts centrally situated in the vicinity of the Old Town, is has been peripheral to the myth of Kraków as the incubator of Polish national and cultural identity.[34] Similarly, the Nazi complex of the concentration and extermination camps in Auschwitz-Birkenau (now a memorial museum), frequently fused with Kraków by travel agencies and journalists as an addition to its sights, never became an extension of Kraków's cultural space and a part of its identity.

Kubicki's list of mythical discourses should be supplemented with the myth of Kraków as Poland's first ancient academic center originated in 1364, when the Jagiellonian University was established by Casimir III the Great—the oldest university in Poland and second oldest in Central Europe. In the course of history the institution has been joined by other excellent schools: the Academy of Music in 1888, the Academy of Fine Arts in 1818, and AGH University of Science and Technology, all highly competitive and prestigious institutions attracting best talent and intellect.

What then are the chances for a dialogue of cultural assumptions, values, and traditions between a British leisure visitor to Kraków equipped with the knowledge of the place communicated by travel journalists, and the locals immersed in their daily reality and bearing—not always consciously—the cultural baggage of Kraków's imagined identity? The incompatibility of the two images is hard to miss. The selective and often shallow texts about Kraków appearing on the travel pages of newspapers do not prepare their readers for meaningful engagement with the destination society. While references to Kraków's historical architecture frequently appeared in the studied sample, its value was acknowledged by analogies to better-known Central European destinations with an already established tourist reputation: Prague, Berlin, and Budapest. While the works of recognized European masters in Kraków art museums were recommended, like da Vinci's "The Lady with an Ermine," no names of best Polish artists, past or present, appeared as worthy of appreciation. Not enough contextual knowledge was offered to the prospective visitors to help them share the historical meanings and aesthetics of Kraków with the host society. The authors tapped the predictable expectations and tastes of their target readers into the coverage by extolling the standards of Kraków's hotels, places for gastronomic overindulgence, and opportunities for the wicked delights of local night-clubs. These strategies may be commercially effective, however they result in insufficient cognitive resources about the unfamiliar foreign culture, and thus did little to stimulate intercultural mindedness in the reading public.

There is no conspiracy of the British papers at work here. On the contrary, the tourist image of Kraków they help construct reflects very accurately the city's own marketing strategies adopted by the public promotion agencies and individual entrepreneurs. However, while the promotion policies pursued by the public and private sectors enjoy widespread support for contributing to the prosperity of the city, they frequently come into conflict with the ethos of the local community. Scanning the local newspapers and blogs, one finds complaints of the Kraków inhabitants, especially the residents of the Old Town "tourist ghetto," about drunken, noisy, and aggressive visitors (foreign and domestic alike). In one calendar year 2010, the city guards imposed 5,000 fines on tourists for causing disturbances and 18,000 fines for drinking in public places.[35] One of the British newspapers reported the disappointing effects of promoting Kraków as a weekend destination for very basic leisure activities:

> Boozy British lads are being told to keep away from Polish stag party hot spot Krakow. Locals are fed-up with the alcohol-soaked antics of Brits who cause fights, molest waitresses and spray the medieval city's streets with vomit. Now most city centre bars and clubs have banned stag parties and local taxi firms say they will refuse to pick up drunken trippers. The move has been supported by Krakow's councillors who want to attract art-loving Europeans to the city.[36]

Another process observed and studied by Kraków sociologists is the inner city depopulation resulting from the nuisance caused by tourists and from landlord harassment. The old residents are being pushed out of attractive property and replaced by the transient population of business operators. Living and spending time in the Old Town has lost much of its attraction to the locals, and the historic part is becoming increasingly isolated from the rest of the city.[37]

The above only adds evidence to the unavoidable conclusion from comparing the two images of Kraków: that commercially informed tourist destination marketing does not necessarily facilitate interculturality, and that, in fact, it may limit and hinder it. If the mediated representations of tourist destinations do not effectively convey the cultural meanings attached to them locally, they will not heighten the awareness of other cultures in the addressees. The visitors' agendas built around culturally selective images are tolerated by the host society as a part of the tourist business, but do not necessarily generate intercultural responses from its members. Similar observations have been made by researchers investigating cultural tourism,[38] authenticity of cultural experience in short-term tourist encounters,[39] and images of natives in tourist brochures.[40] Selling travel destination images only indirectly related to the reality experienced by the visited may work commercially to mutual satisfaction but the media promotion strategies of this kind lay weak foundations for the intercultural process—certainly not robust enough to substantially raise one's epistemological self-awareness or markedly deactivate cultural insularity.

## NOTES

1. The research for this essay was financed from the NCN grant no. 2012/05/B/HS2/04096. "Intercultural Dialogue," Council of Europe, accessed July 1, 2013, http://www.coe.int/t/dg4/intercultural /concept_EN.asp.html
2. "Understanding Tourism: Basic Glossary," World Tourism Organization UNWTO, accessed July 2, 2013, http://media.unwto.org/en/content /understanding-tourism-basic-glossary.html
3. A attempt to counteract the lack of terminological precision in destination marketing theory and research was made in Asli D. A. Tasci, "A Semantic Analysis of Destination Image Terminology," *Tourism Review International*, 13 (2009): 65–78.
4. "The Future of Destination Marketing Tradition, Transition, and Transformation Report of the 2008 Futures Study Conducted for DMAI Foundation by Karl Albrecht International" (DMAI Foundation, 2008), 77, accessed June 25, 2013, http://cvtapartners.com/wp-content/uploads /2013/05/DMAIStudy-CoreReport1.pdf
5. "Interculturality," accessed June 25, 2013, http://www.lmg.ulg.ac.be /articles/intercult_en.html#ancre168186. See also Gerald Bouchard, "What Is Interculturalism?" *McGill Law Journal*, 56 (2010): 435–468.
6. "Intercultural Dialogue."
7. William C. Gartner, "Image Formation Process," *Journal of Travel and Tourism Marketing*, 2 (1993): 193.
8. The sample was obtained in November 2008 by searching the LexisNexis® full-text database providing access to all British newspapers. All quotations from the British papers in the present article come from this digital resource.
9. Gartner, "Image Formation Process," 200–203.
10. Graham Dann, *The Language of Tourism: A Sociolinguistic Perspective* (Wallingford: Cab International, 1996), 145–147.
11. Ibid., 143.
12. See the statistics of the National Readership Survey, http://www.nrs .co.uk; Audit Bureau of Circulations, http://www.abc.org.uk.html

13. Gregory Ashwort and Brian Goodall (eds.), *Marketing Tourism Places* (London: Routledge, 1990), Google Books; Dann, *The Language of Tourism*; Nigel Morgan and Annette Pritchard, *Tourism Promotion and Power—Creating Images, Creating Identities* (West Sussex: John Wiley & Sons, 1998); Olivia H. Jenkins, "Understanding and Measuring Tourist Destination Images," *International Journal of Tourism Research*, 1 (1999): 1–15; Emma Di Marino, "The Strategic Dimension of Destination Image: An Analysis of the French Riviera Image from the Italian Tourists' Perceptions." PhD Diss., University of Naples "Federico II," 2008, http://www.esade.edu/cedit/pdfs/papers/pdf10.pdf; Sérgio Dominique Ferreira Lopes, "Destination Image: Origins, Developments and Implications," *PASOS. Revista de Turismo y Patrimonio Cultural*, 9 (2011): 305–315, http://www.pasosonline.org/Publicados/9211/PS0211_07.pdf

14. Tom Selwyn (ed.), *The Tourist Image: Myths and Myth Making in Tourism* (Chichester and New York: John Wiley & Sons, 1996); Can-Seng Ooi, *Cultural Tourism and Tourism Cultures: The Business of Mediating Experiences in Copenhagen and Singapore* (Copenhagen: Copenhagen Business School Press, 2002).

15. Louise Phillips and Marianne W. Jørgensen, *Discourse Analysis as Theory and Method* (London: Sage, 2004, 1st publ. 2002), 1–23, Google Books.

16. Teun A. Van Dijk, *Racism and the Press* (London and New York: Routledge, 1991), 45.

17. Phillips and Jørgensen, *Discourse Analysis*, 67.

18. Van Dijk, *Racism*, 71.

19. Ibid., 74.

20. In all quotes from the British press, the original spelling—without Polish diacritical marks—has been retained.

21. Duncan Lee, "All Roads Lead to Krakow," *Daily Mail*, December 10, 2005.

22. "Overseas Property: Why Krakow Has Moved into Pole Position as Europe's No. 1 Hot Spot," *The Guardian*, February 10, 2007.

23. "Kracking Krakow," *The Sun*, October 6, 2007.

24. Kate Bohdanowicz, "Winter Breaks; European Breaks; Krakow," *Daily Express*, October 7, 2003.

25. "Poland Is the New Prague…; Krak-er of a City to Discover," *Daily Star*, September 5, 2004.

26. Ian Traynor, "Death of the Pope: Krakow Prays for Heart to Return Home," *The Guardian*, April 5, 2005.

27. "Singing in Ukraine," *The Sun*, April 19, 2007.

28. Clifford Geertz, *The Interpretation of Cultures* (New York: Basic Books, 1973), 10.

29. Pawel Kubicki, *Miasto w sieci znaczeń. Kraków i jego tożsamość* [The city in the web of meaning. Kraków and its identity] (Kraków: Księgarnia Akademicka, 2010).

30. Ibid., 30–31.
31. Ibid., 32–33.
32. Ibid., 40–42, 85–98.
33. Ibid., 37–38.
34. Ibid., 37.
35. "Krakow Tourists Making for Noisy Neighbours," *Polish Radio English Section*, August 29, 2011, http://www.thenews.pl/1/9/Artykul/54121, Krakow-tourists-making-for-noisy-neighbours.html
36. Michael Leidig, "Poleaxed; Boozy Brit Stag Parties Booted Out of Krakow," *Sunday Star*, March 4, 2007.
37. Renata Radłowska, "Coraz mniej mieszkańców w centrum Krakowa," [Fewer and fewer citizens in downtown Kraków], *Gazeta pl Kraków*, July 7, 2010, accessed July 1, 2013, http://krakow.gazeta.pl/krakow/1,35798,8110335,Coraz_mniej_mieszkancow_w_centrum_Krakowa.html
38. Ooi, *Cultural Tourism*, 17–41.
39. John P. Taylor, "Authenticity and Sincerity in Tourism," *Annals of Tourism Research*, 28 (2001): 7–26.
40. Dann, *The Language of Tourism*.

# 12

# DO THE FOLK BELIEVE THAT THEY CAN SPEAK THEIR WAY INTO INTERCULTURALITY?

*Kara McBride and Jingyun Gu*

Some of the most deliberate intercultural events happen in foreign language or second language (L2)[1] classrooms. The professional organizations that set the standards and guidelines for L2 education in the United States (American Council on the Teaching of Foreign Languages) and the European Union (European Council) define as central to the mission of L2 education the development of intercultural competence in the L2 learner.[2] This is a major part of the mission of L2 classes primarily because of the inextricable connection that is believed to exist between culture and language. When L2 scholars and educators refer to this relationship, they do not mean merely that each language is associated to particular cultures for historical reasons; they mean something more elemental.[3] At the very least they mean that some of any culture is expressed through certain linguistic practices which could not be faithfully reproduced in full using different language, and further, that many culturally bound behaviors, perspectives, attitudes and values are expressed, transmitted, and perpetuated through the linguistic practices of each culture's community.[4] To fully participate in a culture, it is necessary to participate in its linguistic practices. Conversely, to fully learn a community's language, it is necessary to master the use of the language as its speakers use it, which means to participate in their particular linguistic practices. This is one of the primary ways of engaging in the cultural practices of a community.

While this connection between language and culture is the philosophical foundation for the explicitly intercultural goals of L2 education, whether, or the extent to which, L2 students believe in this connection is an understudied issue. Students' beliefs about this possible connection can affect how they interpret what is done in the L2 classroom, how they respond to experiences with their language of study both in the classroom and beyond, and what they believe they need to do in order to acquire a new language. This essay presents findings from a study that explored L2 students' folk linguistic beliefs with regards to how they view the relationship between language, thought, and culture. The impact that this can have on learners' experience is discussed in terms of dynamic systems theory. This case study is offered as a model that might be used in exploring folk beliefs and their possible impact in other studies of interculturality, especially where this might have implications for education.

## INTERCULTURAL COMPETENCE

*The Common European Framework of Reference for Languages* describes the development of intercultural competence in the plurilingual speaker through the development of four interconnected types of knowledge or *savoirs*.[5] The first one is called simply *savoir* and refers to knowledge about the self and others. *Savoir-être* requires having a certain kind of attitudinal disposition toward intercultural engagement—one of curiosity, openness, and reflexivity. *Savoir-faire* involves practical skills for socializing and other aspects of living in different contexts. *Savoir-apprendre* is the ability to make discoveries through personal involvement in social interaction. Knowing more information about a culture, acquiring attitudinal dispositions that allow one to relate with members of that culture, and then at some point also doing so are all activities that imply changes within the learner involving both thought and behavior. Intercultural education does not, however, have as a goal to turn the L2 learner into an actor indistinguishable from a monolingual, mono-cultural native speaker of the target language.[6] Intercultural education involves not only knowledge about the target culture (C2) but also a greater understanding of and perspective on oneself and one's own native culture (C1) and an ability to negotiate between the two.

This type of understanding develops over time. Learners can only approach a new topic by beginning to understand it with categories that are familiar to them. Time is required for the learner to create new categories with which to understand new types of information.[7] In the development of intercultural competence, information about the new culture may even go undetected until the learner reaches a certain stage at which he/she is competent enough to recognize the cultural content of an encounter. In McBride's study of L2 Spanish learners exposed to lessons on culture and phonology—delivered primarily in the students' first language (L1), English—, students who had only recently begun their L2/C2 studies were not able to recognize culture lessons for what they were. Second-semester and even more so third-semester students responded on a questionnaire positively about the cultural lessons that they had learned, whereas a full 17.7% of the first-semester students chose the option "I don't know what kind of cultural information was included in the [lessons]."[8]

## DYNAMIC SYSTEMS

Byram and Feng distinguish between scholarship and research on the development of intercultural competence. The latter is primarily concerned with the collection and explanation or understanding of data, whereas scholarship attempts to establish "what ought to be" and is more clearly ideological.[9] Both are needed and inform each other. However, while there has been substantial scholarship covering how intercultural education in connection with L2 education should be, there is little actual research on the development of intercultural competence in L2 learners.[10] Two major reasons for the scarcity of research on the development of interculturality in L2 learners are, first, the difficulty in measuring intercultural competence and second, the complexity of the systems involved. L2 grammatical and lexical choices are fairly easy to judge; even though there are often multiple acceptable answers, incorrect usage is usually easy to identify. This is not however the case with the cultural and emotional sides of language usage, which defy the kind of clear-cut measurement that can be applied to the study of communicative competence. This challenge has kept some issues related to interculturality out of the mainstream discussion of L2 development.[11]

Furthermore, intercultural competence involves multiple complex, dynamic systems. Even work that is limited to tracing the more easily measured development of syntactic and lexical development in L2 learners has increasingly involved the application of what is called both complexity theory as well as dynamic systems theory.[12] There has been a growing realization that development in L2 acquisition is neither linear nor unidirectional. For example, U-curves are common phenomena. Grammatical structures that earlier appeared to be already mastered and stable will later be produced by the same learner with errors—sometimes the same errors from earlier phases, and sometimes with new types of inaccuracies.[13] U-curves are common in cultural adaptation as well. The initial reactions of a person to a new culture may initially be enthusiastic and positive, later quite negative, and later more positive again, all the while shifting in focus and depth of understanding.[14] Changes such as these are ongoing; as the name of the theory emphasizes, complex systems are not static but rather dynamic. The nonlinear nature of something such as a U-curve is not to be taken as an anomaly. Rather, nonlinearity characterizes a great deal of L2 and intercultural development. Causality as well, is frequently not unidirectional in complex systems. Instead we encounter cases of *reciprocal causality*, where factors influence each other, although not always in the same direction over time.[15]

A second language learner's developing linguistic system, which is referred to as *interlanguage*, can also be viewed as a dynamic system, which in turn comes in contact and interacts with other systems. The array of factors that influence a polilingual's L2 performance in a given moment is vast, including not only factors external to the developing system but also factors internal to the system.[16] These factors, proceeding from multiple interconnecting systems, include emotional, cognitive, social, cultural, physical, and linguistic factors.

In dynamic systems, factors may or may not interact in ways resembling the properties of the same factors when experienced in isolation. Frequently entirely new characteristics emerge as a result of the interactions. Such properties, not present in the systems before contact and interaction occurred, are called *emergent properties*.[17] An L2 learner, for example, will sometimes produce forms and structures that are present in neither the L1 nor the L2. Within the realm of culture, objects or phenomena at times take on symbolic meaning that could never have been predicted before the meeting of two cultures.

Because development is affected not only by external factors but also by internal ones, the *initial conditions* of a system tend to have a major effect on development.[18] L2 acquisition has often been studied only by looking at external factors, mostly in terms of teaching methodology, without examining many aspects of the learners themselves other than their level of linguistic competence and their linguistic output during the study.[19] The study presented in this chapter examines factors internal to learners, specifically, their folk linguistics beliefs. These beliefs constitute an important part of the internal factors and initial conditions in the dynamic development of L2 and intercultural competence.

## Folk Linguistic Theories

Young and Sachdev, in calling for more research on the development of intercultural competence, highlight in particular the need to look at learners' beliefs in different contexts. They claim that instructors and scholars of intercultural competence base their classroom practices and scholarly claims on what they believe learner beliefs are, but that this is done almost entirely without testing such hypotheses.[20] The study presented in this chapter begins to address this gap by examining L2 learners' beliefs about the relationship of language to thought and culture. Nonexperts' folk linguistic theories may differ from linguists' knowledge about language from anywhere from only a small degree to, often, quite dramatically.[21] Folk linguistic theories are important to take into account in developing research and scholarship on interculturality because they are elaborate and consistent,[22] and they shape the (folk) theory holders' experience of linguistic phenomena and affect their behavior.[23]

In her study of L2 learners' folk linguistic beliefs, Chavez found a number of ways in which the beliefs of beginning to high-intermediate learners of German as an L2 differed strongly from current theories in applied linguistics.[24] Several of these differences were related to many of the participants' (especially the beginners') fundamentally mechanistic view of language in which rules were seen as rigid and functioning independently of speakers' communicative intentions. While such views contrast with the functionalist perspective that is dominant in applied linguistics—which says that lexical and syntactic choices and changes are fundamentally driven by speakers' communicative goals—Chavez suggests that many textbooks and L2 teaching methods may in fact encourage students to view the target language in a mechanistic fashion in their efforts to simplify the L2 for the students. One negative outcome of students' mechanistic view of language was that the structures that these students viewed as having no communicative value were distinctly resented and resisted. On the other hand, there was one realm in which large numbers of Chavez's participants described the form of German as being a result of German speakers' communicative needs, and this was in the lexical realm. "Learners took great interest in and used as a semiotic device the genetic relationship between English and German," using connections that they believed existed between historic meanings and current forms of words to learn the form and use of those words.[25]

## THE CONNECTION BETWEEN LANGUAGE
## AND THOUGHT

Before considering what L2 students believe about the connections between language and thought and language and culture, let us look at some of the scholarly work that has been done on this topic. In a sense, the question of whether or not thought is shaped by language can never be fully resolved, because most of our thoughts take the form of language itself. Nonetheless, important advances have been made in unpacking the issue. The discussion of this issue inevitably makes some reference to the Sapir-Whorf Hypothesis, which proposes that the language one speaks determines the thoughts one has. Benjamin Whorf was interested in concepts that were fundamental to one culture and easily expressed in that culture's language but difficult to express in another culture's language. In a famous essay, he illustrated this through a discussion of how two language groups understand time.[26] He claimed that the Hopi conceptualization of time fits better with what modern physics has revealed about the nature of time—aspects that are extremely difficult to grasp for those of us who do not speak the Hopi language.

While it is exciting to think that if we were members of a different culture and speakers of a different language, we would have a fundamentally different understanding of the nature of the universe, it turned out that Whorf's arguments were somewhat overstated and relied on investigative methods whose flaws have been since pointed out.[27] Thus, the strong version of the Sapir-Whorf hypothesis—the claim that language *determines* thought—is generally not accepted. Weaker versions of this hypothesis, however, have some support. These range from "language influences perception" to "language influences memory" to "different languages make certain thoughts easier or harder" through relative computational costs.[28] To indicate a weaker version of this family of claims, the term "linguistic relativity" is used.

Some scholars reject even weak versions of linguistic relativity. One rather common sense argument against the idea is to point out that thoughts do exist pre-linguistically.[29] For instance it is common to talk about having difficulty putting one's thoughts into words. This indicates that thoughts can exist independently of language. However, putting thoughts into words often seems to have the effect of clarifying them, which in turn suggests that thoughts are shaped through linguistic expression.

Are thoughts only shaped at the moment of speaking or writing, or does the language that one speaks have an effect on one's thought process even beyond the moment of linguistic encoding?[30] One possibility is that it is not the language itself that affects speakers but rather the exposure to the corresponding culture. A study by Chen and Bond[31] demonstrates that this can occur. In their study, balanced bilinguals of Cantonese and English were found to display different personality traits, depending on which language they were communicating in. Significant differences were found both in their self-ratings and how third parties viewed them. These effects, however do not necessarily indicate a linguistic effect.

Other studies have shown that language itself can have an impact on speakers' thoughts. A number of these studies have focused on grammatical gender. Speakers of languages with grammatical gender tend to use masculine descriptions for objects that have masculine gender in their native language and feminine descriptions for words that have feminine gender.[32] This is true even with seemingly neutral words, such as "pan" or "bridge." Further, the effect still holds when subjects are tested in English, where grammatical gender is not marked.[33]

Similar effects can be induced in monolingual English speakers. In one study, monolingual English speakers were taught an invented language, Gambuzi, that had a noun-marking system similar to grammatical gender. When this feature was constructed like grammatical gender of natural languages—that is, that words for "girl" and "woman" would necessarily be in one category, and words for "boy" and "man" in another—, learners of the invented language were later able to come up with and name significantly more similarities between pictures of objects belonging to the same grammatical category in Gambuzi. Other study participants, however, were taught a version of Gambuzi with a noun-marking system that did not correlate with real-world gender, and these participants were not able to list more similarities for objects that had been assigned the same grammatical category. "Just sharing a category name is not sufficient to significantly increase the similarity between two objects. Only when the category is meaningful, somehow interpretable beyond rote memorization, does the similarity of items within a category increase."[34] By learning a new (even if invented) language, these participants established new conceptual connections. Thus there is evidence for grammatical features affecting thought.

At the lexical level—that is, at the level of words and phrases—this can be even easier to detect. A turn of phrase may provide language learners with a new way of viewing phenomena, which could cause them to think differently about those phenomena in the future.[35] Lakoff and Johnson in 1980 published their book *Metaphors We Live*

*By*, exposing dozens of metaphors entrenched so deeply in the English language that it is difficult initially even to view some of the metaphors they name as metaphors.[36] For example, English metaphorically structures ARGUMENT as WAR, in which we *attack our opponents* and *defend our position*. The dominance of these metaphors in our thinking makes it difficult for us to see them as anything besides natural and necessarily true, and yet they are not.

When a person learns another language, he or she learns about the categories that speakers are required to encode, the hierarchical relations that they must express when planning out sentence structure, and the conceptual metaphors that they are constantly exposed to and constantly employ upon expressing their thoughts. Thus, study of an L2 itself can provide a learner with some insight into the cognitive habits of its speakers. All the more, engaging with speakers of that language and with their spoken and written texts in the original language can give learners insights into the thoughts of the L2 speakers that could not be equaled if passed through the filter of translation. Such effects are likely to be enhanced if the student views his or her study of the L2 in this light, as will be argued next.

## ADVANTAGES TO THE L2 LEARNER WHO BELIEVES IN LINGUISTIC RELATIVITY

The question that we turn to now is whether L2 students do in fact believe in linguistic relativity, and if so, how this affects the experience of their development of L2 and intercultural competence. The hypothesis going into this study was that believing in linguistic relativity would be advantageous to an L2/C2 learner, for five main reasons. One reason has already been illustrated by the Gambuzi example and Chavez's subjects whose etymological beliefs about words served as powerful mnemonic devices. Finding meaning in something makes it more memorable. A great deal of thought takes the form of narrative; framing otherwise abstract information in the form of a story helps people to grasp and remember ideas.[37] This is true even when the story is invented, such as, for example, a chemistry teacher might do when using personification to explain why molecules "want" to act in certain ways.

Believing that language reflects the thoughts and beliefs of its speakers would likely have been useful to those learners in Chavez's study who saw many grammar rules as arbitrary. Had they understood the way that the rules functioned within the larger linguistic system, the rules would not have seemed so arbitrary. If they believed that the grammatical structures of German reflected thought patterns of German speakers, they might have found the grammar intriguing, as many of them found etymological explanations of lexical forms to be. Instead, Chavez reports resentment expressed about structures viewed as arbitrary, and this resentment made some learners resistant to learning those structures.

If an L2 learner believes that L2s reflect differences in the thought patterns of the speakers of those languages, then that L2 learner ought to expect L2s to function in ways that are entirely novel to people who do not (yet) speak that language. This sort of set of expectations would be very useful to an L2 learner, because it would predispose him or her to notice and pay attention to new patterns in the L2 instead of expecting the L2 to be essentially a coded form of his or her L1. This would help the learner because noticing and attention are key to second language acquisition.[38]

Believing in a strong connection between habitual thought patterns of a group of people and the linguistic forms of their language would also help students get beyond the kind of mechanistic view of grammar described previously in some of the participants in Chavez's study. While simplified, mechanistic ways of viewing language can help to avoid overwhelming beginning students with excessive amounts of information before they are ready for it, this same over-simplification locks students into erroneous patterns at later stages in their development.[39] The limitations of inflexible grammar rules have been recognized by a broad range of theorists in applied linguistics, leading many in the field to call for more function- and communication-focused ways of teaching L2s.[40]

One final advantage to mention here that an L2 learner would have by believing in a strong connection between language form and the cultures of the people who speak the language is motivation. Learning about other cultures is of high interest to students, both in and of itself, as well as because of the potential advantages that it has in our globalized society, but many people seek such understanding through other types of studies, without viewing L2s themselves as a possible source of this kind of information.[41] If a learner interested in comprehending other cultures believes that the language itself can provide insight into the habits of thinking of its speakers, this will increase the learner's motivation to master the L2.[42]

## The Study

Two hundred fifty-five L2 students studying at a US university filled out an online survey. The survey asked participants to indicate their level of agreement with items such as, "To learn to speak another language well, you have to learn to see the world in a different way." Elsewhere, students were asked to explain their beliefs and how they came to hold them. Demographic information was also collected. The participants ranged in level and studied any of a number of L2s: Arabic (6 participants), Chinese (12 participants), English as a second language (ESL—71 participants), French (17), German (12), Italian (15), Russian (9), and Spanish (110). In addition to the survey, 11 students were interviewed in depth. There were almost twice as many (153) female participants as male participants (88), plus 14 who did not indicate their gender on the survey. Of the 184 students who were studying a foreign language and not ESL, the spread was fairly even across levels: 70 at the beginner level, 59 intermediate, and 55 advanced.

Looking over the data, it was clear that nearly all participants saw second language acquisition as a way to connect with other people, whether or not they were believers in linguistic relativity. As will be explained in further detail below, most participants tended to believe that there is a connection between language and thought and that changing one's way of thinking is necessary for second language acquisition. It should be noted, however, that a fair number of respondents wrote that these ideas were new to them. Most of these participants added that they felt intuitively that the idea seemed correct but they had not contemplated it before.

One item on the survey was "To learn to speak another language well, you have to learn to see the world in a different way" (Item A in Table 12.1). The overall average for this item was 0.91 on a scale of –2 (strongly disagree) to 2 (strongly agree). That is, the overall

**Table 12.1**  Average responses[a] to questionnaire items, by L2

|  | A) See world differently | B) Experience world | C) Worldview | D) Grammar structures |
|---|---|---|---|---|
| Overall average | 0.91 | 0.88 | 1.06 | 0.87 |
| Arabic | 0.67 | 1.33 | 1.33 | 1.17 |
| Chinese | 1.25 | 1.00 | 1.17 | 1.25 |
| ESL | 1.08 | 0.32 | 1.10 | 0.96 |
| Russian | 0.89 | 0.78 | 1.00 | 1.11 |
| German | 1.17 | 1.17 | 1.25 | 0.78 |
| Italian | 0.93 | 1.20 | 0.93 | 0.80 |
| Spanish | 0.91 | 1.18 | 1.02 | 0.74 |
| French | 0.12 | 0.71 | 1.06 | 0.94 |

[a] On a scale of –2 to 2: "strongly disagree" = –2; "disagree" = –1; "agree" = 1; "strongly agree" = 2.

answer was very close to a solid 1.0 that represents agreement. In Table 12.1 we can see that in general, the groups with the highest averages were groups studying L2s very different from their native languages,[43] although this does not explain all rankings seen here. Participants were also asked to explain their answers. The following quote demonstrates the kind of answers that were provided by participants in agreement with the statement.

> A lot of the time with Russian, your sentences do not need to be in a certain order. It is about modifying the words, not the sentence structure. This allows for a complex fluidity that has forced me to look at the world differently because what I say can be constructed in so many ways.

Some respondents commented that seeing the world in a new way was helpful in learning a new language but was not absolutely necessary.

The overall average response to the item "The way you experience the world is affected by which languages you can speak" was 0.88 (Item B in Table 12.1). The response to this item from the ESL group contrasts sharply with other groups and does so in a manner different from other questionnaire items. Further, these answers tended to contradict ESL participants' written and interview comments. Originally, this item was worded with a double negative ("The way you experience the world is NOT affected by which languages you can speak").[44] It seems likely that many ESL participants misunderstood this item. Taking the ESL students out of the results, the overall average rises to 1.10, expressing firm agreement. When asked for examples of this, one student answered,

> This is probably an over-used example, but I believe the Spanish subjunctive is a major example of grammatical structures reflecting different points of view. Because the language allows, and generally encourages, speakers to form sentences that "could be," I speak with more emotion and tend to be more questioning in general.

There was general agreement with the statement, "By studying another language other than my native language, I am coming to understand the worldview of the native speakers of this language" (Item C in Table 12.1). The average answer was 1.06. Again, we see that students of languages very different from their native language were more likely to agree strongly with this statement. Participants who agreed with this statement sometimes qualified it, as in the following quote: "I don't think that all people who speak the same language think the same way, but I do think that sometimes language reflects the values/ ideologies of a society."

The most radical item on the survey (Item D in Table 12.1) said, "The different grammatical structures of different languages reflect different ways of categorizing and/or seeing the world." Overall, participant responses averaged 0.87—short of the 1.0 of clear agreement across all groups, but much more on the side of agreement than disagreement or neutrality. Students of Chinese, Arabic, and Russian (languages less closely related to the students' L1) were more likely to agree with this than other participants. There was furthermore a sharp difference in agreement with this item between less and more experienced language learners. The answers from the 46 students in the study who were only in their first semester of their first L2 was 0.61, whereas the average answer of the 66 students who were already functionally bilingual and studying additional languages was 1.03. An independent samples t-test showed this difference to be significant $t$ $(110) = 2.27, p = .025$.

The most commonly mentioned evidence for agreement with this statement involved lexical items. One example of this was the following:

> The way certain characters come together to make similar words or even completely different words gives me a different perspective on the way I relate words. An example of this would be the Chinese word for "stuff" which is 东西. When these characters are separated they mean East and West respectively. Without Chinese language courses that is a correlation I would have never made. I expect to make more, and more beneficial, correlations as I progress through my Chinese career.

Many participants talked about words or expressions that exist in one language and not others. Several noted that cultures tend to have more words for those things that are most important to them. Some mentioned the oft-cited example of Eskimos having many terms for "snow,"[45] but even more talked about terms for family relations. Grammatical features were commonly mentioned as well. For example, "I have found in Spanish that the way verbs like *gustar* and *sorprenderse* are used shows a less self-centered worldview. These verbs are not conjugated as 'I like something,' it is conjugated as 'Something pleases me.'" Far less common, although present, were examples in the areas of pragmatics or phonology.

Some participants did not agree with the idea that worldviews are reflected in languages. Those who argued against this idea tended to say that to the extent that this seems to be true, it is only by virtue of the language's association with a particular culture. Some talked about cultural lessons given in language classes and how that alone is what gives students insight into the native speakers. Others insisted that apparent correlations between language and values are only historical and no longer valid.

Among the quantitative items on the survey, there were statistically significant correlations (see Table 12.2) between how motivated the respondents were to learn a foreign language, how well they rated themselves as language learners, how they rated themselves in terms of intercultural competence, and whether they believed that language study leads one to better understand other cultures ("L2/C2" in Table 12.2). A number of the participants themselves spoke of these correlations, as in the following:

> It is hard to say whether or not you have to first see the world in a different way in order to speak another language well, or if learning to speak another language inherently changes the way you see the world. I believe that the two are tied together and augment each other.

One of the open-ended questions asked respondents where they had gotten their information from. Those who wrote that they saw strong connections between thought or culture and language cited a range of sources, most prominently anthropology or cognitive science professors, but, interestingly, not L2 teachers, except among the students of Russian.

The interviews were conducted with eight students of ESL and three students who were residents of the United States. As most ESL students wrote only sparse if any comments on the surveys, the interviews were a way to gather more information from this group. Two of the interviews were done in the students' native language, Chinese. The three US residents who volunteered to be interviewed were

**Table 12.2**   Correlations among survey items

|              | L2 skill | Motivation | IC competence | L2/C2 |
|--------------|----------|------------|---------------|-------|
| L2 skill     | 1        | .444[a]    | .317[a]       | .196[a] |
| Motivation   | .444[a]  | 1          | .258[a]       | .249[a] |
| IC competence| .317[a]  | .258[a]    | 1             | .140[b] |
| L2/C2        | .196[a]  | .249[a]    | .140[b]       | 1     |

[a] Correlation is significant at the 0.01 level (2-tailed).
[b] Correlation is significant at the 0.05 level (2-tailed).

unusually enthusiastic learners. As such, their views were assumed not to be entirely representative of the average L2 learner.

For the most part, the information shared in the interviews echoed trends found in the survey. One major theme that emerged only in the interviews, however, was a belief that the version of the target language taught and spoken in classrooms did not match the way the language was used by native speakers and advanced speakers in non-classroom settings. Local versions of the target language—spontaneously called "Chinglish" by some Chinese ESL students and "Thaiglish" by two Thai ESL students—followed largely target language grammar rules but maintained enough characteristics of the learners' L1 and C1 that it did not allow them to communicate effectively and easily with native speakers of the target language. All participants interviewed expressed a belief that a substantial part of language cannot be learned through studying rules but can only be learned through exposure to and participation in authentic language use.

One of the native English speakers who was interviewed echoed a sentiment felt by some of Chavez's participants: that difficult structures in the L2 that do not exist in the learner's L1 appear to be purposeful attempts on the part of native speakers of the L2 to keep nonnative speakers from entering their speech community. This particular student's main focus was on the subjunctive in Spanish.

## DISCUSSION

The data provide substantial evidence that many learners do read cultural meanings into linguistic forms.[46] Further, a belief that L2 learning is connected to intercultural understanding, self-reported L2 language learning skill, self-reported intercultural competence and motivation were positively correlated among the participants in this study. It is likely that each of these factors promoted the others, through reciprocal causality. For instance, a learner who was convinced of the validity of linguistic relativity would be more motivated to study an L2; this generally leads to more effective learning,[47] which would then result in the student rating him- or herself higher on L2 learning skills. Importantly, these factors do not simply correlate to longer amounts of time spent studying a language. It is not simply the case that studying an L2 longer will lead to an increase in the other factors in this constellation of correlations. This suggests that introducing students to the concept of linguistic relativity—as the data tell us many anthropology and cognitive science instructors but few L2 instructors do—and encouraging L2 students to explore these possible connections[48] could be of linguistic, motivational. and possibly intercultural benefit to L2 learners.

The one questionnaire item that did show a significant relationship with level of L2 studies was the statement, "The different grammatical structures of different languages reflect different ways of categorizing and/or seeing the world." As students advance in their knowledge of other languages and other cultures, their understanding of the differences that exist between L1 and L2 and C1 and C2 deepens. It takes a more advanced level of L2 ability to be able to perceive many of the subtleties of language and culture that make exact translations impossible, as demonstrated in the McBride study mentioned above. In the early stages of this learning, a learner must necessarily interpret the L2 and C2 through categories that he or she already possesses. Only through extended and meaningful exposure to the other systems (the L2 and the C2) can a learner build up an understanding of the categories by which the L2 and the C2 are organized, and only by building up these categories—by reconstructing them within the learner's understanding—can they be fully conceptualized and appreciated as the distinct phenomena that they are.

But how accurate is this conceptualization? When a learner recreates L2 grammar in his/her mind, it differs from native-like use.[49] Likewise, nonindigenous interpretations of a culture typically differ from how members of that culture conceptualize it.[50] Kramsch's shorthand for the reconceptualization of the C2 is *C2'*. To some extent, L2 learners are learning an imagined grammatical system and learning about the culture of imagined communities as conceptualized by themselves, their instructors, their classmates, and the often simplified texts that they are exposed to. For some of the ESL students interviewed, the hybrid nature of the L2' taught in their countries was sufficiently salient as to merit its own name ("Chinglish" and "Thaiglish"), the workings of which include many emergent properties of these occasions of on-going cultural and linguistic contact. Upon arrival to the United States, all ESL students reported, substantial interaction with the locals was necessary to adjust their L2' and C2' so that easier and more constructive communication was possible. Like other aspects of culture, language is constantly reconstituted, expressed, transmitted, perpetuated, and changed through interactions between members of a community.[51] Culture and language are interlocking dynamic systems that shift in form according to local realities. This includes the cultures and language of L2 classrooms.[52] Thus, any cultural actor and speaker will need to make adjustments in specifically linguistic behavior and in other behaviors as well upon entry into a new community.

Such is the learning process: a gradual approximation, beginning with conceptual building blocks that the learner already has. Since these conceptual building blocks form the basis of the learning process, they will continue to influence later development. An L2 learner may, for example, advance fairly far in mastering a particular grammar structure by interpreting examples of this structure through a set of partially inaccurate rules or beliefs that could later hold the learner back in further mastery or cause the learner to fail to detect important patterns in the language that he/she is exposed to.[53] Another culture, as well, may be interpreted by a group of people in ways that do not fit the reality of the target group, but the misinterpretations of the culture may be continually reinforced by what others communicate to each other about that culture. These misinterpretations will continue to filter the other groups' experiences with the culture. This can lead to a distorted view of the L2 or C2 and is likely to keep the person encountering the L2/C2 from being able to grasp the inner logic of the systems. Unable to grasp that, the system may seem senseless. As was seen with some of the learners in Chavez's study and one of the interviewees in the present study, there is a tendency among some people to experience uninterpretable data as deliberate attempts to keep other people from participating fully in a community. Thus, the folk beliefs of actors in intercultural encounters can shape their experiences in an on-going manner. Anyone wanting to study such phenomena, and especially anyone wanting to affect these experiences (e.g., teachers) will be able to understand actors' reactions and behaviors in intercultural encounters better being aware of the actors' (sometimes erroneous) beliefs about how culture and language function.[54]

It should be kept in mind that there exists the possibility that inaccurate interpretations may serve the learner's gradual approximation to the target language or culture in a positive way. If a fictitious mnemonic device helps a learner master a concept, it can aid learning. Depending on the nature of the invented story, the strength with which it is held to be true, the learner's openness to noticing information that contradicts it, and the type of understanding of the L2 or C2 that the story touches upon, the mnemonic device may continue to serve its purpose, may later be a cause for misinterpretations, or may be shed.

There are many possible directions for L2 and intercultural development to go in, and these are complex, dynamic, and largely unpredictable systems. How development proceeds depends a great deal on the initial and internal conditions. What the learner believes and how these beliefs evolve over time can change what the learner notices and how that is experienced. The actors' personal interpretation of an experience may affect outcomes as much as the external objective facts of the experience. In L2 and C2 pedagogy, this means that it is important for scholars and teachers to know about learners' folk theories throughout various stages of development, and to engage students in ways that encourage them to be open to constructing new categories. In intercultural scholarship in general, this means that information about actors' beliefs, reactions, and feelings—in the original language as much as possible—is essential for the interpretation of events and for understanding the development of surprising emergent properties.

## NOTES

1. When it is important to distinguish between studying a language in a country where that language is not widely spoken versus studying the language in a country where the language is commonly used, the term "foreign language" is used for the former and "second language" is used for the latter. Where this distinction is not important, the term "second language" is preferred, even in cases where it may in fact be the learner's third (or greater) language.
2. American Council on the Teaching of Foreign Languages, "Standards for Foreign Language Learning: Executive Summary," http://www .actfl.org/public/articles/execsumm.pdf; Council of Europe, "Common European Framework of Reference for Languages: Learning, Teaching, Assessment" (2011), http://www.coe.int/t/dg4/linguistic/Source /Framework_en.pdf
3. Karen Risager, *Language and Culture: Global Flows and Local Complexity* (Buffalo, NY: Multilingual Matters, 2006).
4. Srikant Sarangi, "Culture," in *Culture and Language Use*, ed. Gunter Senft, Jan-Ola Ostman, and Jef Verschueren (Amsterdam: John Benjamins, 2009), 81–104.
5. Council of Europe, "Common European Framework." The American Council on the Teaching of Foreign Languages describes the development of intercultural competence in very similar terms.
6. Monika Chavez, "The Diglossic Foreign Language Classroom: Learners' Views on L1 and L2 Functions," in *The Sociolinguistics of Foreign-Language Classrooms: Contributions of the Native, the Near-Native, and the Nonnative Speaker*, ed. Carl Blyth (Boston: Heinle, 2003), 163–208; Robert W. Train, "The (Non)Native Standard Language in Foreign Language Education: A Critical Perspective," in *The Sociolinguistics of Foreign Language Classrooms: Contributions of the Native, Near-Native and Non-Native Speaker*, ed. Carl Blyth (Boston: Heinle, 2003), 3–40.
7. Allan Luke, "Two Take on the Critical," in *Critical Pedagogies and Language Learning*, ed. Bonny Norton and Kelleen Toohey (New York: Cambridge University Press, 2004), 21–29.

8. Kara McBride, "Vídeos *mashup* para enseñar pronunciación y cultura," *Hispania*, 95, 2 (2012): 316–332.

9. Michael Byram and Anwei Feng, "Culture and Language Teaching: Teaching, Research and Scholarship," *Language Teaching*, 37 (2004): 150.

10. Michael Byram and Anwei Feng, "Culture and Language Teaching: Teaching, Research and Scholarship"; Tony Johnstone Young and Itesh Sachdev, "Intercultural Communicative Competence: Exploring English Language Teachers' Beliefs and Practices," *Language Awareness*, 20, 2 (2011): 81–98. However, there has recently been a fair amount of research done in this direction within the context of study abroad.

11. Merrill Swain, "The Inseparability of Cognition and Emotion in Second Language Learning," *Language Teaching*, 46, 2 (2013): 195–207.

12. Kees de Bot and Diane Larsen-Freeman, "Researching Second Language Development from a Dynamic Systems Theory Perspective," in *A Dynamic Approach to Second Language Development*, ed. Marjolijn H. Verspoor, Kees de Bot, and Wander Lowie (Philadelphia: John Benjamins, 2011), 5–23.

13. de Bot and Larsen-Freeman, "Researching Second Language Development."

14. Barbara F. Freed, "An Overview of Issues and Research in Language Learning in a Study Abroad Setting," *Frontiers: The Interdisciplinary Journal of Study Abroad*, 4 (1998): 31–60.

15. de Bot and Larsen-Freeman, "Researching Second Language Development."

16. Ibid.

17. Ibid.

18. Ibid.

19. Swain, "The Inseparability of Cognition and Emotion." This short-coming, however, has recently been addressed in the form of a number of studies that have come out on individual differences.

20. Young and Sachdev, "Intercultural Communicative Competence," 96.

21. Nancy A. Niedzielski and Dennis R. Preston, *Folk Linguistics* (Berlin: Mouton de Gruyter, 2000).

22. Dennis R. Preston, "Language Teaching and Learning: Folk Linguistic Perspectives." Paper presented at the Georgetown University Round Table on Languages and Linguistics, 1991.

23. Monika Chavez, "Learners' Descriptions of German Pronunciation, Vocabulary, and Grammar: A Folk Linguistic Account," *Die Unterrichtspraxis/Teaching German*, 42, 1 (2009): 1–18.

24. Ibid.

25. Ibid., 13.

26. Benjamin Lee Whorf, "The Relation of Habitual Thought and Behavior to Language," in *Language, Thought and Reality*, ed. John B. Carroll (Boston: MIT Press, 1956), 134–159.

27. Iman Tohidian, "Examining Linguistic Relativity Hypothesis as One of the Main Views on the Relationship between Language and Thought," *Journal of Psycholinguistic Research*, 38, 1 (2009): 65–74.

28. Ibid., 70–72.

29. Steven Pinker, *The Language Instinct* (New York: W. Morrow and Co., 1994).

30. Dan I. Slobin, "Learning to Think for Speaking: Native Language, Cognition, and Rhetorical Style," *Pragmatics*, 1, 1 (1991): 7–25.

31. Sylvia Xiaohua Chen and Michael Harris Bond, "Two Languages, Two Personalities? Examining Language Effects on the Expression of Personality in a Bilingual Context," *Personality and Social Psychology Bulletin*, 36 (2010): 1514–1528.

32. Toshi Konishi, "The Semantics of Grammatical Gender: A Cross-Cultural Study," *Journal of Psycholinguistic Research*, 22, 5 (1993): 519–534.

33. Lera Boroditsky, Lauren A. Schmidt, and Webb Phillips, "Sex, Syntax, and Semantics," in *Language in Mind: Advances in the Study of Language and Cognition*, ed. Dedre Gentner and Susan Godin-Meadow (Cambridge, MA: MIT Press, 2003), 61–79.

34. Boroditsky, Schmidt, and Phillips, "Sex, Syntax, and Semantics," 74.

35. Randal Holme, *Mind, Metaphor and Language Teaching* (New York: Palgrave Macmillan, 2004).

36. George Lakoff and Mark Johnson, *Metaphors We Live By* (Chicago: University of Chicago Press, 1980).

37. Jerome Bruner, *Actual Minds, Possible Worlds* (Cambridge, MA: Harvard University Press, 1985).

38. Richard Schmidt, "Attention," in *Cognition and Second Language Instruction*, ed. Peter Robinson, Michael H. Long, and Jack C. Richards (Cambridge, UK: Cambridge University Press, 2001), 3–32.

39. Eduardo Negueruela and James P. Lantolf, "Concept-Based Instruction and the Acquisition of L2 Spanish," in *The Art of Teaching Spanish: Second Language Acquisition from Research to Praxis*, ed. Rafael Salaberry and Barbara Lafford (Washington, DC: Georgetown University Press, 2006), 79–102.

40. Diana Larsen-Freeman, *Teaching Language: From Grammar to Grammaring* (Boston: Thomson Heinle, 2003).

41. Byram and Feng, "Culture and Language Teaching: Teaching, Research and Scholarship"; Jo Carr and Anne Pauwels, *Boys and Foreign Language* (New York: Palgrave Macmillan, 2006).

42. Zoltán Dörnyei, "Researching Motivation: From Integrativeness to the Ideal L2 Self," in *Introducing Applied Linguistics: Concepts and Skills*, ed. Susan Hunston and David Oakey (London: Routledge, 2010), 74–83.

43. This is based on the relative amounts of time needed for a speaker to master the language, as defined by the Foreign Service Institute (FSI) of the US State Department. Table 12.1 displays the languages in this

order. ESL is in the position it is in because most of the ESL students were native Chinese speakers.

44. Some items were phrased negatively so as to force participants to read the questionnaire items carefully. Negative items were then reverse coded so that the results were easier to read.

45. Laura Martin, "Eskimo Words for 'Snow': A Case Study in the Genesis and Decay of an Anthropological Example," *American Anthropologist*, 88, 2 (1986): 418–423.

46. Since data were collected from only one university, these data are not necessarily generalizable to other situations. Further studies could shed some light onto the extent to which these results are typical.

47. Dörnyei, "Researching Motivation."

48. For example as illustrated extensively in Holme, *Mind, Metaphor and Language Teaching*.

49. Neguerguela and Lantolf, "Concept-Based Instruction."

50. Claire Kramsch, "Teaching Along the Cultural Faultline," in *Culture as the Core: Perspectives on Culture in Second Language*, ed. Dale L. Lange and R. Michael Paige (Greenwich, CT: Information Age, 2003), 19–36.

51. Risager, *Language and Culture*.

52. Kim Griffin, "La relación entre *input*, interacción e *intake*," in *Lingüística aplicada a la enseñanza del español como 2/L* (Madrid: Arco Libros, 2005), 115–138.

53. Neguerguela and Lantolf, "Concept-Based Instruction."

54. Niedzielski and Preston, *Folk Linguistics*.

# CONTRIBUTORS

**Brien K. Ashdown** is Assistant Professor of Psychology at Hobart and William Smith Colleges in Geneva, New York. He holds undergraduate degrees from Weber State University and a doctorate from Saint Louis University. His research interests include the influence of group identity on health decisions and behaviors, the psychology of religion, and other issues related to cultural, ethnic, and gender identity. His research takes a cross-cultural perspective, with a particular interest in Latin America.

**Yetilú de Baessa** is Director of the Department of Psychology in the University Francisco Marroquín in Guatemala. She graduated from Universidad del Valle in Guatemala in 1980 with a *Licenciatura* in General Psychology, and in 1981 with a Master in Measurement, Evaluation and Research in Education. She holds a PhD in Educational Psychology from the University of Texas. She has published several articles, and has worked at del Valle University where she was in charge of National Testing for the Minister of Education, as well as at the Research Project on Child Development, funded by IDRC in a marginal area in Guatemala City.

**Michael D. Barber, S. J.** (PhD Yale, 1985) is Professor of Philosophy and Dean of the College of Arts and Sciences at Saint Louis University. He is the author of 6 books and over 60 articles generally in the area of phenomenology of the social world. He has written on the work of Edmund Husserl, Max Scheler, Alfred Schutz, Emmanuel Levinas, and Enrique Dussel. He is the author of *The Participating Citizen: A Biography of Alfred Schutz* (SUNY 2004) and most recently *The Intentional Spectrum and Intersubjectivity: Phenomenology and the Pittsburgh Neo-Hegelians* (Ohio University Press, 2011).

**Nilanjana Bardhan** is Professor in the Department of Communication Studies at Southern Illinois University, Carbondale. She is the author of several journal articles and book chapters and the coeditor of books *Identity Research and Communication* and *Public Relations* *in Global Cultural Contexts.* She is also the coauthor of *Cultivating Cosmopolitanism for Intercultural Communication.* Her current research focuses on critical cosmopolitanism and on issues of identity, culture, and communication, specifically within the conditions of postcolonial globality.

**Tracy L. Brown** is Professor of Anthropology and Director of General Education at Central Michigan University in Mount Pleasant, Michigan. She has published widely on Pueblo and Spanish interaction in eighteenth-century New Mexico. Her book, *Pueblo Indians and Spanish Colonial Authority in Eighteenth Century New Mexico* was published by the University of Arizona Press in 2013.

**William P. Childers** is Associate Professor at Brooklyn College and CUNY Graduate Center. He is the author of *Transnational Cervantes* (Toronto, 2006) as well as numerous articles on Cervantes and other aspects of early modern Spanish cultural history. He is currently working on a book on the Moriscos of Granada during the last decades of the sixteenth century. He is also part of an international team of scholars putting together an anthology on the under-utilized Inquisitorial sources known as *libros de testificaciones* in Spain, and *cuadernos do promoter* in Portugal and Brazil.

**Judith L. Gibbons** is Professor Emerita of Psychology and International Studies at Saint Louis University. She is the president of the Interamerican Society of Psychology and the editor of the American Psychology Association Division 52 journal *International Perspectives in Psychology: Research, Practice, Consultation.* Her research interests include intercountry adoption and adolescent development in the majority world.

**Jingyun Gu** is a doctoral student in Education at Saint Louis University. She is also a lecturer in the College of Foreign Languages, Shanghai Maritime University, China. Her research interests include language teaching and learning strategies, language policy, and curriculum evaluation.

**Jennifer Hale-Gallardo** is a postdoctoral research fellow at Saint Louis University, St. Louis, Missouri. She is a medical anthropologist whose interests include cultural alterity and subaltern healing, the sociodeterminants of health and health disparities, and the democratization of healthcare.

**Mun-Cho Kim** is Professor of Sociology at Korea University in Seoul, South Korea. He has written extensively on work and occupations, information society, science and technology, culture and social theory. He served as the president of the Korean Society of Social Theory, Korean Association of Science and Technology Studies, and Korean Sociological Association. Currently he is the head of the Program in Science, Technology and Society Studies at Korea University and the president of Korean Association for East Asian Sociology. His recent publications include *Class Disparity of Korea* (2008), *The Coming of Convergence Civilization* (2013), and "Dialectics of Risk, Security and Surveillance in a High-Tech Society" (2011).

**Paul Kollman, C. S. C.** is Associate Professor of Theology at the University of Notre Dame, Indiana, and Leo and Arlene Hawk Executive Director of Notre Dame's Center for Social Concerns. A Catholic priest and member of the Congregation of Holy Cross, he is the author of *The Evangelization of Slaves and Catholic Origins in Eastern Africa* (Orbis, 2005). Kollman's research focuses on African Christianity, mission history, and world Christianity, and he has carried out research in eastern Africa, Nigeria, and South Africa, as well as in archives in Europe and the United States. He has published articles and reviews in a wide variety of journals in theology, religious studies, and African studies. He is currently studying the Catholic Charismatic Renewal in Africa; investigating archival records on the origins and growth of the Catholic Church in Uganda, Kenya, and Tanzania; and preparing a textbook on Christianity in eastern Africa.

**Henrik Gert Larsen** holds an MA in East European Studies and Social Science from Copenhagen University, and a PhD in International Psychology, Systems and Organizations from the Chicago School of Professional Psychology. He has gained broad experience with acculturation issues during more than ten years of working with China. He is affiliated with the Chicago School of Professional Psychology and The Nordic International Management Institute in Chengdu, where he is teaching global social responsibility, social marketing, and theoretical perspectives on acculturation and assimilation.

**Kara McBride** has a BS in Philosophy (University of Oregon), an MA in Spanish (Purdue University), and an MA in Applied Linguistics (Indiana University). After teaching English as a second language in Chile and the United States for some years, she got her PhD in Second Language Acquisition and Teaching at the University of Arizona (USA). She is an Associate Professor at Saint Louis University. She trains foreign language teachers, and her research focuses on L2 oral language development and interculturality.

**Michal Jan Rozbicki** is Professor of History at Saint Louis University. He has authored 5 books, including the award-winning *Culture and Liberty in the Age of the American Revolution* (University of Virginia Press, 2001), and held fellowships from several global institutions, including the Rockefeller Foundation, American Council of Learned Societies, Oxford University, and the Kennedy Institute for North American Studies in Berlin. He had served as Chair of the History Department, and currently is Director of the Center for Intercultural Studies which he founded in 2011. It is devoted to systemic research on the interactions between different cultures, and to developing interdisciplinary methodologies of interpreting the relationships of otherness.

**Miriam Sobré-Denton** received her PhD from Arizona State University in 2009. After five years as Assistant Professor in the Department of Communication Studies at Southern Illinois University at Carbondale, she started Intercultural Connections LLC, a company designed to connect intercultural scholars with practitioners. She has published in numerous peer reviewed journals and is coauthor of *Cultivating Cosmopolitanism for Intercultural Communication.*

**Teruyuki Tsuji** is former Postdoctoral Research Fellow at Saint Louis University, and currently holds the position of Diplomat-in-Residence at the Institute of International Relations at the University of the West Indies (St. Augustine, Trinidad). His research has focused on the implications of religious expressions and ritual practices for social capital development and civic engagement among the African and South Asian migrant and diaspora populations in South Florida and the Caribbean.

**Irmina Wawrzyczek** is Professor of Anglo-American Cultural History at the Department of English, Maria-Curie-Skłodowska University in Lublin, Poland. Her interests involve the theory of popular culture, and the cultural study of the British print media. Her main publications in this latter area include the coauthored book in Polish *The Representations of Poland and the Poles in the British Press 2002–2010* (2007), and the essays "Remembering Women in *The Times* Obituaries of 1920s and 1980s" (2012), and "The Discursive Construction of National Identities in the Polish Sports Press 2004" (2007). Her current research is on interculturalism, sports, and the media in Europe.

**Leslie Wolowitz**, PhD, is a clinical psychologist. She served as faculty in clinical psychology doctoral programs for 20 years, and chaired the International Psychology doctoral program at the Chicago School of Professional Psychology. She has written and taught on issues of cultural context and difference. Dr. Wolowitz is currently in private practice in Chicago, Illinois.

# INDEX

Printed and bound by CPI Group (UK) Ltd, Croydon, CR0 4YY